A GREEN AND PERMANENT LAND

DEVELOPMENT OF WESTERN RESOURCES

The Development of Western Resources is an interdisciplinary series focusing on the use and misuse of resources in the American West. Written for a broad readership of humanists, social scientists, and resource specialists, the books in this series emphasize both historical and contemporary perspectives as they explore the interplay between resource exploitation and economic, social, and political experiences.

John G. Clark, University of Kansas, Founding Editor
Hal K. Rothman, University of Nevada, Las Vegas, Series Editor

A GREEN AND PERMANENT LAND

Ecology and Agriculture in the Twentieth Century

Randal S. Beeman
and James A. Pritchard

 University Press of Kansas

Portions of this work have previously appeared in *Environmental History Review* and the *Journal of Sustainable Agriculture*.

Published by the University Press of Kansas (Lawrence, Kansas 66049), which was organized by the Kansas Board of Regents and is operated and funded by Emporia State University, Fort Hays State University, Kansas State University, Pittsburg State University, the University of Kansas, and Wichita State University.

Library of Congress Cataloging-in-Publication Data

Beeman, Randal S., 1963–
　　　A green and permanent land : ecology and agriculture in the twentieth century /
Randal S. Beeman and James A. Pritchard.
　　　　　p. cm. — (Development of western resources)
　　　Includes bibliographical references and index.
　　　ISBN 0-7006-1066-9 (cloth : alk. paper)
　　　　　1. Agriculture—United States—History. 2. Sustainable agriculture—United
States—History. 3. Agricultural ecology—United States—History. I. Pritchard,
James A., 1954–　II. Title. III. Series.

S441.B36 2001
333.76'16'0973—dc21　　　　　　　　　　　　　　　　　　　　　　　　　00-063334

British Library Cataloguing in Publication Data is available.

Printed in the United States of America
10 9 8 7 6 5 4 3 2 1

The paper used in this publication meets the minimum requirements of the American National Standard for Permanence of Paper for Printed Library Materials Z39.48-1984.

For
Monica Quirarte-Beeman
and
Diane Marie Debinski—
two wonderful women

Contents

Acknowledgments

The authors wish to thank readers of the manuscript through its various phases over the past five years, including R. Douglas Hurt, Alan Marcus, Jim Sherow, Donald J. Pisani, and Andrew Hurley. We also wish to thank our many friends and colleagues who have expressed interest in our topic and discussed ecology or agriculture with us, including Tony Thompson, George Naylor, Dick Thompson, Ron Rosmann, Rick Exner, Matt Liebman, Bill Hohman, Kay Niyo, and David and Lin Zahrt. The opinions and interpretations we express are entirely our own, remaining here despite the good advice these fine folks offered.

We acknowledge the invaluable assistance we received from archivists all over this great land. Special thanks go to our families. We are grateful to our spouses for their support and indulgence of our obsessions during this project. Our kids helped with some of the typing of the manuscript, so we will attribute any typos to their valiant efforts. Last but not least, we want to express gratitude to our editor, Nancy Scott Jackson, for her faith in the project and her efforts to bring this work to print.

Introduction

In November 1999, the World Trade Organization (WTO) met in Seattle to establish an agenda for future discussions. While delegates wrestled over the details of international trade, an estimated crowd of ten thousand individuals protested in the streets and blocked access to buildings. Unfortunately for the perceived legitimacy of the nongovernmental organizations that helped organize the protest, a few members of the crowd vented their frustration at being excluded from meetings, and the protest turned violent, with demonstrators smashing windows and throwing bottles at police equipped with space-age protective gear. While some columnists labeled the protesters "infantile," a more accurate characterization of those waving signs or chanting slogans would portray them as people who felt they had little or no voice at the table of negotiations. Those people in the street represented popular concerns, including environmental issues, affairs of social justice, the rights of labor, and resentment against the pervasive influence and power of multinational corporations. Inside the hotels and other venues, the WTO talks continued largely unaffected, eventually ending in stalemate nonetheless. Lesser-developed countries (LDCs) felt excluded and took offense when the major trade leaders, in an apparent effort to move the proceedings forward, held closed sessions at which only a few countries were represented. LDC negotiators were concerned that developed nations would impose unreasonable environmental standards or labor regulations that would impair their competitiveness. The Clinton administration, for its part, had a different set of chestnuts to roast.

Growing resistance among European consumers to genetically modified crops resulted in firm demands for labeling American food products derived from genetically modified organisms (GMOs). European consumers, traditionally more particular about taste and quality than their American counterparts, seem more concerned about human health and food purity as well. American policy makers and opinion makers reacted brusquely, suggesting that insistence on GMO labeling was nothing but a cover for protectionism aimed at keeping European and Japanese farmers in business. Americans wanted to increase grain shipments to Europe (thus buoying price levels) because recent commodity prices in America had dropped precipitously. Average farm income also had collapsed—in Illinois, for example, falling from $62,000 in 1996 to $11,074 in 1998. Although

1

Americans celebrate consumer choice when buying a motor vehicle or detergent, opinion columnists and policy spokesmen seemed to resent the idea that European consumers might be anything less than utterly rational in their choices at the market, decrying the unscientific nature of market-place resistance to GMOs. Yet, supported by respected people such as Prince Charles, most Europeans remain suspicious of what they call "Frankenstein food." American government and corporate officials pushed European representatives to accept nonlabled food products, arguing that science had not proved GMOs harmful. Yet when delegates boarded their homeward-bound aircraft, Europeans had not agreed to discuss the issue at the next round of WTO talks.[1] The collapse of the talks in Seattle and the attendant protests illustrate how since the 1930s, agricultural issues have remained central in public discourse on human and environmental health.

Agriculture is more important than most suburban and city folks real-ize. There are several good reasons to care about agriculture and about what happens to farmers both in the United States and abroad. First, despite the abundance produced by modern agriculture, we are never more than two or three crop years away from devastating food shortages. Should some unexpected pestilence sweep through an entire soybean crop, helped on by the genetic similarity of the plants, or a cycle of severe drought limit crop production, a period of scarcity (well known to ancient peoples) might well ensue. Second, the health of our families is reason enough to be concerned about how our food is produced. According to the Environmental Working Group, infants in forty-four Midwestern towns receive a lifetime dose of the herbicide atrazine from drinking water before they reach one year of age. According to a 1987 National Academy of Sciences (NAS) study, pesticide residues in food may cause anywhere from four to twenty thousand cases of cancer each year in the United States. Pesticides have been linked to sup-pression of the human immune system, and organophosphate pesticides are classified as neurotoxins, which damage human nerve cells. Traces of synthetic chemicals from various sources have been found to accumulate in infants, passed to them through breast milk. Any parent should be pro-foundly disturbed by the implications of this sort of information because, despite the assurances of manufacturers, we are not sure what long-term risk of cancer or other disease is associated with minute yet continuous long-term dosages of chemicals originating in pesticide and herbicide use. The insidious and disturbing part of all this is the pervasive reach of syn-thetic chemicals in our environment, with long-term effects on individuals, biodiversity, or the human race that are unknown and unknowable.[2]

The third reason to care about agriculture has to do with people and communities. Average sorts of people, neither working class nor white-collar, modern "small" farmers still constitute a viable and important seg-ment of American society.[3] The independent farming family is important to our culture partly because it represents a powerful mythical image that we refuse to let go. Ideologues of every sort look to the farmer to embody "American" values such as honesty and hard work. Perhaps we invest the farmer with the last vestiges of the dignity of productive toil, when the value of work for millions of other Americans has been debased by the assembly line and by massive layoffs following mergers and corporate "streamlining." If the honest laborer in the most necessary of all industries loses independence, home, and hearth to the processes of modernity and industrialization, why should anyone maintain hope that their labors will yield the just reward of economic security and the dignity of a useful contribution to the community? That is the subconscious fear that drives our society toward efforts to preserve the family farm.

In episodic cycles from the late nineteenth century through the present day, American farmers have been going broke. During the last quarter of the nineteenth century, the Populist movement rose in the heartland, protesting the power of industrialists, bankers, and railroad owners that worked to the disadvantage of the small producer. By the 1880s, high debt loads and low grain prices already plagued farmers. Distrusting the established political parties, Midwestern farmers carried considerable momentum into the 1892 presidential election, when the People's Party ran James B. Weaver for president. The party later fused with the Democrats, and in 1896 and 1900 William Jennings Bryan attracted over 45 percent of the popular vote, yet ultimately the agrarian agenda lost out to William McKinley's promises of stability, order, and integrity. During the 1930s, the Great Depression meant another round of hard times and economic crisis for American farmers. During the 1980s and again in the late 1990s, commodity prices tumbled, more storefronts closed in small towns across the nation, and banks foreclosed on farmers who could not connect the separate strands of capital, markets, weather, technology, and practice.[4] While greedy bankers and undemocratic industrialists certainly did exist in their era, the Populists could not understand events in the same way that we can today, looking back on a century of history and farmers' experience.

The century-long process that has moved people off the land and driven countless farmers out of business can be summed up as a "structural transformation" of farming toward an industrialized model.[5] Various trends and forces play into this larger process, of course, including mechanization, the growth of corporations, the consolidation of capital and land, the development of mechanical and seed production technologies, and the widespread adoption of synthetic agricultural chemicals used as herbicides, pesticides, and fertilizers. While modern agricultural techniques have yielded the great benefit of vastly increased production of food and fiber, the process also created wrenching and extensive social change. Some historians claim that technology is neutral, deployed by humans for better or for worse; other historians, farmers, philosophers, and some rural economists see technology as a more active agent, carrying with it ethical implications. Marshall McLuhan and Lewis Mumford, for example, observed how societies shape themselves around their tools. Technologies change their users, sometimes in unexpected ways. Biotechnology, the latest revolution in agricultural tools, combines the processes of industrialization and increasing corporate control with vexing moral issues and troublesome environmental questions.[6]

Improvements in agricultural technology began with primitive seed drills used in Mesopotamia, but for our purposes the mechanization of agriculture began alongside the industrialization of America. In 1870, James Oliver began commercial production of a plow made with hardened cast iron. From the 1860s through the 1880s, various farming implements such as grain drills, reapers, wire binders, and threshing machines came into mass production. The manufacture of tractors started around 1902, and after World War I this now familiar symbol of the farm came into widespread use.[7] The mechanization of agriculture promised relief from hard labor, faster completion of tasks, and the compelling possibility of increased production and therefore more profit. Bigger reapers, efficient binders, plows with multiple shares, larger tractors to haul wider harrows and cultivators, updated sprayers, and hybridized seeds all held the promise of more profit through greater crop yields. Yet higher levels of technology, such as bigger and more efficient combines, usually meant obtaining another bank loan to buy upgraded equipment, thus using up the increased profits on the debt treadmill.

Ironically, the very success of agricultural mechanization helped create a chronic problem of overproduction that depressed commodity prices, along the way bankrupting many of those who embraced the goals of "progress." More "efficient" farmers made it through cycles of depressed prices, buying out their neighbors and expanding their operations. With larger farms, they found full utilization of their equipment or invested in larger farm machinery. Yet many farmers found that adopting the methods of modern industrialized agriculture kept them in a cycle of debt and dependence on expensive chemical inputs. Not only mechanization but also culture played a role in creating the problem of overproduction. Our belief in free markets, the independent outlook of individual farmers, and the sheer number of producing units have worked against effective production controls. Finally, the culture of farmers is relatively competitive. As Iowa farmers Dick and Sharon Thompson have observed, "What a farmer won't do to beat his neighbor by one bushel per acre!" These factors have produced a perennial problem of commodity overproduction. Farmers have paid a price for failing to control levels of production, going out of business by the thousands.[8]

During the 1980s alone, about 20 percent of Iowa farmers went out of business. For every six farms that expire, calculated one economist, a business in a rural town also goes bankrupt. So it is not just individual farmers losing out; it is the entire fabric of America's rural population that is being transformed. Since the 1940s, the farm-based population in the United States has dropped from 30 million to 5 million. Those left behind, such as aging residents of rural towns, face restricted essential services and declining community economies that prompted Osha Gray Davidson to call today's heartland "America's rural ghetto."[9] Such a grand transformation of an entire economic sector reverberates through the nation.

The remaining farmers have relied on advancements in technology and science) to keep them in business.

Two main strategies of hope have sustained farmers in times of crisis. First, many farmers found continual promise in technology and science. The allure of modernity is extremely compelling. Modern technology developed by farm implement and chemical manufacturers promised to help the farmer solve vexing and immediate problems. The adoption of modern techniques seemed, at least for a time, to deliver. The land-grant colleges also helped create scientific and technological advances in agriculture. While farmers always had an ambivalent relationship with the extension agents, doubting the expertise of men who seldom left the laboratory, they also embraced many of the techniques science brought. Scientific advances since World War II have carried a mantle of legitimacy that inspired confidence in technology. For better or worse, science served as a technical assistant to larger trends and the agendas of other actors, namely, the industrialization of agriculture. Despite the heavy and obvious burdens of financing new equipment required by industrialized techniques, many farmers could see no other way to carry on. Given a lack of production control in commodities, it seemed that the only way to make more money was to produce ever more grain or livestock, which required expensive new technologies. Modern agriculture produces the absurdity of the largest independent farm producers going broke. Many farmers today stay with the industrial model only because they are so far down the road of mechanization and debt that their options have become limited by their need to maximize income flow. Others stay with the industrial model because it effectively delivers high yields, and if the weather holds and the rains come at the right time, if the management team (the farm family) can push the efficiency of the farm and judge the market with some luck, things will work out for another year. A fortunate few have learned how to beat the system, farming on an industrial model but, through very tight budgeting and unusually efficient management over several generations, remaining free of debt.

The second major vision for American agriculture can be seen in the movement for alternative agriculture. This movement occurred in two main phases, during the 1930s and again since the 1970s, advertising itself under several names, including permanent, sustainable, organic, biodynamic, and alternative farming. It was not so much an organized, coherent movement as a spectrum of approaches to the problems posed by modern agriculture, ranging from the eminently practical to the cosmologically inspired. This continuum of technique and practice joins into a wider array of agricultural practice that includes a variety of "conventional" farming methods. A good example of mixing and matching across the spectrum is a farmer who may have some acreage in organic production and other parts of the farm employing ridge-till techniques that require synthetic fertilizer and a reduced, yet continued, use of herbicide.

The story of how ecological thought has altered agricultural theory, practice, and policy since the 1930s is an underdeveloped chapter in the agricultural, environmental, and technological history of the United States. Our book about agriculture in the age of ecology is primarily a history with ideas at its center, yet it is also a tale of colorful personalities, changed institutions, and innovative people introducing specific farming practices and policies. From the mid-1930s to the present, proponents of what we label "ecological agriculture" were in the vanguard in communicating to the general public what would now be called "environmental" messages, usually framed as warnings and advice laced with ecological thought. While traditionally viewed as "conservation," their thinking about agriculture embodied ecological notions. We suggest that the two distinct movements of ecological agriculture served as important elements in the coalescence of American environmental ethics. Finally, the history of ecological agriculture illustrates changing American conceptions toward farming, technology, and environmental health. We hope that this work will foster a better understanding of the centrality of food production in the history of American civilization and of how agriculture has shaped, and in turn been shaped by, its physical and intellectual environment.

The permanent and sustainable agriculture movements may be most significant for providing a beacon of hope for farmers seeking alternatives to modern-day industrialized agricultural practice. For many farmers, organic agriculture presents a viable way to reduce the costs of high-tech inputs and a better way to fulfill their obligations of stewardship. For the consumer, organic agriculture promises healthy produce for the table that is more savory than that produced by industrial agriculture. A booming market for organic food signifies possibilities for modern farmers to adopt methods that are more environmentally benign. Consumers' concerns about healthy food may yet coincide with farmers' desires for economic stability and with larger concerns about conserving natural resources to create what Rexford G. Tugwell envisioned as "a green and permanent land."

PART 1: PERMANENT AGRICULTURE

CHAPTER ONE

Soil and the Crisis of American Civilization

We often say that the farmer feeds all the people. He must do more than this: he must leave his part of the earth's surface in more productive condition than when he received it. This will be accomplished by a better understanding of the powers of the soil and means of conserving them, for every well-managed soil should grow richer rather than poorer; and, speaking broadly, the farm should have within itself the power of perpetuating itself.
—Liberty Hyde Bailey, 1908[1]

CRISIS AS AN AMERICAN AFFLICTION

A notable feature of the American condition is the historical trait of reacting strongly to real and perceived crises rather than acting preemptively to avert them, as Liberty Hyde Bailey would have preferred. As Page Smith and other historians have noted, Americans have alternated between prideful accomplishment and lamentation over disappointing failure. Smith and others have documented several episodes in this historical legacy of "anxiety and despair." Writing in 1942, anthropologist Margaret Mead cited this periodic retreat to crisis mongering as residual in the American preoccupation with "success" as a personal and societal virtue. Mead wrote of the American character as "geared to success and movement; invigorated by obstacles and difficulties; but plunged into guilt and despair by catastrophic failure and wholesale alteration in the upward and onward pace."[2]

During the depression and war years of the 1930s and 1940s, "despair" pervaded the American landscape and lexicon. Economic collapse, portentous international machinations leading to the crusade against fascism, and the appearance of ecological catastrophes in the form of floods and dust storms compounded lingering concerns regarding the general prospects of future civilization, expressed in the writings of Fritz Lang, Lewis Mumford, and others during the 1920s. A new era of mass culture and mass consumption challenged many things once held dear, and required new systems of ideas and technologies to ensure the nation's survival amid a series of crises in an increasingly complex and intertwined world. As one rather typical author noted at the time, that world abounded with "impoverishment, revolutions, wars, migrations, and the social decadence of billions of peoples" awaiting the "oncoming desolation of their lands." Many Americans during this time felt their value system was under attack from the pervasive forces of urbanization, foreign immigration, and the creation of a mass consumer society.[3]

For many farmers, agricultural issues embodied this deep sense of crisis during the 1930s. Agriculture had been in a state of disrepair for years, with some farmers unable to cope with technological change, fluctuating commodity prices, and the general loss of prestige that rural life had once enjoyed. Following the Civil War, farmers faced financial troubles due to mortgage debt, excess production, and the high shipping rates charged by the railroads. The perennial appearance of farmers' organizations indicated continuing economic problems. Formed in 1867 for educational and social purposes, the Patrons of Husbandry (or the Grange) quickly shifted to pursue cooperative business arrangements during the 1870s. The Grange faded after the mid-1870s but was followed during the late 1880s by the more militant and political Farmers' Alliance. Like the Grange, the Alliance movement advocated cooperative marketing and buying strategies. In 1880, farmers in Kansas founded the People's Party, based largely on Alliance goals. The Populist Party used political means to pursue its agrarian agenda, including antitrust legislation, government ownership of the railroads, a progressive income tax, and direct representation through the referendum and initiative. The Populist movement lost momentum after the party's defeat in the election of 1896. From 1909 through 1914, commodity prices rose faster than farm expenses, and thereafter "parity" referred back to price levels during that era. During World War I, European demand for American grain helped buoy prices, but recovery following the war and competition from Russia and Argentina caused falling prices and severe financial distress for American farmers, many of whom had expanded their operations on credit. Prices fell dramatically in 1920, reaching only 67 percent of parity by 1921. After the stock market crash of 1929, the U.S. agricultural economy crumpled as the nation entered the Great Depression. During the 1920s, the Farmers' Union took up cooperative marketing and buying to improve farm economics, while a faction also tried to control marketing and sought government help in price stabilization. From 1915 to 1922, the Non-Partisan League in North Dakota argued for state-owned banks, grain elevators, flour mills and meat-packing plants. In 1919, Midwestern farmers who were not in financial crisis found representation in the American Farm Bureau Federation, which opposed government ownership of the railroads, disliked labor unrest and radicalism, supported the privately held Federal Land Banks, and supported the extension services of the U.S. Department of Agriculture (USDA) and the land-grant colleges. While the

Farmers' Union wanted to withhold commodities from market and install production controls, the Farm Bureau argued that better domestic and foreign marketing would improve the farmers' position.[4]

As foreclosures escalated during the 1920s, many members of the Farmers' Union began to think in terms of a strike, or "holiday," during which farmers would not sell their produce. They hoped federal intervention would guarantee farmers their production costs plus a modest profit. In 1932, Milo Reno organized the Farmers' Holiday Association at the state fairgrounds in Des Moines, Iowa. The complete closure of markets was impossible to maintain because farmers needed to support their families. The holiday turned violent in Wisconsin, where the National Guard beat striking farmers. From 1932 to 1936, the Farmers' Holiday movement effectively blocked many foreclosure sales by bidding mere pennies at auction, threatening bank officers should they fail to accept sale proceeds as payment in full for debt. This was the economic backdrop that the administration of Franklin Delano Roosevelt faced as it considered agricultural policy during the early 1930s.[5]

SOIL AND THE FATE OF SOCIETY

In numerous soil jeremiads throughout the 1930s and 1940s, and in speeches, broadcasts, and writings, several erosion apostles warned Americans about the fate of past civilizations that had allowed deterioration of their soils. Pointing to numerous perceived villains that created the soil crisis, the critics of poor land management called for the rejection of excessive individualism and the recognition of the need for planning and cooperation in a modern society rife with complex interrelationships. The erosion apostles were led by Hugh H. Bennett, Rexford G. Tugwell, and Morris L. Cooke, all prominent New Dealers committed to the idea and reality of a planned, permanent agriculture to avert chaos and ensure a future for American civilization.[6]

A sense of crisis was not a new phenomenon in American agricultural history. Even prior to the Civil War, observers such as George Perkins Marsh, in a fashion that presaged ecological critiques of society, expressed concern over the decline of agriculture and the threat of soil erosion. Agriculture endured other "crises" in the late nineteenth and early twentieth centuries, giving birth to such disparate groups as the Grange, Liberty Hyde Bailey's Holy Earth Society, the country life movement, the cooperative movement, the USDA and land-grant college–experiment station–extension service network, and other ideas and institutions seeking to bring "uplift" and "equality" for agriculture. During the 1920s, agricultural prices remained weak in most regions of the country. A dominating urban culture that assigned low status to farmers also burdened agrarians in the period. Farm groups, social planners, legislators, and others offered remedies for the agricultural anxieties of the 1920s, calling for increased cooperative efforts, expanded technology, increased efficiency, soil conservation, and the removal of so-called marginal farmers from the land. All this would make rural life "more satisfying and beneficial" and would serve as a bulwark against "industrial serfdom." Additional examples of attempts to lift up agriculture in the 1920s range from state support of small farmers in California to Henry A. Wallace's promotion of the industrial uses of farm crops in the period. Thus, even prior to the soil crisis of the FDR era, individuals and governments had begun work to build a more prosperous agriculture that halted the wastage of topsoil and rural life.[7] Fanned by the Great Depression, an emergent sense of crisis during the early 1930s increased in scope with the appearance of ecological disasters, notably rampant flooding along the nation's river systems and the dust bowl in the Great Plains. Part of a deepening agricultural crisis, the pervasiveness of topsoil erosion in the United States intensified the overall state of despair in the period.

In essence, the individuals describing the soil crisis linked agricultural problems to the larger human crisis of the period. In *New Frontiers* (1934), Henry A. Wallace, secretary of agriculture and a luminary agricultural theorist, opined that "human beings are ruining land, and bad land is ruining human beings, especially children." Morris L. Cooke, the social reformer–engineer and later administrator of the Rural Electrification Administration, likened the soil crisis to a national case of "tuberculosis" or "cancer." Cooke wrote: "America is doomed agriculturally unless the problems of drought, dust storms, floods, and worst of all, erosion are taken seriously." Ecologist Paul Sears, in his typically poignant manner, illuminated the human dimensions of the soil crisis for readers of the *American Mercury* in 1937. Sears warned that "the soil is our national meal ticket. It is also a marvelous and intricate phenomenon which the ordinary person understands about as well as a Colonial barber understood the germ theory of disease." Sears continued, stating, "Soil is truly a measure of abundance so far as living things are concerned. This fact is as vital to the city dweller as to the farmer." Hugh H. Bennett, the father of soil conservation and a central figure in this history of ecological agriculture, echoed the sentiments of Sears, arguing that "the soil is indispensable not merely to the farmer but to everyone else as well. A source of trouble in the past and a danger in the future is that too often the land is thought of as an end itself, rather than a means toward greater ends." Bennett, Sears, and like-minded people spoke with a sense of urgency commensurate with the scale of the perceived threat. As contemporary writer Charles D. Jarrett commented, the problems of agriculture required an erudite description of the crisis: "Drama in presentation is the most effective tool that any speaker, teacher, or salesman can use in reaching the thinking process of the uninformed. Soil erosion control is a vital problem that concerns every living man, woman and child. . . . it is imperative that we employ every ethical means to impress them with the peril of continued indifference."[8]

LESSONS FROM HISTORY

In numerous soil jeremiads or lamentations of American soil abuse produced from the mid-1930s through the early 1940s, Hugh Bennett and others also linked the soil crisis to the larger problems of American civilization by taking "lessons" from history regarding civilizations that had perished or declined because of ill treatment of the soil. The erosion apostles conducted investigations of the human record in the hope that history might reveal sources of abusive husbandry and provide a road map to a future of stewardship and permanence.

In a number of books, articles, and public comments, leaders of the permanent agriculture movement also looked to other cultures for messages about care or neglect of the soil. They identified a variety of American cultural traits that fostered a particularly destructive form of agriculture. This list of America's soil villainy included an arrogant and exploitative attitude toward the land, ruinous farming practices, misguided leadership from agricultural scientists, farm organizations, and policy makers, as well as general greed that the erosion apostles associated with an unplanned, speculative, and shortsighted economy. After singling out past mistakes and lessons of soil neglect, the authors of these tracts inevitably offered prescriptions for the future, which they indicated would be built on the principles of interdependence and societal permanence. While sometimes including agrarian or back-to-land exhortations, most soil jeremiads were imbued with a faith in technology and progress, such as the New Deal emphasis on dams as a tool of conservation. While some of the most significant permanent agriculture advocates were social planners associated with New Deal governmental activism, critiques of poor stewardship emanated from a wider range of national and international sources, including people opposed to New Deal social engineering.

Fundamental to the "soil" interpretation of history was the stark consensus that civilization was at risk, a conclusion derived from a faith that "when governments disappear, they do so because they have reached crises for which they are unable to find solutions." More often than not, according to these texts, the crises that crippled and destroyed past civilizations were crises of the soil. Hugh Bennett, speaking at a conservation conference in Tyler, Texas, in July 1935, asserted that "history has shown time and again that no large nation can long endure the continuous mismanagement of its soil resources. The world is strewn with the ruins of once flourishing civilizations, destroyed by erosion." Bennett punctuated his point with the admonishment that "the very fact you are met in a conference to consider the problems of soil and water conservation shows an understanding of the nature and extent of the task before us." Bennett later compounded this sense of urgency with the suggestion that, with erosion, it was "not just the land which goes. The people, the cities and towns, and the civilizations decay with the land. That's history. Not the kind of story you read in books, but the history you read on the land." Filmmaker Robert Flaherty even used a historical approach in his 1941 film, *The Land.* Accompanied by scenes of eroded land, Flaherty's narrator told viewers: "Something has happened to the soil. When the soil moves, people move. When the soil fails, life fails. . . . the ancient Chinese knew this; they wrote books about it forty-six centuries ago." For the apostles of the new ideology of soil conservation and restoration, history offered messages, meaning, and mission.[9]

With a vested interest in illuminating the soil crisis, the Soil Conservation Service (SCS) sent an "operative" into the field to discern present and historical lessons regarding human relationships with the soil. Walter C. Lowdermilk, one of the more committed erosion apostles, later described his mission for the USDA. "In 1938," he wrote, "in the interest of a permanent agriculture and of the conservation of our land resources, the Department of Agriculture asked me to make a survey of land use in olden countries, for the benefit of our farmers and stockmen and other agriculturists in this country." Lowdermilk spent the next two years touring Europe, North Africa, and the Middle East. He had also spent a number of years in China observing soil conditions. In his historical-geological observations, Lowdermilk felt that he had literally toured a "graveyard of empires." He was not alone in his perceptions. In his 1936 book, *Rich Land, Poor Land,* Stuart Chase noted that Saint Paul had chastised the city of Antioch for "its pride of wealth and sins," but that Antioch's glory had passed "not from its sins but from the erosion of the Taurus and Lebanon rivers. Protective terraces were neglected, forests were cut off, and the silt and gravel streamed down." Chase, Lowdermilk, and several more authors in the period also cited the history of other civilizations for lessons on the soil. For example, Mayan society had "choked itself to death . . . with mud from its hillside corn patches" in "half a century." North Africa, "once a famous wine region," had fallen victim to "creeping deserts."[10]

China, in particular, served as a wellspring of historical lessons on the soil and human-soil relationships. Lowdermilk and cohort discussed

the long history of soil erosion problems in China, where periods of neglect and the overtaxing of resources had created hills "devastated and
slashed with gullies," exacerbating already rampant seasonal flooding
that in turn created barren wastelands on the sites of once-prosperous
cities, villages, and farms. Yet China, as well as other past and contemporary civilizations also learned from past abuses of the soil and worked
to correct them, thus imparting a positive historical lesson of positive
husbandry. Despite an ongoing struggle with erosion and a burdensome
population problem, over centuries the Chinese developed a culture of
stewardship and a system of land management that emphasized terraces,
dikes, forest preservation, and the use of composts and night soil (human
waste). According to Pearl S. Buck, the Chinese example of stewardship
was said to have emanated from a "sense of belonging to a particular
place on earth." Paul Sears, in a chapter entitled "The Wisdom of the
Ages," expressed an admiration for Chinese agriculture, which in his
view was "almost unique in bringing forth as heavy yields today as it
ever has." Sears cited contoured terracing and the incorporation of
organic material into the soil as the most successful methods of Chinese
soil stewardship.[11]

The histories of other lands and people also provided insight into
proper relationships with the soil and with nature in general. Louis
Bromfield, who was influenced by the simple yet productive husbandry
he had witnessed in France and India, praised "the rule of agriculture in
Denmark, Holland, Belgium and most of France where each acre produced the potential maximum without loss of fertility." Other commentators praised the Japanese as a people that "love the land and hope to
keep it permanently productive." Within the United States, the authors
describing the historical roots of the soil crisis noted that Amish and
Mennonite minorities "generally combined the ancient practice of stewardship with common religious bonds" that produced an "obligation to
the land [that] is fundamentally a matter of faith" and "spiritual fellow-
ship." Even with these positive examples of permanence, however, the
soil historians of the period still viewed disaster as the historical norm in
the soil life of civilizations. G. V. Jacks and R. O. Whyte, in the 1939 work
The Rape of the Earth: A World Survey of Soil Erosion, noted that all too often
"the soil upon which men have attempted to found a new civilization"
has "disappeared, washed away by the water and blown away by the
wind . . . on a scale unparalleled in history."[12]

Certainly, America's brief history offered few positive examples of
proper soil stewardship. In the historical assessment of the roots of the
soil and human crises in the 1930s and 1940s, many participants in this
critique blamed the problem of the soil on a number of recurring American cultural traits, such as expansiveness and acquisitiveness, that led to

exploitation of land and people. Critics of past farming conventions chided excessive individualism while noting additional cultural problems that contributed to the soil crisis, including bad farming habits, poor leadership and training, and misguided scientific and technological endeavors. These critics also attacked what they viewed as an unplanned rush to embrace new tools, despite the rural transformation then under way fostered by a farming regime increasingly characterized by "bigness" and business rather than "balance" and longevity.

In the view of individuals such as Paul Sears and Hugh Bennett, American practices typified a modern yet dysfunctional, soil-destroying agriculture. Bennett, Sears, and others presaged the "New Western History" by four decades by tarnishing the previously heroic record of the pioneers. The pattern of expansion onto and domination of the new soils was not the inspiring, Turnerian epoch of yore; rather, it was a story of arrogance and foolish use of the land. Sears depicted the pioneers as purveyors of a "lustful march . . . across a virgin continent, strewn with ruined forests, polluted streams, gully-laden fields, stained by the breaking of treaties and titanic greed." This American callousness regarding the soil resource, a mixture of ethnocentric and anthropocentric attitudes, eventually resulted in what Bennett called "the fundamental cause of soil erosion—the reckless denudation of the soil, the removal of the integument of vegetation which serves as a protective covering of the earth." Bennett, speaking to fellow conservationists in 1935, stated that "the time has come . . . when we must make concessions to nature. The kingdom of Nature is not a democracy; we cannot repeal natural laws when they become irksome. We have got to learn to conform to these laws or suffer severer consequences than we have already brought upon ourselves." Noting that "any successful program of erosion control must provide the means of making production compatible with protection," Bennett was one of many Americans who concluded that the crux of the soil problem was the desire to dominate nature for production and profit, regardless of the cost to the topsoil, which he considered "the true basis of wealth."[13]

The soil jeremiads of the 1930s and 1940s criticized the American preoccupation with short-term profits and prideful domination of nature. Promoters of the concept of a soil crisis tried to persuade their fellow citizens that "ours is a record of heedless land abuse and needless exploitation seldom, perhaps never equaled in the history of civilization." But why had this pattern of abuse become so engraved in the American farming character? According to Bennett, the chief soil prophet, "unconcern for the land had its root . . . in a national illusion of abundance. White men found America a continent more lush and fertile than they had dared imagine. For a century they pushed the frontier westward, and always found virgin land." Yet "gradually," according to Bennett, "a national land philosophy evolved. It was a philosophy of exploitation . . . a philosophy that permitted a man, in good conscience, to destroy his land and move onward to new and fertile fields."[14]

Organic farming advocate Louis Bromfield likened the westward expansion to "a plague of locusts," which "moved across the continent leaving behind here and there men who found the soil so deep and the mining so inexhaustible that there was no necessity for migration." For Bromfield, technological ingenuity and the immensity of America's soil resource implanted the notion that "man is the lord of creation—that he dominates the earth." The tremendously accelerated rate of soil erosion apparent in the 1930s was, the critics said, "due to primarily one factor— human interference." Although a major reevaluation of technology would not appear until after World War II, even prior to the war the proponents of soil stewardship had begun to see technology as a nefarious force.[15]

Several films echoed this theme of heavy-handed human technology and human error in the onset of the soil crisis. Government-produced films such as Pare Lorentz's *The River* and *The Plow That Broke the Plains*, both of which appeared in the late 1930s, presented examples of how human folly was linked to the soil crisis. In *The Plow That Broke the Plains*, the "great plow-up" of World War I and thereafter was especially damning, as was the advent of power farming and tractors, which were symbolized as mighty tanks conducting an attack on the unbroken sod. In Robert Flaherty's film *The Land* (1941), a view of gullies in Stewart County, Georgia, highlighted the theme of mismanaged technology. The accompanying sound track lamented: "This was a beautiful farm once on a land of marvelous vigor. Soil that it took weather fifty centuries to make—gone now, gone, in a century or less."[16]

Cultural traits, critics thought, both led to and resulted from bad farming practices. Mistaken farming practices included the improper use of science and technology, poor cropping patterns (monocultures), and a lack of terracing, cover crops, and other conservation methods. Technology, labeled a "seductive force," had brought increased yields and cheaper labor costs, but the horizontal expansion of farming also disrupted rural life and the health of the soil.

For agricultural critic and organic farming advocate Edward Faulkner, American farming suffered needlessly from the improper use of technology. For example, Faulkner criticized the use of the moldboard plow as an instrument of soil preparation and advised farmers that their plows were heavyhanded instruments operating in an intricate web of life. Moldboard plows, while historically necessary for breaking the prairies, were, in Faulkner's opinion, destroying capillary connections and burying organic mass that would have been better left as soil cover or integrated into the topsoil as green manure, via the disc plow. Faulkner also lambasted the effect of tile drainage on land and waters and questioned the use of "artificials"—manufactured fertilizers, herbicides, pesticides, and insecticides then being introduced on a massive scale in American farming.

Faulkner thought that a "machine mentality" in American agriculture was central in the crisis of the soil. He wrote, "The easy money to be made in the world food and cotton trade dictated the universal use of machines in farming. So long as the land remained naturally productive, machine farming gave us still further advantages in trade." Rather than build their soil for long-term production, American farmers, judged Faulkner and his supporters, sought to increase production by expanding the number of acres they could "mine," often losing their neighbors and their topsoil in the process. Bromfield wrote that "one of the most striking evidences of the poverty and inefficiency of our agriculture has been the almost universal tendency of our farmers to expand horizontally rather than vertically when they seek to expand production." For Faulkner, the history of American agriculture sounded "a continuous series of disappointments." Sadly, Americans never "remained to solve the problems of the area [farming] has worn out." Instead, wrote Faulkner, "they sold out, or left the land to its successors and moved on to richer fields."[17]

For Bromfield, bad farming was the product of bad farmers. He thought "a great many of them actually hate the soil which they work, the very soil which, if treated properly, could make them prosperous and proud and dignified and happy men." From his perspective in the early to mid-1940s, Bromfield estimated that "not 10 per cent of our agricultural population today could seriously be called good farmers." Yet they stayed on the soil because, in his opinion, "they never had the gumption to get off it." The oft-rankled writer charged that "the philosophy that anybody can farm has cost us billions of dollars of taxes, in high prices, and the destruction of the soil which is the fundamental and ultimate basis of wealth of every nation." Again, history had revealed a strong message to the erosion apostles; bad farming arose from an unsound culture that featured an arrogant attitude toward nature and an unquestioning posture regarding technological change.[18]

CRITIQUES OF THE ESTABLISHMENT

As major leaders in agricultural theory and technological information, the USDA and the nation's land-grant colleges found themselves the subject of strident criticism. "Distributist" agrarian Ralph Borsodi, in his typically bombastic style, put the land-grant colleges and the USDA on "trial" in a 1945 essay entitled "The Case Against Farming as a Big Business." Borsodi wrote: "I accuse them of teaching the rape of the earth and the destruction of our priceless heritage of land, of impoverishing our rural communities, wiping out our rural schools, closing our rural churches, destroying our rural culture, and depopulating the countryside upon which all these depend." For Borsodi and fellow travelers, the USDA and the land-grant colleges (and by implication their supporters in agriculture-related industries and the American Farm Bureau Federation) fostered "big farming" by promoting capital-intensive scientific and technological innovations without regard for their impact on rural people or the ecology of the land. Professors of agriculture and agricultural researchers, so went the argument, had lost their connections to the soil and to their constituents, the farmers. Borsodi and Bromfield saw many other ominous offshoots of the allegedly misguided leadership of the USDA and the agricultural colleges, including excessive devotion to cash-crop monoculture and the perceivably urbanized, acquisitive culture that allegedly profited from a "colonial" relationship with the soil and rural people. Charles E. Kellogg, a soil scientist whose views often supported the concept of permanent agriculture, later remarked to his colleagues that prior to the early 1940s, the vast changes in agriculture resulting from science and technology had led to confusion and duplication in research.[19]

Bromfield led the way in his trenchant critique of the USDA/land-grant record. After arguing with his farm manager for a diversified farm as opposed to a monoculture-commercial operation based on corn raising, he sent the young man away with the chastisement "I can't really blame you, I suppose, for those half-baked ideas. . . . Where'd you go? Ohio State?" Bromfield opined, "I've seen quite alot—a hell of a lot more than any of your autocratic college professors. . . . what they know about economics you can put into a USDA pamphlet and chuck it in the waste basket." He led the assault against the agricultural "establishment," stating that "the whole commercial fertilizer theory represented both the ignorance and arrogance of limited or greedy men, manufacturers, farmers, and professors, who are perpetually seeking a short-cut or a means of outwitting nature and the laws of physics, of chemistry, and even economics." A story in *Science News Letter* in July 1943 depicted Bromfield as "deploring" the "factory methods" validated by the USDA, the land-grant schools, and other proponents of "business" farming. "Especially pernicious," according to the article, was the danger monoculture cropping posed to the soil. Hugh Bennett also castigated the decline of crop rotation and diversified farming when he stated that "planting an entire region to a single cash crop is usually as precarious to soil resources as to economic welfare." Bad policy decisions also added weight to the tiresome American soil legacy. As Henry A. Wallace pointed out, "We have permitted our livestock men of the West to overgraze the public domain and so expose it to wind and water erosion. Much of the grassland of the Great Plains has been plowed, exposed and allowed to blow away."[20]

As Morris L. Cooke summarized the soil history lesson, "The pioneer was the first villain. For the sake of his own generation he sacrificed the future. He leveled forests, mined the soil, impoverished resources. Water engineering on false principles helped carry the process farther." Yet these depredations had caught up with a nation that was no longer an immature country. Americans had dominated the continent agriculturally, but Cooke suggested "this 'conquest' of nature is . . . a short-lived one. Man, in truth, does not conquer nature. At best, he has the privilege of cooperating on terms and conditions set by nature." History presented many clear messages and warnings about the soil and societal permanence to the erosion apostles, yet the contemporary preoccupation with assessing blame for the soil and human crises also served as a starting point for planning a permanent agriculture.[21]

If history offered lessons, it also was useful in guiding future conduct, and the critics of past husbandry always offered a scenario of salvation at the end of their soil jeremiads. Two essential messages emanated from these scripts. The first expressed the need to recognize the interdependent reality of the modern world that meant agriculture must be viewed as part of an interconnected set of components. The erosion apostles also called for a society based on permanence as opposed to the past conditions that inculcated a short-term, exploitative, and unplanned land management system. The call for interdependence and permanence also led to the articulation of a new type of farming based on the principles of planned ecological harmony, a system that by 1940 became known as *permanent agriculture*.

THE CALL FOR INTERDEPENDENCE AND PERMANENCE

The soil apostles reasoned that if the soil crisis was a human crisis, then with enough knowledge, Americans could adopt a more thoughtful attitude toward the land. A crucial element in provoking a new soil mentality was the need for Americans to recognize the pervasive interconnections of their rapidly changing world. After World War I, Americans began to reconceptualize how their society operated. Historians Alan Marcus and Howard Segal argue that a new conceptualization of systems was "predicated on a much more complex relationship among the parts. Each part seemed to acquire a share of its definition from interrelationships with other parts of the system." Agriculture was certainly not immune to this new understanding of systems. The authors who wrote about the soil crisis sought to establish multidimensional solutions, for it was a crisis with many roots and one whose solutions would come from many seemingly disconnected sources.[22]

While "interrelations" between agriculture and other endeavors had long been recognized, the concept of "interdependence" enjoyed virtual cult status from the 1920s throughout the 1940s. Henry A. Wallace proclaimed a "declaration of interdependence" in 1934, and the emerging science of ecology validated this approach by studying "the interrelationships between life forms and their environments." In the developing ideology of the "permanent agriculture" phase of the history of ecological agriculture, interdependence was fundamental to understanding the social and biological dimensions of the soil crisis.[23]

On the social plane, the concept of interdependence helped Americans at all levels of society become more cognizant of the vast dimensions of the soil crisis. Hugh Bennett constantly invoked the theme of interdependence throughout the 1930s and 1940s. In speeches, in pamphlets, and on radio programs, he asked Americans to observe the omnipresent linkages in society. "The ability to support and produce, plentifully, made America great," claimed Bennett. "It must be sustained if America is to stay great." He told his audience that this greatness could be sustained only if "the fountain of production—the soil—is guarded and preserved." Bennett thought that "the problem is by no means solely agricultural, it effects the urbanite as surely as it effects the farmer. Its solution is of as much importance to the industrialist as to the agriculturist. It is of vital concern to all America, because all America must have food and clothing taken from the soil." Thirteen years later (1948), Bennett still preached the gospel of interdependence, claiming that "every man, woman and child throughout the country depends on productive land for virtually all their food, as well as a large part of their clothing and all their wood, leather and many other necessities." Similarly, Paul Sears warned against repeating the mistakes of the past: "Scholars (and here I include scientists) may themselves, through preoccupation with a particular segment of a problem, fail to see the whole."[24]

For Bennett, Sears, and company, the methods for solving the soil crisis arose from the condition of interdependence and ran "the gamut of agronomy, biology, engineering, forestry and geology," to imply "the maximum possible restoration of vegetative cover—nature's own method of soil stabilization, and the only one that affords any true permanence." Again, the permanent agriculture cohort perceived the soil crisis as a human crisis with human causes, primarily the human disruption of nature's process of "self-stewardship." To correct past abuses and halt the soil crisis, those proposing "holistic" plans had to show the citizenry that it lived under the reign of biological, as well as social, interdependence. Although it mentioned the word *ecology* only once, the founding manifesto of the conservation organization Friends of the Land (1940) is a particularly telling example of the ideology of biological interdependence. It reads in part:

> Any land is all of one body. If one part is skinned, bared to the beat of the weather, wounded, not only the winds spread the trouble, dramatically, but the surface veins and arteries of the nation, its streams and rivers, bear ill. Soiled water depletes soil, exhausts underground and surface water supplies, raises flood levels, dispossesses shore and upland birds and animals from the accustomed haunts; chokes game-fish, diminishes shoreline seafood, clogs harbors, and stops with grit and boulders the purr of dynamos. . . . We too, are all of one body. We all live on, or from, the soil.[25]

The new concept of biological interdependence represented the beginnings of a shift away from the old values of the Teddy Roosevelt–Gifford Pinchot conservation era, with its purely utilitarian and anthropocentric emphasis on the "wise" and efficient management of resources for human use, toward a new era of seeing life as a vast web of interconnections, with human beings simply one of many delicate strands. This recognition of biological interdependence was in many ways an ethical reawakening. Stuart Chase elaborated on this new way of thinking, telling his readers, "We are creatures of this earth, and so are part of all our prairies, mountains, rivers, and clouds. Unless we feel this . . . we may know all the calculus and all the Talmud, but have not learned the first lesson of living on this earth." Science could assist humanity, wrote Chase, "only if it recognizes basic realities and the unified order of enduring life." Fairfield Osborn added an ethical imperative to the message of Chase and others, cautioning, "There would seem to be no real hope for the future unless we are prepared to accept the concept that man, like all living things, is part of one great biological scheme." Clearly, the new attitude regarding human interactions with nature revered the complex relationships of soil and water, the fundamental supporters of human and nonhuman life.[26]

Although humanity formed part of an interdependent world and "great biological scheme," in the final sum the soil crisis was a human crisis. Concern for other species of life emerged in the permanent agriculture movement, but human concerns remained the focus. Still, looking to history and the call to interdependence fostered a broader definition of stewardship, as well as a call for societal permanence. "The human race can destroy itself on this planet," wrote Chester C. Davis, "unless we can meet and solve some of the problems that confront us. The one is, can man master and control the industrial machine he has created? The other is, can man so organize his activities on the land that he can hand on to future generations a heritage, a resource not only unimpaired but increasing in groundline productivity?" J. E. Noll, a farmer and conservationist from Missouri, continued in the vein of luminaries such as Chase and Davis, telling readers of their periodical, the *Land*: "We are not going to be here long as individuals. We have to see that the support of future generations is guaranteed."[27]

The call for permanence not only expressed a demand for new soil conservation techniques but also involved a societal makeover along lines envisioned by the legendary social critic Lewis Mumford. Antagonistic toward the pallor, squalor, and uncertainty of the industrial-urban "megamachine," Mumford asked his contemporaries to "visualize a new framework of farms and villages and cities and regions, which will make industrial organization subordinate to the demands of nurture and education and living." For Mumford, the complexities of modern society demanded a new way of social organization, based on a "systematic spiritual culture, a body of common ideas that will make social cooperation possible once more throughout civilization." Mumford's voice was one among many in the period, all calling for a new epoch of planning, cooperation, and rural-urban/agricultural-industrial balance.[28]

Ideas for permanent agriculture included "the essential qualities of balance, order and reserve," with goals such as "opportunities and security, a better way of life." Rexford G. Tugwell, a New Deal brain truster, noted the sources of this new ethical imperative for permanence—a soil crisis and a human crisis, as well the new recognition of interdependence and the need to plan for the future. Tugwell wrote: "The shock of the depression has at last awakened us to a new attitude. We no longer regard land as land alone; we regard it as one of the central and controlling elements in our whole national economy. The recovery program brings us finally face to face with devising a plan which shall draw together our divergent efforts and look forward as far as possible toward permanent policy." Tugwell was at the center of a growing group of individuals from many walks of life who were convinced that disaster was imminent yet avoidable. Their sentiment expressed the notion that "soil is a natural heritage. As such it should be safeguarded by the government. A good citizen regards himself not as an absolute owner of the soil but rather a manager set in charge of using it wisely. His duty is one of passing on to succeeding managers a soil which is as good as, or better than, when he found it."[29]

While Bennett, Davis, and Tugwell had personal, professional, and bureaucratic interests in publicizing the soil crisis, the fact is that a crisis existed outside of Washington, D.C., and New York City, and it was not merely a creation of power-mongering social planners. Indeed, a number of people outside of New Deal social planning circles also saw the potential threat of an eroded and destabilized soil. Solving the riddle of a poor economy or defeating overseas enemies would mean little if America lost its vital force, the topsoil, fundamental to the health and life of the nation. Walter Lowdermilk invoked the missionary zeal needed to build a permanent, ecological agriculture. Noting the crucial nature of stabilizing soil and water resources, he called for an "11th Commandment," which would read: "If any shall fail on this stewardship of the land thy fruitful fields shall become sterile stony ground and wasting gullies, and thy descendants shall decrease and live in poverty or perish from the face of the earth." Clearly the time had come for a civilization based on an enduring husbandry, a "permanent agriculture" that promised to save humanity from the long night of crisis.[30]

The dust bowl phenomenon of the 1930s, with its attendant human misery and dislocation on the Great Plains, gave intellectual leaders pause. Hugh Bennett explained the need to bring about a plan of action regarding the soil. "Past negligence is water over the dam," he stated. "The important thing is that we have finally come to a cognizance of the problem of erosion, and an understanding of the physical land crisis so definitely at hand. . . . Out of that understanding the forces which will shape a new era of land conservation are arising." Bennett was one of many soil conservationists calling for surveys and land use studies, multidisciplinary research, and coordinated planning between farmers, federal officials, and academic investigators.[31]

Henry A. Wallace, Rex Tugwell, Hugh Bennett, Ralph Borsodi, and others perceived connections between the physical farm and the human condition. They urged Americans to recognize the interdependent nature of their world and implored them to take steps beyond merely discussing the idea of societal permanence. Permanent agriculture, they argued, demanded an entire cultural makeover, not simply new techniques on the farmstead.

A PLANNED AND PERMANENT AGRICULTURE

Overcoming a national heritage of antagonism to planning was a major difficulty for Hugh Bennett and other reformers. Their loosely assembled ideology for a permanent agriculture based on ecological principles required a shift in American attitudes toward planning and cooperation. In the intellectual and institutional preparation for permanent agriculture, the authors of the concept rejected excessive individualism and the decay and squalor inherent in what they viewed as the unplanned, unbalanced, and undemocratic economy of their time.

Although the planning idea was not new to American society, the supporters of the permanent agriculture movement overcame several cultural, political, and economic barriers to planning. New Deal relief and recovery programs provided initial opportunities for the permanent agriculture movement to advance its agenda. Legislation and agencies such as the Agricultural Adjustment Administration (1933) and the Soil Conservation Service (1935) helped institutionalize government intervention in the marketplace and support for soil conservation programs. Other New Deal programs, such as those in the Resettlement Administration (RA), supported the notion of planning for a permanent agriculture. These programs, including the Subsistence Homesteads Division, arose partly from appeals for a better balance between agricultural and industrial, and between rural and urban worlds.

Building upon the urgency created by the soil and human crises and an ascendant planning ethic, the authors of the permanent agriculture idea honed their concept during the early years of the New Deal era, both within and outside of governmental circles. Although aggressive programs promoting prototypes of planned and permanent agriculture emerged in the USDA during the 1930s, organized agriculture and individual farmers still displayed a hostility toward what they saw as the heavily bureaucratic and centralized New Deal agriculture program. Farm groups, especially the Farm Bureau, successfully promoted less rigorous programs to fight the soil and human crises, as well as decentralized decision making in conservation plans and other agricultural programs. While the New Deal conservation and stabilization programs helped a crippled agriculture survive until the rejuvenating days of World War II, the permanent agriculture program lingered as a diffused ideology that gradually developed a guiding force—ecology—and an effective communications strategy to promote itself.

Throughout the life of the permanent agriculture concept, from its initial stages in the 1920s through its relative decline in the early 1950s, one individual's efforts characterized these first stages of ecological agriculture. A central figure of the permanent agriculture movement, Rexford Tugwell had an exceptional ability to grasp and synthesize ideas and communicate new concepts to political allies and the larger public, but he often was criticized as arrogant, radical, and communistic for his role as a New Dealer. His voice resonated above the chorus hailing a planned and permanent agriculture. Tugwell echoed what many of his contemporaries, both famous and unknown, were discussing. His ability to stir up controversy, his willingness to champion and implement the planning idea, and his national audience made him an important voice in a movement that included luminous figures such as Aldo Leopold, Hugh Bennett, Paul Sears, and Louis Bromfield.

Tugwell is one of the most notable and least understood of the "personalities" in the New Deal. His career placed him at the center of the soil and human crises in the period. Prior to his life as an FDR brain truster, Tugwell had been a controversial economics professor at Columbia University, influenced in part by the social activism of his former professor, exiled academic Scott Nearing. Tugwell served as the highly influential and controversial assistant secretary and then under secretary of agriculture at the USDA from 1933 to 1939, and in 1941 (after a brief tenure as a city planner in New York City) he began a four-year stint as governor of Puerto Rico, where he focused on soil erosion problems. He also taught during the postwar years and continued to expound on the concept of ecology at the University of Chicago in the 1950s.[32]

From his days at Columbia University in the 1920s through his halcyon years in the New Deal, Tugwell preached a gospel of planning, cooperation, and societal permanence laced with increasing portions of interdependence and ecological ideas. Tugwell scorned a society operating for the benefit of self-serving, shortsighted "plutocrats" whose pursuit of individual interest drained the nation of its ability to provide comfort and sustenance for all its members. He chastised the prevalent American "belief in rugged individualism," which in his view led to "the conclusion that society is best served by the pursuit of individual interests in production." Tugwell argued that ominous results would follow continued individualism in agriculture. To convey this thought, he created a fictional English traveler in the year 2135. Having crossed a nearly dry Mississippi River, this future Tocqueville approached the once-mighty Missouri River, where he recalled "there was once a considerable city [presumably Kansas City] and that this was a country devoted to the cultivation of grain." The traveler noted that the grain belt farms were "now only moving piles of dust for a least a thousand miles. Of the city little remains except some skeletons of twisted steel."[33]

Tugwell joined others in agriculture who were calling for planning and permanence from World War I onward, many of whom were associated with the land-grant colleges and the USDA. Planning in this pre–New Deal period focused on ways to promote "a better rural life" through improved management, collective action, and governmental intervention. Price supports for wheat during World War I, the establishment of statistical services in the Bureau of Agricultural Economics, and the Federal Farm Board exemplify these efforts.

Even though a soil problem had emerged along with other agricultural concerns prior to the New Deal, Americans content in the growing urban-oriented mass-consumer economy were criticized by the permanent agriculture group for having neglected the need for planning throughout the 1920s. Tugwell and Harry Carman, writing for an educated audience in 1938, elaborated on the continued pressing need for a planned, balanced economy when they wrote: "We do not know what a permanent agriculture is, to say nothing of ways to insure it. While the shadow of industry lengthened from east to west, a decline of interest in country things has taken place. The center of our attention was the city. We were learning to build and govern it, to manage its economic affairs, to enjoy its pleasures." Tugwell indicated to his fellow citizens that because of this urban focus, "We are beginning to pay, in the 1930s, for seventy-five years of agricultural neglect. . . . Farmers are unwise because they have supposed their status to be permanent; the rest of us are unwise because we have lost any sense of intimacy with the rich arts of agriculture."[34]

Obviously, for Tugwell and other planned agriculture advocates, organization and cooperation provided necessary elements in attacking individualism and embracing permanence. Tugwell harped against what he labeled the "moralists who created an individualistic ethic" for their "identification of capitalism with democracy." For him, freedom and democracy entailed responsibility to society and to nonhuman life, not simply a right to make profits. "If the race is to survive with freedom," he wrote, "it must have a majority of men who will choose ways which will lead to survival," and not pass decisions to the few who traditionally had been "allowed to dominate policy." Again, the planning idea was more than a set of techniques; it was a new ethic. Tugwell's call for planned permanence recognized that "man is earthbound, soilbound, seabound, but no longer in any simple ways which any individual may determine for himself. He has got to live with others in a very social world. It is time he learned to do it and make a virtue of his learning." Indeed, Tugwell's call for a new stewardship seems prescient. A decade later Aldo Leopold published his writings, illuminating his famous "land ethic." Speaking to graduating seniors at the University of New Mexico in 1935, Tugwell set this theme, saying, "Now if ever your generation is required to assume the full stature of Americans, regard not only your rootedness but also the sun, the air, the water, and the soil of your environment as your sphere of interest." He also told the young graduates, "You can have a system of institutions which is as modern as the concrete and steel of our architecture, as flexible and efficient as the science of factory management, and they can be turned to the uses of liberty, democracy and good living which are the canons of our tradition. But you cannot have these things by default, you will have to create them, . . . protect and nurse them, and perhaps recreate them as conditions change again and again."[35]

Tugwell portrayed "speculative competition" as the "sickness of our system" that opposed planning. Yet planning, he thought, had to disengage from both a blind faith in profit and a fear of dictatorial control. He suggested that "measuring prosperity by profits" was a poor economic indicator, feeling instead that "we ought to measure it by our people's living standards. Then we could find a way to permanent prosperity." In other words, permanent and planned agriculture required a fresh definition of "efficient" farming. According to the noted contemporary agricultural economist Sherman E. Johnson, "For the individual that does not necessarily mean the highest profitable combination of land, labor and equipment it would be possible to devise. Nor does it necessarily mean maintenance of land and buildings at a high standard of physical productivity, nor following the best-known technical production practices. It means rather the estimating of the highest possible in a given situation and a balancing of present and future incomes." Johnson went on to say: "In the public interest it may be desirable to prevent soil depletion which results in the extreme need for present income by individual operators. The group as a whole is better able to strike a balance in favor of future income than is an individual."[36]

For USDA economist Bushrod Allin, farmers and other citizens required assurances "not only that planning is compatible with democracy, but that democracy cannot be preserved without planning." Although critics railed against the allegedly heavy-handed programs of the New Deal, for the most part the plans for permanent agriculture consciously sought to balance the rights of individuals against the duty of society to effect a program of permanence. To adhere to humane and democratic principles, the land program tried to develop "an economic policy in line with physical necessities. As such, the method appropriate for dealing with it must include economic and social techniques which provide adequate inducements for or remove existing handicaps to the adoption of proper physical techniques." In 1936, this included professional land management, government purchase of marginal land, and a dedication to nondictatorial planning that still conceded an increased interventionist power to the federal government in agriculture.[37]

Henry A. Wallace and other agrarian scientist-philosophers hoped that a planned and permanent agriculture would rise from a multidimensional understanding of the soil problem. In a memo to Hugh Bennett in 1935, Wallace cautioned his subordinate that in order to be "effective, permanent and economically feasible," the plan to end the soil crisis would involve "more than the use of vegetative and engineering methods," including general land use planning, proper crop rotations, and "the application of other sound farm management practices." Hence, for the secretary of agriculture, "every branch of the Department is concerned, should be called on, and should cooperate at all times in shaping and carrying forward a practicable program."[38]

Clearly, the concept of a planned and permanent agriculture infected the top level of national leadership in the 1930s. In a 1937 address, Franklin Roosevelt, who liked to call himself a farmer, asked Congress to sponsor a "prudent husbandry." "Nature has given us recurrent and poignant warnings through dust storms, floods, and droughts," stated the president, "that we must act while there is yet time if we would preserve ourselves and our posterity the natural resources of a virile nation." Morris L. Cooke, an engineer, planner, and social reformer, added weight to FDR's challenge to create planned permanence. In a 1938 article titled "Is the United States a Permanent Country?" Cooke told readers that "unless there is a marked change in our present agricultural methods, we have, as a virile nation, perhaps less than 100 years to go. The United States is not a permanent country unless we make it so." Cooke and others suggested that the permanent agriculture program should be "wisely and vigorously applied, not merely talked about." The alternative seemed a future where "we may wake up some bleak dawn to find ourselves indeed a poor nation, our chances for abundance vanished or seriously impaired."[39]

In the 1930s, schemes for a planned and permanent agriculture evolved with varying degrees of success. New Deal programs, such as the Soil Conservation Service and the Resettlement Administration, offered ambitious but essentially piecemeal attempts using the ideas of permanent agriculture. Additionally, critics outside of government offered ideas on what would bring a new and enduring husbandry. Eventually these efforts merged with the more cohesive guiding ideas of ecology, yet the 1930s attempts at permanent agriculture did attract a newfound reception in all quarters regarding planning for permanence and abundance. Nonetheless, concerns over commodity prices, worries about centralized control by Washington bureaucrats, and a lingering devotion to individualism all worked against the permanent agriculture program. That resistance, however, set the stage for a greater incorporation of holistic ecological thought into the permanent agriculture camp.

PERMANENT AGRICULTURE

Apparently, the term *permanent agriculture* was coined by University of Illinois agronomist Cyril G. Hopkins around the year 1868. Hopkins's views on soil fertility were quite different from those presented by advocates of ecological agriculture in the 1930s. The idea of planned and permanent farming practices grew from its embryonic stages with the onset of the soil and human crises in the 1930s. Proposals for agricultural permanence, championed by individuals from diverse political persuasions, emerged prior to the far-reaching agricultural legislation of the New Deal. The first specific plans for permanent agriculture emerged in the late 1920s and continued to escalate in scope and complexity through the 1940s. Critics of past practice and policy from outside of government were among the first to offer a platform for the new husbandry.[40]

"Distributist" agrarian-intellectual Ralph Borsodi helped foster an agricultural ideal linked to the Back-to-the Land Movement of the 1920s and early 1930s. Despising the city and the mass culture that it appeared to produce, the Borsodi clique favored a decentralized, subsistence agriculture antagonistic to capital, capitalism, science, and technology as they then existed. Borsodi agrarianism was eventually joined with the rhetorical impulses of other groups such as the fabled Nashville Agrarians (or Twelve Southerners), who enjoyed brief notoriety in the early 1930s. These fundamentally conservative agrarians called for an attack on "irresponsible" agriculture through such measures as stiff inheritance taxes (except for inheritors who passed successful husbandry reviews from a "soil court"); a ban on mortgage foreclosures that failed to pass a "court of equity"; rights of escheat (forfeiture of land to the state); a ban on "speculative" land purchases and land sales to real estate firms, insurance firms, or banks; fines for not halting erosion; and a denial of credit to noncooperating farmers. Much in the vein of Henry Ford's Village Industries concept, Nashville Agrarian Frank Owsley believed that society had to be balanced between agriculture and industry if America's farms were to continue feeding and clothing the nation. Owsley called for "a modified form of feudal tenure where, in theory, the King or state has a permanent interest in the land." Significantly, the state would incorporate an interventionist role in the quest for permanent agriculture. The program of Owsley and cohort called for the creation of stronger regional governments, based on geographic and economic parameters, that had the power to impose land policy on states, counties, and localities. These methods would lead to the creation of an enduring society. Agrarians like Owsley based their program on their own assumptions of agrarian life. Owsley idealized the advent of a society where "art, music and literature could emerge into the sunlight from the dark, cramped holes where industrial insecurity and industrial insensitiveness have driven them."[41]

While people outside the government promoted state intervention to preserve the soil and promote rural life, New Dealers also fostered the rise of permanent agriculture. While the initial focus of Roosevelt's USDA was to cut agricultural surplus and alleviate the general crisis of the depression, the concept of a soil crisis and a permanent agriculture also animated the New Deal agenda. Rexford Tugwell's theories epitomized a shift away from simple issues of prices and allotments toward a comprehensive land program geared for permanence. Speaking to a group of economists and statisticians in 1933, Tugwell said that the federal government would "perform two functions with respect to our land in the future. It will directly hold and administer, as public forests, game preserves, grazing ranges, recreation centers and the like, . . . and it will control the private use of the areas held by individuals to whatever extent it is found necessary for maintaining continuous productivity." Tugwell sought to legitimize his stand for federal interventionism, stating, "It is only by conceiving the government in this double active and supervisory role that we can expect to attain a permanent system of agriculture. . . . past developments . . . have demonstrated the ineffectiveness of a land system which depends on private management."[42]

During the early to mid-1930s, the idea of planned permanence seemed ascendant. The sense of crisis had stripped down old barriers to governmental invention in the nation's economic life. Tugwell indicated that "the shock of the depression has at last awakened us to a new attitude . . . the necessity for devising a plan which shall draw together our divergent efforts and look forward as far as is possible toward a permanent policy." Tugwell finally positioned himself to implement ideas he had advocated as far back as the 1920s. While acknowledging the immediate need to correct the surplus and provide rural relief, his ideas went far beyond manipulation of production and markets. For Tugwell, agriculture had to be profitable without being attached to monoculture and cash crop farming, which the erosion apostles thought caused both market imbalance and soil depletion. Tugwell lamented monocultures of corn, cotton, and wheat that facilitated tenancy, which he equated with modern serfdom. He called for a withdrawal of public lands from public entry (still in place from the 1862 Homestead Act), prevention of the "familiar abuse" of overgrazing on public lands, and "careful investigation and planning" for the retirement of "submarginal" lands in three select regions—Appalachia, the Michigan to Minnesota "cutoff" area, and the Great Plains. Tugwell's outline of permanent agriculture called for a devotion to cooperative planning and the employment of scientific expertise to attack the problems of farming and farm life. While he saw no quick or simple solutions, Tugwell envisioned a system of rural-urban balance, arising from new, smaller-scale manufacturing technologies and better transportation, and predicated on semiagricultural "rurban" villages where part-time employment in industry or forestry would be supplemented by five-acre family subsistence plots. He fiercely advocated highly effective soil conservation and a switch in land use from regional monocultures to regionally designated tree, fruit, or grassland agriculture.[43]

As an intellectual voice, Tugwell formed part of a faction in the Roosevelt administration that believed the time had come for permanent agriculture. Academics such as Howard Tolley and M. L. Wilson supported the idea. In 1934, Tolley considered it "imperative that we think ahead of the present stage of agricultural reorganization and set up a permanent land program." Wilson suggested that restoration of the soil presented "the opportunity for expressing our best instincts" and "the key for better standards of rural living." Higher-ranking supporters of planned permanence included Secretary of Agriculture (later Vice President) Henry A. Wallace and President Roosevelt himself. In 1934, Wallace wrote in *New Frontiers* that "we should outline a [land] policy to continue over many administrations, and stick to it for the sake of our children and their grandchildren." For Wallace, the alternative to interventionist land policies was to "maim and misuse our heritage." By 1937, he reported to his boss that "our government is engaged in a vast land use program looking toward wise husbandry of our land resources, both public and private."[44]

Generally speaking, the New Deal's vast, oft-changing, and sometimes paradoxical plans for agriculture offered short-term relief in terms of price supports or production allotment programs, midrange plans for recovery, including increasing the amount of credit available to farmers, and long-term reform ideas such as soil conservation or the "ever-normal granary" that sought to stabilize agricultural communities. Many New Deal programs were associated with the concept of planning for permanence. It is revealing to note how major supporters of permanent agriculture, including Bennett and Tugwell, presented and employed their ideas once they attained greater status and power as World War II approached.

Under Bennett's leadership, the Soil Conservation Service plan eventually coalesced into the watershed approach, a "coordinated plan of correct land use" that sought to juggle the rule of experts, local decision making, and nationally mandated soil conservation policy. This general approach often was linked to other USDA price programs, such as the Soil Conservation and Domestic Allotment Act of 1936. Despite difficulties, the SCS program for restoring the soil was farsighted and effective. It called for cooperation between farmers, the SCS, and the land-grant colleges that would provide the knowledge for creating "new farm operations." The program included retirement of erosion-prone soils from production and the use of conservation measures such as reforestation; replanting cropland to grass; using grass strips between crop rows, cover crops, basin listing, and contour furrowing; building ponds and terraces; and improving crop rotations. Although the SCS by no means perfected its efforts, its employees displayed zeal and expertise as they helped save the soil. The leader of the SCS, Hugh Bennett, used the issue of soil conservation to attain a national audience for his views on permanent agriculture. [45]

Rexford Tugwell also implemented many concepts for planned permanence during his days at the USDA. Most notably, his leadership of the

Resettlement Administration represented the opportunities as well as the limitations of the "planned permanence" idea during its formative years. The RA sought to buy out, relocate, and retrain rural people who lived on land deemed submarginal. Behind the resettlement idea was the notion that the soil crisis and the human crisis could be countered through education, planning, and creating an ideal rural-urban balance. The RA's Subsistence Homesteads Division (transferred from the Department of the Interior) supported the construction of model communities based in part on the ideas of individuals like Ralph Borsodi, who eventually participated in one of the RA projects. The RA also sponsored the fabled Greenbelt Cities program, another attempt at achieving rural-urban and economic-ecological balance. Although a crucial chapter in the early quest for implementing the permanent agriculture idea, the radical social reform aspects of the New Deal were far less successful than the more tangible progress of more "practical" programs, including the Tennessee Valley Authority and the Rural Electrification Administration. The RA sometimes worked at odds with other policies intended to remove marginal farmers from the land, and it suffered from a lack of support by labor, which felt threatened by the idea of a dispersed labor force. Tugwell felt that the RA lacked money and congressional support and suffered from its "experimental" status, opposition from the press and the American Farm Bureau Federation, falling public interest in conservation issues, and the general reign of "sentimentalism" and "prejudice" in the rural community.[46]

Clearly, the bolder social reform programs of the New Deal were not as successful in implementing ideas of permanent agriculture as were the more practical programs of the SCS. The SCS drifted away from a focus on planning and permanence because of calls for decentralized control of the decision-making process that reflected a challenge from the farm states to the perceived heavy hand of Washington's bureaucracy. The SCS attack on the soil crisis also suffered from the oft-changing farm program, the vagaries of a market influenced by overseas affairs, problems related to "local variations in physical and economic conditions," difficulties in coordinating federal, state, and local officials, and lack of communication between the SCS and the land-grant schools. The SCS program also sustained damage because its rapid implementation offended many, and because the prodigious scale of the soil problem defied politically timely solutions.

Although planning and permanence were given an effective trial during the early New Deal, the soil crisis lingered. Thus, Morris Cooke was forced to tell President Roosevelt in 1937 that, though "more has been done in the last three years to curb accelerated runoff and erosion than in all previous history," the "damage is undoubtedly spreading faster than control measures are being applied." Cooke asked the president to approve a plan that would hit problem areas within fifteen years and complete a total soil restoration of the country within forty years. Obviously, the concept of a permanent agriculture was not radically reshaping American farming, despite successes in the soil conservation program. Still, the evolution of permanent agriculture in the 1930s helped bring some changes in the theory, practice and policy of agriculture. The putative attempts at a planned and permanent agriculture converted many to the idea that "farms must be treated as organic, integrated units," interdependent with the greater physical, social, and economic environment. Yet in 1940, the faith in a planned and permanent agriculture seemed to be floundering amid the many issues and concerns of the period, such as the international crisis and debate over farm policy, including Henry Wallace's call for an "ever normal granary." [47]

The concept of permanent agriculture clearly needed a more defining science to describe its planned world. As a reformist-utopian ideology, it also required a more fundamental guide than planning for permanence. Like a religion, permanent agriculture needed an animating spirit and a new evangelical zeal that would take the idea beyond a call for logical planning. Ecological ideas proved effective in providing the scientific guidelines as well as the missing philosophical animus for permanent agriculture. Over the next twenty years, its adherents effectively proselytized the new religion of permanent ecological agriculture to the American people.

CHAPTER TWO

An Ecological Basis for Culture and Agriculture

As soil washes downhill, down the streams, down to the wastes of the ocean, so goes opportunity, security,—a gradual wasting away of the chance for men to make a living on the land. In a very real sense, the man of the land is our national backbone. Permit his base to wash out beneath him and we leave the whole economic and social structure undermined, threatened.

—Hugh H. Bennett[1]

The movement for permanent agriculture involved more than soil conservation and production allotments, price-support programs, or bold social engineering. While these programs and techniques were steps toward permanent agriculture, the new farming system also incorporated an ethical, almost spiritual, ideology. It required a rejection of past assumptions regarding the land and a new governing cosmology for agriculture. Increasingly, from the late 1930s through its decline in the 1950s, the loosely assembled permanent agriculture school placed the science and philosophy of ecology at its vortex. As a science, ecology based itself on then-prevailing currents such as interdependence, balance, and harmony. As a philosophy, ecology was easily adapted to the social and biological dimensions of the soil crisis. Ecological ideas both scientific and philosophical permeated the message and method of permanent agriculture, offering a foundation for both culture and agriculture.

Advocates of a planned and permanent agriculture drew on ecology in several ways during the 1930s. First, they drew on ecology for their movement's ethical base. Ecology presented a new way of looking at society. Humanity no longer enjoyed a privileged seat at the center of the table of creation. Instead, humans were revealed as an influential element in a delicate, intricate web of life. To the movement's advocates and investigators, the ecology of the interwar years offered a guide to organizing society in a more harmonious fashion, in ways suggested by observing nature's enduring balance. In other words, ecological thinkers found ways to understand humans' interactions with each other and with the biological universe that surrounded and supported them. This viewpoint entailed a greater respect for life and a greater understanding of the environmental consequences of human activities.

Second, ecology informed holistic thought employed by some of the advocates of permanent agriculture. To the most committed advocates, the new ecological agriculture went beyond simple changes in farming methods and machinery. To them, the new agriculture embodied part of a more general awakening of holistic and organicist thought, and ecology was as much a philosophy as a physical science. Ecology's central ideas for describing nature—harmony, balance, and stability—also served as key words in fighting the general societal crises of the time, including depression, war, and the difficulties of urbanism and mass production.

Third, a cross-section of permanent agriculture's adherents drew on ecology to inform their technical prescriptions for agriculture. Within the academy, some scientists began to use ecological concepts in their work. Yet many of the basic notions and most dramatic demonstrations of ecological agriculture came from outside the established scientific world of the land-grant institutions. Specifically, the exponents of permanent, ecological agriculture championed such ideas as soil restoration via humus-building cover crops and composts, multiple cropping and crop diversification (as opposed to monocultures), terracing and other soil-saving techniques, biological (versus chemical) control of pests, and the use of farm-produced fertilizers (as opposed to purchased chemicals). Proponents hoped these changes on the farmstead would transform the culture of waste and soil exploitation into a new husbandry that mirrored the perennial bounty of nature. They argued that the new farming would save and rebuild soil and create dynamic increases in crop yields per acre, with lower costs for the farmer and better, cheaper food and fiber for the consumer.

Various promoters of permanent agriculture mixed together elements of science, ethics, and a few mystical notions in unique ways. While advocates used ecology in different ways as they developed their own ethics, holistic approach to problems, or agricultural technique, ecologically based ideas provided a common element among the various faces of permanent agriculture. A vision for the successful future of rural agricultural communities also unified the various factions of the permanent agriculture movement.

For the proponents of permanent agriculture, whether they were small farmers, powerful bureaucrats, noted scientists, or conservationists, an ecologically based agriculture promised hope for a world that appeared near ruin. The alleged benefits of permanent agriculture were sundry: by farming "vertically," producing more per acre rather than increasing output by expanding the amount of land under cultivation, efficient small-scale farmers could survive economically and thus help preserve rural culture. Furthermore, a permanent and ecological agriculture promised to bring "true efficiency," sparking giant yields of traditional and new market crops, used partially for inexpensive food and partially for low-cost and renewable supplies of raw materials via chemurgic processes. The new abundance would also mean that "marginal" land could be retired for forestry, grasslands, and wildlife preserves.

Crops produced under ecological guidelines also promised to be healthier for humans, according to advocates, and the new tillage systems promised to help revitalize the nation's waterways. By creating a rural-urban and agricultural-industrial balance, and by producing incredibly inexpensive supplies of food and fiber, permanent agriculture also promised to usher in a new era of permanent peace and prosperity. Among the most idealistic members of the permanent agriculture camp, the new ecologically inspired farming system promised to create a world with such abundance that people would simply have no reason to go to war. For a brief culminating period during the war years of the 1940s, the apostles of permanent agriculture effectively broadcast their message to a surprisingly interested public.

SCIENTIFIC ECOLOGY

Coined in 1866 by the German zoologist Ernst Haeckel, the term *ecology* literally means "household economy," but it has been defined over the years as the science dealing with the interrelations between life-forms and the interactions between life-forms and their environments. While ecology has been built on the study of biological and social interrelationships, exactly what ecology means and what ecologists do have shifted subtly over the years. Several currents led to the development of ecology as an academic discipline around the turn of the twentieth century. First, natural history had matured. A vast amount of taxonomic and biogeographic information had been gathered during the heyday of nineteenth-century natural history, yielding the insights of Charles Darwin and Alfred Russell Wallace. During the late nineteenth century, natural history began to fracture into more specialized disciplines such as entomology, mammalogy, and limnology. Scientists pushed biology toward an emphasis on experimentation, with embryology leading the way. Those interested in experimental work believed their method was superior to the descriptive work of natural history. Reductionistic and experimental approaches, because they resembled techniques used in the physical sciences, enjoyed greater academic and budgetary prestige. Descriptive work, although important in evolutionary theory, was left to the taxonomists in museums.[2]

Ecology derived from studies in both botany and zoology. By the 1890s, American botanists, including Henry C. Cowles, Charles Bessey, and Frederic Clements, began to pursue ecological research, although the term *ecology* was still absent from most dictionaries at the turn of the century. In the first decades of the twentieth century, American plant ecologists and animal ecologists such as Victor Shelford and Charles C. Adams superseded European and English theoretical advances. By the onset of World War I, British scientists had formed an ecological society, and in 1915 the Americans followed suit by establishing the Ecological Society of America (ESA). In 1920, the ESA began publishing its journal, *Ecology*. While those studying the ecology of plants and animals found some common ground, ecology still lacked theoretical unity and disciplinary identity after World War I. Critics of ecology attacked the lack of quantitative or biochemical analysis, as well as the tools and mission of the field. During the 1920s and 1930s, ecologists successfully distanced the field from taxonomy and description and forced a new focus on quantitative analysis.[3]

Barrington Moore, editor of the first issue of *Ecology*, saw the need for a synthesis between plant, animal, and human ecology. Moore expressed his desire for ecologists to rise above internecine squabbles and expand their discipline by offering some threads of theoretical unity, as well as practical, applied research that would allow ecology to catch up with its burgeoning academic competitor—the field of genetics. A few early American ecologists sought to give their work a practical hue by integrating ecological research into the burgeoning revolution of agricultural science in the United States. Ecology also became an important part of fields such as meteorology and wildlife management.[4]

During the early years of the twentieth century, two main ideas dominated plant ecology. The first notion was the succession model of vegetation change, introduced by the work of Henry Cowles and Frederic Clements. Plant communities eventually developed from simple units to complex, evolved systems that reached a stable state, or climax. Many scientists today recognize a dynamic equilibrium, where populations and species composition fluctuate over time within wide and general boundaries. Yet for Clements and the climax school, the course of nature was a more directed process, always advancing toward an eventual state of balance and general stasis. Second, Clements saw vegetation types as interdependent plant communities. Indeed, these scientists defined ecology as the science of communities. Clements and his supporters tended to emphasize biotic interactions more than environmental effects on the vegetation, and they tended to interpret the vegetation type as a whole unit, as an organism-like entity acting differently than the individual parts would do on their own. Clements used the term *complex organism* to describe the character of climax vegetation. Others saw this organismic character in nature, too. In 1910, Harvard biologist William Morton

Wheeler used the term *superorganism* in describing groups of social insects acting together.[5]

Although the climax school dominated ecological investigations during the first decades of the century, beginning in the 1920s critics questioned and modified this unifying theory of ecology. In 1926, Henry Gleason argued that the community concept was flawed. His essay "The Individualistic Concept of the Plant Association" suggested that assemblages of plants were the result of particular circumstances and history, not the product of an orderly process of succession or an organism at work. From 1926 to 1935, A. G. Tansley of Oxford University disputed the notion of a monoclimax, suggesting that many different types of vegetation appeared more or less permanent and deserving of the name climax.[6]

Part of the dispute over the Clementsian school concerned scientific method. Scientists rightfully described the limitations of attempts to study whole systems. Put simply, natural systems are so complex that attempts to describe the entire system fall short or grossly oversimplify nature. On the other hand, selecting out smaller parts of the system for study risks overlooking causal connections with the larger system. A second piece of the puzzle was philosophical. Critics of Clements felt uncomfortable with the way he infused organicist notions into his discussion of plant associations. The metaphor of the prairie as an organism struck too closely to old arguments over vitalism and idealist notions that some questions could not be answered by science. During the early twentieth century, a majority of life scientists subscribed to materialist agendas and a reductionist philosophy suggesting that all biological questions might be answered if split into manageable parts. In 1935, Arthur Tansley proposed a way to get past some of these semantic and philosophical difficulties. He advanced the notion of an *ecosystem* to bridge the gulf between the holism of Clements and the reductionism of his critics. Later critics of the ecosystem concept overlooked Tansley's intention to solve the philosophical puzzle, making the mistake of placing the ecosystem in the holist camp.[7]

Although the discipline of ecology remained divided over theory and method, during the interwar years Frederic Clements, Victor Shelford, and others offered a definition of ecology that synthesized plant, animal, and eventually human ecology. *Bio-ecology* (1939), written by Clements and Shelford, attempted to merge plant and animal ecology. Just as plants fulfilled roles in a habitat, so, too, animals played their parts in creating this environment. The authors used the terms *biotic community* and *biome* in describing plant and animal communities. The book also elaborated on field, laboratory, and classroom techniques. *Bio-ecology* represented an attempt to find a new synthesis that would qualify as "ecology in the widest sense."[8]

Several ecologists, notably Tansley, were uncomfortable with the way the climax concept seemed to suggest that a primordial state of nature represented an ideal standard against which human activity should be measured. Tansley suggested the notion of an *anthropogenic climax,* a modern landscape shaped by humans, yet as balanced as Clements's grassland climax. The study of human ecology grew in fits and starts, notably within the discipline of geography. Charles Adams was among those who became interested in human activities and their environmental impacts, hoping that human ecology might yield some clues and remedies for a relationship with nature that appeared increasingly exploitative and destructive.[9]

Partly because of its technical information about interrelationships in nature, and because some ecologists strove to understand complex biological systems, ecology also supplied the raw materials for building metaphors that aided (or obscured) public understanding, substantiated holistic points of view, and contributed to a new ethical program.[10] While ecology as a science provided specific and practical information for farmers and "land management biologists," it also provided a philosophical underpinning for what could best be labeled the holistic, or *organicist,* side of permanent agriculture. For some, this aspect manifested itself in a quasi-spiritual attitude about ecological agriculture, but for most intellectuals and the general public, an ecologically inspired ethic and a holistic way of thinking solidified rational argument and broadened the significance of permanent agriculture. Ecology contributed to the new agricultural-environmental ethic during the interwar years. While historians emphasize Aldo Leopold's elegantly stated "land ethic," many other people of this era grasped the ethical dimensions of ecological concepts and their relationship to farming and the livelihood of the human species.

The general crisis of the 1930s fed an ethic of interdependence and created a nurturing environment for the concept of permanent agriculture. As historian Donald Worster noted in his book *Nature's Economy,* "In the 1930s, largely as a direct consequence of the Dust Bowl experience, conservation began to move toward a more inclusive, coordinated, ecological perspective. A concern for synthesis and for maintaining the whole community of life in stable equilibrium with its habitat emerged." But the new ecological ethic dictated more than just manipulating fields and forests with new, less intrusive farming techniques. It also revealed that "conservation is not a subject which can be taught. It is a way of life into which we must grow as a people." The tense international situation and the need to mobilize and secure America's future also added to the message of the new ecological ethic. In the frontispiece of Sears's *Life and Environment,* an illustrated flowchart offered this simple but effective rationale for adopting an ecological point of view. With a soldier saluting an American flag at the top, the chart read: "Flag needs man, man needs beef, beef needs clover, clover needs bee," and so on down the food chain.[11]

The proponents of permanent agriculture drew on a history of linking ecological ideas with the farmer's spiritual responsibility for the earth. In his books, Liberty Hyde Bailey called for an ethical relationship with the land, and Sir Albert Howard, the patron saint of organic farming, echoed similar Albert Schweitzer–like "reverence for life" admonitions in the 1930s. Howard and his second wife, Louise, profoundly influenced the American permanent agriculture movement with their construction of an ethical tie to the soil. Writing in 1947, Louise Howard spoke of human cultivation as one, albeit important, component in "the earth's green carpet." She asked her readers to envision the earth as a living and delicate landscape that operated on such principles as inalterability, persistence, regeneration, the "law of return," stored reserves, and "the principle of mixed existence." She also tried to give her readers an understanding of the Buddhist concept of a "wheel of life" as opposed to the Western construction of linear, ladderlike progress.[12]

For SCS biologist Edward Graham and his boss, Hugh Bennett, attempting to establish a soil conservation ethic meant "more than wise use of resources. . . . It may well be the foundation of a new social philosophy." Ecology, as Paul Sears pointed out, could help make society more aware of its natural resources and serve as a tool for political decision making. Conservationists also attacked the "triumph over nature" attitude Americans displayed in their long battle to control nature. Graham compared traditional American ignorance of nature with the Romans' misdiagnosis of malaria as the result of "night air." Other advocates of a new agricultural-ecological ethic described the Christian sacraments of wine and bread as symbolic of the fact that life had material resources at its root, and that "spiritual survival, no less than physical, rests upon compliance with the order of the universe." A physician involved with the Friends of the Land suggested that ecological diagnoses for agriculture helped him learn to think "in terms of soil, health, population and human weal," leading to recognition of "a profound dependence of Man, even in his intellectual and perhaps spiritual outlook, on what he gets from the soil."[13]

Ecology also informed the holistic approach used by some advocates of permanent agriculture. In "What Is Ecology and What Good Is It?"—an article that appeared in *Ecology* in 1936—Walter P. Taylor echoed then Secretary of Agriculture Henry A. Wallace's call for a "Declaration of Interdependence," as he defined ecology in the holistic sense as "the science of all the relations of all organisms to all their environments." Ecology already guided game management and had increased the scope of ethical consideration beyond humans. In the realm of soil conservation and land management, ecology became a crucial element. In his article, Taylor wrote, "Harmonious and satisfactory land use and efficient conservation of natural resources can be obtained only through programs based on a sound ecological foundation." If heeded, the lessons of ecology would "help assure the basic essentials of a more abundant life." Ecology would thus provide "a unifying point of view" regarding the use of resources and their effect on the biological universe and "upon our own social structure."[14]

ECOLOGY AND ETHICS

In modern times and particularly since Darwin, many individuals and schools of thought have used science, or what they labeled as science, as the basis for constructing systems of personal and societal ethics. Social Darwinism (or, more correctly, social Spencerianism) and the eugenics movement present two cases in which people employed "science" to justify misguided and ignoble endeavors such as imperialism and institutional racism. In contrast, the science of ecology became a foundation for a proposed new ethical system devoted to the individual dignity of all life, mutual cooperation among individuals and species, and the increase and perpetuation of a prosperous, peaceful civilization. As historian Anna Bramwell suggested, German romanticism and the British rural folk heritage, including early work on urban ecology and city planning by Scotsman Patrick Geddes, also contributed to the more holistic, social reformist, and political aspects of ecological thought in its early stages.[15]

Although Aldo Leopold is often lauded by historians and environmentalists for his original and clear elucidation of a "land ethic," he was one of several scientist-philosophers in the interwar period who recognized that humanity's survival hinged upon recognizing the delicate and vital interrelations among life-forms. For the practitioners and proponents of permanent agriculture in the 1930s and 1940s, ecological thought nurtured the adoption of a new mentality geared toward plenty, permanence, and aesthetic beauty.

For academic ecologist and noted conservationist Paul B. Sears, writing in his *Life and Environment* (1939), the "social function" of ecology was to "provide a scientific basis whereby man may shape the environment and his relations to it, as he expresses himself in and through his social pattern." Sears and colleagues used ecological concepts to form an ethical system that incorporated both anthropocentrism and biocentrism, as well as a range of ideas that would embody the environmental ethic as it emerged over the postwar years. On one hand, ecology suggested a new respect for the nonhuman world, illuminating the notion that humanity posed the greatest threat to life on earth. On the other hand, ecology presented an avenue for salvaging a nearly bankrupt human society by harnessing the "economy of nature" for ends such as societal permanence, physical beauty, and overall human health and prosperity. Although Sears found many like-minded thinkers in his push for an all-encompassing ecological worldview, he thought that presenting the new ethical system to the public at large would be an arduous endeavor because Americans "with a few notable exceptions . . . despise the earth upon which [they] depend." Following in the footsteps of Russia's eminent biologist, geographer, and anarchist Prince Kropotkin, Sears saw Darwin's evolutionary theory in a different light than the followers of social Darwinism. For Sears, the "highest opportunity for eventual human freedom and dignity lie[s] precisely in the fact that we are products of evolution. As responsible units in the great web of life, we can be guided by an infinitely long inherited experience, built into our bodies and minds and shaping our decisions in the interest of our own species."[16]

For Sears, Leopold, and others, ecology presented "a way out" of the troubled state that humanity found itself in during the 1930s and 1940s. Competition and imprudent attitudes toward natural resources, as well as misguided scientists, industrialists, and farmers, had led to a soil crisis, again a manifestation of the overall human crisis in the period. If ecology taught that nature dictated an eventual state of harmony, then certainly humanity, particularly as influenced by rising mass production, mass consumption, and mass culture, was the greatest contributor to disharmony in the overall scheme of nature's economy. Sears suggested that as "the sensitive and intimate relationship to the natural world characteristic of indigenous culture is lost or obscured," the task for the ecologist becomes documenting the "disastrous maladjustments" of humanity and offering "laws of community development and behavior in such a way that they may be applied not only within the human community but to the wider community of living things . . . whose control he has assumed."[17]

Ecology implied a biocentric message that "we're all in this together," but it also implied that as the main player in the environment, humanity needed to "work toward a new equilibrium of nature fitted to [its] own survival" and stop "the waste of our natural resources, soil, forest, grassland, fish and game, water and minerals." Humanity demanded an enforceable new ethic that priced goods and services to the scale of their "social cost," with individuals no longer "permitted to find it profitable to work against the interests of society." For Sears, Leopold, and many others, ecology offered not only an opportunity for human understanding of the natural world but also a chance "to better understand each other." One prominent example Sears used to illustrate the practical results of the new ecological ethic was his call for engineers to receive ecological training, hoping they would become more sensitive to the biological ramifications of their projects, such as the effect of highway development on streams or the impact of a dam on a river system.[18]

Sears expressed his version of a "land ethic" at the conference "Food and the Future," held in 1946. Sears's speech tied agriculture to the realities of an ecologically interpreted world. Crediting Darwin and Kropotkin's "biological basis for human ethics," Sears told his audience, "Our responsibility now has two facets—we are custodians of ourselves and our environment as well. We did not make and cannot change the laws under which we must work, but at least we can understand them." He reminded his audience that "the stuff that life is made of must be used and re-used by succeeding generations and shared among many forms of life." The system "maintains itself," wrote Sears, "but when man takes over the system is disrupted. Too often he sustains himself by mortgaging the future instead of maintaining true economy." Sears asked farmers to look to other occupations for a guide to cooperating with nature. "Man has conquered the sea by learning to live with it—not by violence and self-will, but with patient wisdom in shaping vessels to meet the waters and ride them." He continued, "Perhaps the sea, which so quickly engulfs our failures to deal with it, is a better tutor than the land, which protracts its penalties through the years, even generations."[19]

Author and agrarian iconoclast Louis Bromfield brought the ethical imperatives of ecology home to a large public audience. Bromfield, whose restoration of his Malabar Farm in Ohio focused national attention on permanent agriculture, expressed his almost spiritual view of ecology frequently in the 1940s. Bromfield's ecological orientation centered on "the premise that God and Nature have produced an orderly universe governed by immutable laws, the most obvious of which is the life cycle, and that man violates them only at his own peril." For Bromfield, "the secrets of life" were "combined in a cubic foot of soil." He thought farmers were receptive to ecological messages because of their close contact with nature. He wrote: "The men and women of no other profession are as content to die when their time is come. . . . they know by living with the earth and sky and in companionship with their fellow animals that we are all only infinitesimal fragments of a vast universe in which the cycle of birth, death, decay and rebirth is the law which has permitted us to live."[20]

THE MODEL OF NATURE

As the science and ethic of ecology merged with the notions of a planned and permanent agriculture, various specific and often well-publicized visions of permanent agriculture emerged in the 1940s, all with the "model of nature" as a central component. In essence, basing ecological agriculture on the model of nature meant that agriculturists needed to mirror nature's process of soil building, in turn crafting a new type of farming that would eventually evolve into a state of perpetual, low-maintenance fertility. Understanding the lessons of nature required both scientific knowledge and the use of personal observation of conditions on any particular parcel of land. Hence, the guideline of nature infused permanent agriculture with both scientific empiricism and mystical-intuitive deductions, imbuing the movement with what present-day observers might call a New Age quality.

Paul Sears illustrated the desire to build permanent agriculture via a scientific understanding of the model of nature. In his many literary offerings during the late 1930s and 1940s, he championed the old notions of "directed" ecology, using the terminology of "climax communities" and "balance" in nature. In his frequent attacks on America's poor stewardship record, Sears suggested that the mechanized and unplanned agriculture that emerged in the United States broke the equilibrium with nature. The American farmer, by not recognizing and acting upon the evidence ecology provided, "failed to develop his artificial plant cultures in a way to simulate nature in holding and building soil." Sears reminded his sundry audiences that "the idea of balance—of a flexible system of give-and-take—seems implicit throughout nature." This erstwhile member of what would grow to be a large group of ecological literati warned his audiences that the idea of balance was fundamental to biology and to physical and chemical theory and that there was "no reason to think that human activities are exempt" from nature's model. Although science was already being cited as "a monster which may turn on man and destroy him," in 1946 Sears proclaimed the contrary, noting that "knowledge of natural forces can be utilized to promote a new equilibrium which will make the landscape efficient."

Permanent agriculture based on the model of nature required three essential components: the building of humus through the incorporation of organic material into the topsoil, maximum diversity or mixed farming, and providing a permanent cover of vegetation as a "skin" for the soil. Humus-building and soil-holding procedures were ancient techniques that in the late 1930s and 1940s became canonical components of the permanent agriculture idea. Many individuals verified the efficacy of humus building and providing a vegetative cover for the land, but none was more instrumental than Sir Albert Howard, a British colonial and mycologist whose research and writings on crops in the 1920s and 1930s extensively developed the idea of emulating nature.[21]

Indeed, although the permanent agriculture movement was essentially an American phenomenon, Howard's ideas (as well as those of other British agricultural reformers and the farming systems of the Orient) provided the foundation for many of the tenets of permanent agriculture. Howard asked fundamental questions, such as how nature manufactured humus and built reserve fertility and "What does she do to control such things as insect, fungus, and virus diseases in plants and the various afflictions of her animal kingdom?" He thought traditional agricultural science had neglected nature's "great law of return," and his "Indore Process" sought to mirror and expand upon nature's power to regenerate fertility and build soil. Howard linked his scientific pronouncements with claims that would resurge in the holistic agriculture systems of permanent agriculture. He claimed that what he called "healthy" soil would produce healthy crops, disease- and pest-resistant crops that, in turn, would provide the same qualities to humans who consumed them. Howard served as a constant source of reference for the American champions of permanent agriculture and, along with his second wife, Louise, often added to the rhetorical and social construction of permanent agriculture.[22]

ECOLOGY AND AGRONOMY

Those in the milieu of permanent agriculture hoped that their movement would provide a unifying force for scientists and farmers who would try to build a "permanent system of farming." It is essential to recall that the ecological consensus in the interwar years hinged on such ideas as the climax concept, which taught that communities (including people and nations) evolved from rudimentary to complex systems, eventually reaching a stable state of harmony and equilibrium. Ecology taught that society, especially its linchpin, agriculture, had to become symbiotic with other biological communities in the eventual development of a stable-state world biotic community. As Hugh Bennett and his colleagues often suggested, ecological awareness showed the need for "adjustment of agriculture to its environment."[23]

The science of ecology eventually contributed a good deal to the science of agronomy, especially in the land-grant colleges under the tutelage of Charles Bessey and others. Ecology provided information about the overall interrelationships between such things as predators and range control, insects and vegetative cover, and the effects of erosion on the overall productivity of the land. Still, as ecologists and others often lamented, the majority of ecological research prior to the 1930s focused on nonagricultural topics such as undomesticated plants and wildlife. The human-fostered erosion problems of the 1930s prompted ecologists to call for more research in the field of agriculture.[24]

In December 1938, Herbert Hanson, president of the Ecological Society of America, promoted the need for an "invasion" of ecology into the realm of agriculture and conservation. Hanson noted that while ecological researchers had focused on wild plants and animals, agronomists, geographers, sociologists, and economists incorporated ecological ideas and tools with a great degree of success. Asserting that ecological thought had also benefited such areas as soil conservation, range management, and forestry, Hanson called for ecologists to enter the practical realm of agriculture, asking them to explore topics such as the flax plant, which responded quickly to environmental conditions. He also thought ecology could help solve many problems in the American West, including insect infestation and drought. For Hanson, ecology provided the "concepts and tools that are needed" for "achieving harmonious relationships of organisms between themselves and to their environments, the concept of natural tendency toward stabilization of the environment, and the need for natural areas as checks, or standards, by which the values and effects of tillage, irrigation, drainage, grazing, lumbering, and other uses may be measured."[25]

Hanson went on to quote British ecologist Arthur Tansley, who advocated the use of ecology to counter "the forces which are making for the wholesale destruction of our civilization." Hanson suggested that "man is inherently ecological" and hence has "a commonalty with nature," and that the academy need not "dub as 'agroecologist' the man working in these fields" or use any other terminology. He simply wished for ecologists to enter into the fray of constructing permanent agriculture and to teach people to "use all available scientific information in order to adapt their modes of living to the environment." For Hanson this would probably result in restrictions on cultivation in ecologically sensitive areas, more land devoted to grazing, larger farms, "regrouping" of people outside of marginal land, and the use of planning for "greater stability and higher standards of living" and for the "building of a culture far beyond our present dreams." For Hanson, permanent agriculture could be defined as a way to adjust humanity's relationship with the environment so that past mistakes with the land could be avoided as American civilization passed from "its pioneering stage to more advanced stages."[26]

Apparently the desire for the infusion of ecological thought and ecological research into the realm of agriculture was a sentiment shared by many of Hanson's contemporaries. In the 1940s a number of articles appeared that linked ecology and the call for a permanent agriculture system. Edward H. Graham, chief biologist of the Soil Conservation Service, led the way in establishing the validity of ecology for understanding agriculture. He provided several specific examples of how ecological ideas could help reform the abusive practices of American farming. For example, he noted that the old practice of keeping the ground "clean" around orchards, which was thought to reduce problems with insects, with mice eating the tree bark, and with weeds or ground cover compet-ing for irrigation water, was actually a bad idea. Ecological research, according to Graham, showed that a vegetative cover of legumes and grass actually harbored predatory insects and birds that helped control pest infestations, provided food for the mice so they would not consume tree bark, and helped preserve soil moisture. Hence, ecology provided lessons that would increase agricultural productivity while accounting for the health of the overall environment. For Graham, the ways of nature "were not easy to learn"; hence, "a sound agricultural program" would arise from "a balanced condition where crops and soil, rainfall and run-off, birds and insects, yields and markets, and all other components of the farm as a habitat, are in adjustment." Graham and fellow scientists found that ecology provided lessons for agriculture that ranged from the causes and impact of erosion to the relationship between agricultural practices (like strip-cropping and range management) and wildlife populations. Ecology also proved useful in land classification schemes necessary for building a planned and permanent agriculture.[27]

Edward Ackerman, an ecologically oriented geographer, indicated that the principal practical lesson ecology offered agriculture "probably lies in the more widespread adoption of humus-building cultivation, and less dependence on commercial or mineral fertilizers." Ackerman, while considering the prospect of a worldwide ecological farming regime, recalled his visit to a sugarcane estate in Cuba that used crop residue and leaves as a compost mulch. This system produced high yields over a long period with no need for manufactured fertilizers. This led Ackerman to conclude that this particular plantation was essentially emulating the process of nature. On a more general level, Ackerman indicated that eco-logical lessons were going to bring tremendous changes, which would "disturb politicians, economists, and plain citizens for a long time." He wrote: "Resettlement, education, large-scale engineering, and world-wide integration of crop production may be involved." Thus, for some, incorporating ecology into agriculture had little to do with preserving small-scale farming enterprises but everything to do with technique. For Edward Graham, ecology showed that "a great deal of our physical and material well-being depends upon our ingenuity of thought. Not only ecologists, but politicians who lose sight of this fact let slip from their grasp one of the most potent influences in the human prospect."[28]

THE ORGANIC MOVEMENT

Although Sir Albert Howard's substantial influence on the technique of the new farming derived from his experimental work, and while Edward

Ackerman, Edward Graham, and Paul Sears sought to build agriculture from the science of ecology, less empirical proponents of organic agriculture such as Louis Bromfield and Edward Faulkner made some of the most significant contributions to the permanent agriculture movement. While New Dealers provided considerable energy and practical applications of permanent agriculture, the tenets of organic farming provided an indispensable part of the rationale for permanent agriculture, particularly the notion of building "healthy," humus-laden soil. Sir Albert Howard's work deserves the most credit for introducing organic farming to America, but others also made important contributions. For South African J. P. J. Van Vuren, soil erosion was symptomatic of a "specific disease of the soil, caused mainly by a humus-deficiency." Other proponents of organic farming and humus building championed harnessing the earthworm to build humus, using composts and green manures, and treating the topsoil like a precious, delicate life-form, unlike "your scientific agronomist, who should know better, but who recklessly throws a monkey- wrench into this microbial universe, by dousing it with strong corrosive chemical fertilizers. He believes that the conveyor-belt method must be introduced into every aspect of farming. He even applies it to cows who wearily yield five times the quantity of milk Nature intended them to, only to discover that it contains less vitamins than the milk obtained in smaller quantities from scrub animals."[29]

The culture of organic farming in the late 1930s through the 1940s hinged on several central ideas derived from land use planners, ecologists, the "biodynamic" school of the anthroposophists, Sir Albert Howard, and American observers of peasant agriculture. Essentially, the organic farming philosophy sought to see the topsoil and crops from the viewpoint of ecological interrelatedness, which would allow the organic farmer to emulate the natural growing conditions and fertility creation of nature. Again, by incorporating composts, green manures, and even recycled sewage into the soil, a healthy humus might be produced, and this productive soil would grow sturdy, pest- and disease-resistant crops and pass these vigorous qualities to humans who ate the organically produced food. Many of the grand claims made by the organic farmers fueled the drive for permanent, ecological agriculture, including the proposed farming regimes of two of permanent agriculture's chief stalwarts, Louis Bromfield and Edward Faulkner.[30]

LOUIS BROMFIELD AND MALABAR FARM

Although twentieth-century social movements honor particular events and a few individuals for initiating significant historical trends, in reality complex ideas emerge over time and from a variety of sources. Such was the case of the permanent agriculture idea, as noted in 1945 by Louis Bromfield (1898–1956), who hailed the "new agriculture developing slowly in America for the past thirty or forty years." In hundreds of places, he wrote, "observant and intelligent farmers, school teachers, bureau or academic men, men and women in back gardens or on an acre or two of land, have been *watching* their soil, living with it, *feeling* it under their feet, learning from it." For Bromfield, permanent agriculture represented an "evolution in methods, seething beneath the surface, waiting to take form."[31]

Ever the student of Sir Albert Howard, Bromfield sought to emulate the laws of nature while restoring a worn-out thousand-acre patch of land that "represented hundreds of millions of acres of once-rich agricultural land reduced to this condition over the whole country." Bromfield envisioned himself as a "Michelangelo" of the earth, reshaping and restoring "a desolate farm, ruined by some ignorant and evil predecessors." Much in the spirit of Lewis Mumford, another iconoclast of his day, Bromfield became a self-anointed knight waging battle against what he saw as the pervasive and destructive "illusions of prosperity" and the "ambitions, greed and intricate mechanical ingenuity" of a crass industrial-urban society that he labeled the "Age of Irritation."[32]

Bromfield became the most effective voice for permanent ecological agriculture, at the same time pursuing his quixotic Jeffersonian dream of perpetuating a nation of small, independent farmers to serve as a permanent anchor for the Republic. A Pulitzer Prize–winning novelist, expatriate, and World War I ambulance driver, Bromfield returned from Europe in 1939 and established Malabar Farm in his native state of Ohio. That collection of worn-out fields represents one of the most unique agrarian experiments in American history. Bromfield's experiment and his fight against ruinous farming gained national attention, and Malabar Farm became a clearinghouse for agricultural conservation, ecological agriculture, and the ideology of the independent farmer.[33]

Bromfield's life experiences formed his vision of proper agriculture. He grew up in and near Mansfield, Ohio, the son of a local businessman and politician who aspired to return his family to its agrarian roots. As a young man, he enrolled in the College of Agriculture at Cornell University in 1914, only to be forced to return to Ohio to help manage the newly reoccupied family farmstead. Bromfield returned to college in 1916, this time (at his mother's urging) in the distinctly urban environs of Columbia University. Bored with college and enticed by the war in Europe, he joined the French Ambulance Service in 1917 and served meritoriously, finding French life suited to his taste for a blend of the rural and the cosmopolitan.

After the war, he returned to the States, married, and began a productive and lucrative career as a novelist, eventually receiving a Pulitzer Prize in 1927 for his book *Early Autumn*. With several of his books converted into Hollywood films and with substantial revenues flowing in from royalty checks, Bromfield and family removed to a pastoral village outside of Paris in 1927, remaining there until 1939, with occasional jaunts to ski in Switzerland or to explore India's bucolic Malabar Coast. Bromfield often expressed his intense attraction to the simple but fruitful lives of the peasantry surrounding his French home, but when war arrived in 1939, he and his family were compelled to return to America, where he began his luminous career as an agricultural commentator, experimental farmer, and prophet of permanent agriculture.

Upon his return to America, Bromfield first stopped in New York City but soon after found himself in the Ohio community where he was raised, hoping to establish a farmstead that would provide the means to rectify the errors of modern farming and be a successful investment, both in financial terms and in rebuilding a sense of rural community in the region. Bromfield, his wife, and his agent-manager-friend George Hawkins arrived in Ohio on a dreary winter day. As he passed the once prosperous farms of his youth, Bromfield recoiled at the apparent neglect of farmsteads that formerly enjoyed "a rich, well-painted appearance." Buildings had fallen into disrepair, and many fields suffered from erosion and were sparsely vegetated. Bromfield found the farm of an old neighbor and later recalled, "All these great memories came flooding back during the short walk from the house to that great barn. Then I pushed open the door and walked into the smell of cattle and horse and hay and silage and I knew that I had come home and never again would I be separated from that smell because it meant security, stability . . . it had reclaimed me. It was in my blood and could not be denied."[34]

Bromfield's system of ecological agriculture borrowed from numerous sources and expressed many of the contemporary currents in the permanent agriculture milieu. In building permanent agriculture, the new agriculturist needed to reconcile the forces of nature with the knowledge provided by ecology, chemistry, economics, and nutrition. Characteristics of the new farmer included not only a mastery of science and technology but also qualities such as love, respect, intelligence, and a notion of usufruct (using without harming). Bromfield's version of permanent agriculture sought to combine a peasant's intuitive stewardship with American notions of efficiency and independence.

Bromfield used Malabar Farm to implement and test his ideas for a productive and ecologically sound agriculture and to promote the benefits of rural life. The author, along with his wife, two children, and entourage, moved into an older farmstead on his property and began to draw the blueprints for Malabar, which included an impressive new thirty-two-room home. Bromfield was excited to be back among familiar friends and territory, but the land he had purchased, as described by his daughter Ellen, was "worn thin by years of bad, unimaginative farming. Deep gullies slashed its hills and remained like open wounds kept festering by wind and rain and never allowed to heal. . . . the final stage of land which had been abused by foolish, thoughtless men who have no business calling themselves farmers, keepers of the precious land." Bromfield claimed that some of his acreage was not rentable even at five dollars per acre per year. He established a plan to rectify the destruction and restore the farmland, woodlands, and pastures of what he christened Malabar Farm.[35]

While entertaining an endless stream of visitors, including his friend Humphrey Bogart, who married Lauren Bacall at Malabar in 1945, Bromfield began to apply his multidimensional prescription to the ills of his debilitated farm. Practical application of ecology at Malabar meant restoring the land and streams to a pre-1800s condition by halting erosion, using a minimum of manufactured agricultural chemicals, rebuilding the pastures and grasslands by planting grass or nitrogen-fixing legumes, using generous amounts of green manures, organic mulches, and composts, and gaining an overall scientific and psychic knowledge of the intricacies of the land so that, in Bromfield's words, "we could restore the soil infinitely more quickly [working] with nature rather than against her as our predecessors had done." Bromfield, via his reading, publicity status, and participation with Friends of the Land, was personally acquainted with individuals like Paul Sears and Aldo Leopold, who taught him that "hard" scientific information should be coupled with personal observation of local conditions. In accordance with this thinking, Bromfield divided his time between the library, where he read authors such as Selman Waksman and Sir Albert Howard, and taking walks around Malabar to check plant, soil, and water conditions and plant willow switches along the creek beds. He wrote: "Expansion into the whole field of ecology became inevitable, as indeed it must become on any well-managed farm. We discovered very early that trees, water, and soil do not exist merely as isolated factors in a specialized study. They were hopelessly involved with the very basic welfare of man and the conditions of his daily life."[36]

Bromfield employed many techniques to bring ecological agriculture to Malabar. He experimented with imported strains of grass to hold the soil against erosion, planted crops that he claimed "matched" the soil, and pursued the aforementioned humus-building "organic" techniques espoused by Howard, organic advocate J. I. Rodale, and others. Many of his ideas defied empirical proof and were based primarily on personal observations and the unproved claims of the cultish adherents of organic farming. Bromfield planted test plots to "discover the relationships of given soil balances suited to given plants in their resistance to both disease and insects" and indicated that "by 'sorting out' crops into different gardens and parts of gardens where soil composition suited a specific plant, we have arrived at a high degree of resistance to both disease and insects." Bromfield claimed that his farm, which incorporated surface residues, green and animal manures, composts, and mulches into the topsoil, had drastically increased the productive capacity of the land with virtually no reliance on manufactured chemicals (he did briefly use some fertilizers on his replanted pastures). He reported that fields yielding a paltry five bushels of wheat per acre in 1940 yielded thirty-three bushels two years later and fifty-two bushels in 1944.[37]

In Bromfield's description, Malabar became a mighty compost heap teeming with fertility by emulating and enhancing the recycling abilities of nature. Bromfield also worked to capture water via ponds and natural (untiled) drainage areas. He was particularly proud of his restoration of Kemper's Run, a dirty channelized creek that had once been a clear fishing and swimming hole for a younger Louis Bromfield. After planting Babylonica willow along the stream's banks and slowing the flow of water and soil running into it by careful, effective land management, Bromfield could report that Kemper's Run had recovered by the late 1940s and was once again well stocked with bass and other fish. He also cited a return of wildlife to his little valley as signatory of his restoration of ecological balance. His ideas and accounts are verified by the remarks of others in the period and by the fertility apparent at the Malabar site today.[38]

NO GENERAL UTOPIAS:
EDWARD FAULKNER'S TRASH FARMING

While Louis Bromfield's experiment at Malabar Farm provided a dramatic episode in the early stage of ecological agriculture, many of Bromfield's ideas were infused with the messages preached by another focal figure of the permanent agriculture movement of the 1940s, those of self-labeled experimental farmer and best-selling author Edward Faulkner. Faulkner, whose ideas regarding a permanent ecological agriculture garnered national attention amid the great crisis of World War II, created a system that became the most publicized and representative of the sundry proposed systems of permanent agriculture.

Faulkner's controversial 1943 book, *Plowman's Folly*, formed the basis for his national notoriety, but his ideas regarding permanent agriculture crystallized over several decades. Born in Kentucky in the 1890s, Faulkner claimed that his father's stewardship ethos influenced his own later deliberations. He studied agriculture at the University of Kentucky and became a county agent in that state for a number of years until he was apparently forced from that position for his nonconformist ideas. By 1930, Faulkner settled in suburban Elyria, Ohio, where he pursued a career as a businessman. He continued his study of agriculture, poring over extension station reports and a variety of works, including those of Sir Albert Howard. He maintained contact with the soil by attempting to create a garden in the hardened clay of his suburban plot. During the 1930s, as his garden grew larger and more productive, Faulkner's agricultural ideology began to solidify—a vision that, in his mind, offered a chance at ecological harmony, permanent prosperity, and enduring peace to a world wearied and threatened by war, economic strife, and hunger of potentially catastrophic proportions. Despite these lofty goals, Faulkner claimed he offered "no general utopias."[39]

Faulkner's ideology of farming incorporated the tenets of permanent agriculture that had evolved in the 1930s. He offered a critique of farming practices and the misguided use of science and technology, and he presented a "way out" of the problem via an ecologically based husbandry that featured societal permanence as an eventual goal. Faulkner claimed that the shortsighted agriculture practiced by farmers and propagated by the agricultural colleges had sapped the "cream of fertility" from the land, thus eroding the principal basis for societal wealth and fostering a reliance on expensive and possibly unhealthy manufactured agricultural chemicals. Faulkner thought farmers actually worked against nature and were forgetful that "the earth is self-sufficient. . . . its failure to deliver to its plants everything they need can be traced to the manner in which we handle the land . . . in part from the unnecessary disturbance of the upper layers of the soil." Faulkner's diatribes regarding the heavy-handed use of machinery and science heralded a new era in which technology, formerly hailed as a solver of problems, increasingly became viewed as a source of problems in society.[40]

Faulkner's main attack on the tradition of American soil abuse centered on the use of the venerable moldboard plow as a tool for soil preparation. While the moldboard had been a necessary pioneer in the era of breaking sod, Faulkner argued that its continued use led to a decline in fertility, increased erosion, and impoverishment of land and people. He argued that the moldboard's action created "an explosive separation of the soil mass [that] wrecks temporarily all capillary connections; the organic matter sandwiched in further expends the period of sterility of the soil because of dryness." Faulkner noticed that plowed fields, when left fallow, grew few plants the next year, whereas adjoining unplowed areas produced flora in abundance. In Faulkner's view, deep plowing

trapped undecayed organic material underneath the topsoil, which in
turn "leeched" or poisoned the ground, thereby creating a hard surface
layer that released moisture instead of absorbing it into the ground, leading to runoff, erosion, evaporation, and climatic change. The result of the
moldboard's battle against "nature's process" of soil building was an
increased dependence on manufactured chemicals, a need to expand the
amount of land under cultivation, and highly inefficient crop yields,
judged by bushels per acre and by the amount of investment needed to
sustain yields. In Faulkner's description, American agriculture had failed
to develop "self-sufficiency of the soil" and "permanence in soil productive power" by neglecting the "almost automatic provisions of nature for
supplying plants with complete rations." Furthermore, farmers were
becoming hooked on quick but expensive technological "fixes" instead of
solving their problems permanently.[41]

Faulkner labeled his plan to correct past abuses and provide for an
abundant future *trash farming*, or *trash mulch culture*. His system was
derived from other concepts of the period, including conservation tillage,
humus farming, and organic farming. Simply stated, Faulkner proposed
to emulate organic farmers and ancient peasant agricultural systems by
incorporating large amounts of organic material into the topsoil. Unlike
the organic farmer who spaded or rototilled barnyard waste, composts,
and mulches into the soil bed, the trash farmer would stir green manures
and crop and weed residues ("trash") into the topsoil using the disc plow
instead of burying the natural or planted organic material underneath the
surface layer via the deep plowing action of the moldboard. The result
would be a humus-building topsoil teeming with "trashy" residue that
Faulkner claimed would assist in "restoring the conditions which pre-
vailed upon the land when it was new, [and which] will cure erosion and
restore productiveness in a single stroke."[42]

By incorporating organic matter into the soil, more water could be
infiltrated into the soil, thus providing more nutrients to plants and
working against water erosion. Additionally, "decayed vegetable growth,
trash, and dead and living roots of all kinds . . . [created] a poor field for
the forces of wind erosion." Trash farming purportedly created what
Faulkner described as "real soil," which was "black, crumbly, loose
enough to be springy when walked over, free from crusts in all circumstances, and may be worked almost at once after a rainfall." Real soil, he
claimed with characteristic bombast, would produce up to five times the
yield per acre as standard American farms, without the expensive pesticides, fertilizers, herbicides, and other manufactured agents that
swamped American agriculture. Like Sir Albert Howard and J. I. Rodale,
Faulkner railed against these "poisons," claiming that healthy soil would
nurture healthy, disease-resistant crops, which in turn would nurture

healthy people and societies. Faulkner also offered ideas for new machinery to effect trash mulch culture, suggestions regarding the correct angles for working "trash" into the ground without mucking up planter shoes and other machinery, and advice on the best green manure crops (usually rye or legumes).

After Faulkner's ideas were widely circulated, many machinery manufacturers began to produce equipment that would assist in mixing "trash" into the soil. For instance, advertisements for large-scale roto-tillers (an idea that had existed since at least the 1850s) started appearing in farm magazines in the years after the publication of *Plowman's Folly*. In late 1945, *Farm Journal, Wallaces' Farmer,* and *California Cultivator* printed advertisements for an "amazing new implement" called a Till-Master that assisted in working green manures and surface rubbish into the soil. A West Virginia farmer named John F. Hensler described for readers of the *Land* a machine he called "my Faulknerizer"—a device that rolled down a cover crop, chopped and pulverized it, and mixed the crop residue with the topsoil.

Again, while claiming "no general utopias," Faulkner recognized that his vision of trash farming went beyond simple techniques. His ideology offered a dramatic shift in American agriculture toward a new era of stewardship and ecological and societal harmony. Many people opposed Faulkner's highly generalized and scientifically dubious plan. Nonetheless, this self-described experimental farmer found many influential supporters, including Hugh Bennett, who noted, "By personal observation, by the results of scientific study and by the practical experiences of farmers, I believe it is becoming increasingly evident that the passing of the turning plow from general use in our cultivation would be a boon. Some day it may be regarded as a notable event in history."[43]

THE BENEFITS OF PERMANENT, ECOLOGICAL AGRICULTURE

Both the organic and the New Deal wings of permanent agriculture thought that, beyond its promise of ecological health and rural-urban balance, permanent agriculture offered an array of agrarian, economic, and other societal benefits. Especially in the mid-1940s, proponents believed the new agriculture offered an opportunity to salvage the small farmer and the Jeffersonian, agrarian ideal. It also afforded the chance to bring long-term stability and prosperity to a national economy emerging from two decades of domestic and civil strife. Most fantastically, the advocates of permanent agriculture portrayed their various systems as brightly lit avenues leading toward a future America endowed with health, abundance, and permanent peace.

First, permanent agriculture promised to restore ecological harmony between people and the land. After all, "cooperation" with nature formed a central tenet of permanent agriculture. "Once this collaboration with nature is accepted, and a program of biologically sound planning is undertaken," wrote a new farming proponent employed by the Tennessee Valley Authority, "we will realize at once that our traditional cash accounting has given rise to fundamental error." In other words, permanent agriculture helped establish the idea that societal wealth was more than economics and was part of a greater complex of ideas that included a reckoning with the environmental costs of exploitative agriculture. William Vogt wrote that the ideal of permanent agriculture represented the onset of a new "recognition and acceptance of the responsibility that [humanity] adjust properly to [its] total environment."[44]

A second general benefit promised with the adoption of permanent agriculture included the salvation of rural life and the revitalization of the oft-resurrected Jeffersonian ideal. Historian David Danbom labels this ideal romantic agrarianism, while others have called it agricultural fundamentalism. In basic terms, it pictured a nation of small, independent, prosperous farmers rewarded by the economic and psychic values of country life. Louis Bromfield's experiment epitomized this agrarian aspect in the general ideology of permanent agriculture. Bromfield's nonfiction books in the 1920s and 1930s invoked the American agrarian tradition, and his later work continued this theme of the farmer as guardian of republican virtue.[45]

In his many attacks against the "Age of Irritation," Bromfield proclaimed permanent agriculture as an alternative to a future of urban industrialism. He wrote: "The farm, the earth, appeared to be the sound base from which man, especially one who was weary and disillusioned through too much experience in the modern, complex, industrial, imperialist world, could re-examine his own significance." The truculent Ohioan also asserted, "There is in all the world no finer figure than a sturdy farmer standing, his feet well planted in the earth, looking over his rich fields and beautiful, shiny cattle." Bromfield considered himself part of a "natural rural aristocracy," a superior "soil being" who could enlighten both urbanites and the small-scale (read peasant) farmers in his locale, which in Bromfield's case was the entire nation. He subscribed to the view that "the vast majority of the great men and women of the nation and those who have built it come from farms or hamlets." Indeed, for many Americans in the 1940s, agriculture was "a special social order" with distinctive "moral, intellectual, and cultural points of view." These claims were echoed by others in the period, including A. Whitney Griswold, president of Yale University, who would write of the "soft spot we have in our hearts for farming. Who talks of saving business or manufac-

turing as a way of life? Who does not lament an abandoned farm?" Griswold, while noting that "the Jeffersonian ideal is a hardy perennial,"
agreed with Franklin Roosevelt's concern that the "agricultural ladder
has become a treadmill." Thus, in the permanent agriculture worldview,
"If agriculture is sick, the whole structure is affected. If agriculture col-
lapses, all else goes with it—health, banks, insurance companies, cur-
rency, high standard of living—everything."[46]

Bromfield's message of a permanent and ecological agriculture featured his devotion to the agrarian ideal. He invited thousands of people
to visit his farm to witness the "terrifying" fertility of his land, where
"there is no smell quite so good as fresh-turned sweet earth . . . tinged
with the vanilla-like smell of sweet clover being crushed by the moving
wheels of the tractor." Special visitors invited to the grand table of the
Bromfield home enjoyed the proprietor's bounty, detailed by "King
Louis" as "young White Rock broilers, mashed potatoes, gravy, cauli-
flower and sweet corn fresh from the garden, quantities of fresh butter
churned Thursday, tomatoes like beefsteak and the first limestone lettuce,
newly made peach butter and freshly made pickles, . . . ice cold can-
taloupe, watermelon, big bunches of Niagara and Concord grapes and
fresh peaches, . . . Guernsey milk, . . . everything . . . produced on the
place."[47]

E. B. White, an occasional visitor to Malabar, wrote a tribute to Bromfield's attempt at a pastoral utopia. White's lengthy poem, published in
the *New Yorker*, read in part:

> Malabar Farm is the farm for me,
> It's the greatest place in the whole countree,
> It builds the soil with stuff organic,
> It's the nearest thing to a planned panic.

Even the cosmopolitan and defiantly unsentimental Rexford Tugwell
coupled the concept of permanent agriculture with mythical agrarianism.
While criticizing the backwardness of the back-to-the-land element in
permanent agriculture, Tugwell thought Americans had "everything to
gain from the recovery of lost companionship between men and women
who have a common task, to the renewal of the joys of sound appetites
and healthy bodies which come from tending gardens and making honest flour." Tugwell envisioned a countryside laced with "the wide-shoul-
dered house surrounded by edible and fragrant growing things, . . . hills
to rest the eyes, . . . and there is the slow rhythm of natural succession,
day and season and year, turning toward a ripe and fruitful age. There is
a place to put down roots, with people and animals to care deeply and
permanently about."[48]

Permanent agriculture's alleged agrarian benefits merged with this period's oft-expressed desire for a better balance between rural and urban, and between agricultural and industrial worlds. At the end of Tugwell's description of a prosperous countryside, he noted that this dream had "all been lost." The causes of social dislocation in the period were as varied as the commentators who belabored the problems of modern civilization, but there was general agreement in the permanent agriculture camp that a sound agriculture was fundamental to a balanced, prosperous, and peaceful civilization. For Louis Bromfield, Edward Faulkner, Hugh Bennett, and others, the true gauge of a nation's wealth was productive land, the vital element needed to build a vigorous rural society that could counter industrial urbanism. The permanent agriculture camp thought a nation of cities left unchecked in their growth would "produce tensions, prejudices and bitterness which would scarcely exist at all if industry were dispersed into smaller communities over the whole of the nation." Also, by farming "vertically," America's farmers could produce more on less land, thus eliminating the need to displace neighbors as occurred when they farmed "horizontally."[49]

Permanent agriculture also promised a third general benefit: an economic prosperity that would support the revitalization of rural life. Edward Faulkner's remarkably simple reasoning best illustrates the economic claims made by the proponents of permanent agriculture. Faulkner, who offered "no general utopias," claimed that his system would allow farmers to take "full advantage of the productive power of real soil" while "maintaining their mechanical lead over other farmers the world over." Hence, American farmers could "undersell the rest of the world" in a program of planned abundance and deflation of prices. Because they would be producing more per acre while lowering costs via the Faulkner system, farmers could accept reduced prices for their products. Highly erosion-sensitive land would then be retired, planted in perennial grasses, reforested for commercial use, or set aside as wildlife preserves and refuges. Additional acres could also be devoted to fruit and vegetable production and could be farmed for chemurgic purposes, thus creating a supply of renewable raw materials for industrial use and further padding the farmer's wallet. Faulkner's idealistic side predicted that abundance would make food and industrial products extraordinarily cheap for consumers, eliminate economic competition and war, and create farmers who were gratified "middle class consumers" enduring fewer "tensions of civilization" and living more comfortable lives.[50]

Like the organic wing of the movement, the New Deal section hoped for social benefits from permanent agriculture. Hugh Bennett suggested that the new farming was "not limited in its effects and benefits just to the farm on which it is practiced. It is closely related to the profitability of industry, the well-being of municipalities, and the health and welfare of all the people." The chief of the SCS constantly reminded bankers and farmers, industry and labor, professional people, and "everybody else" that they had "a vital stake in the permanent welfare of the country's productive land." Bennett constantly linked a federal program for permanent agriculture to concerns over postwar unemployment and depression. In late 1943, the SCS claimed that its plan for permanent agriculture could employ 470,000 people for one year at $1,200 to $1,600 per person, or 117,000 people for four years at a cost of $831 million plus $100 million for hiring engineers. Bennett would always claim that no matter the cost, his soil conservation and rebuilding program was a sound financial investment in the future. "Economic stability grows from good soil used intelligently" was one of his favorite slogans. In 1947, the stalwart Georgian, already hailed as the father of soil conservation, claimed that he could put America on a program for permanent agriculture for the cost of $5.5 billion over seven years. While this was a steep outlay, Bennett asserted that his program would result in a $50-per-acre dividend over ten years when accounting for increased productivity and reduced costs.[51]

Faulkner's and Bennett's claims of economic rejuvenation via permanent agriculture were echoed by others in the period, including Louis Bromfield, who presented a loud and needlesome voice in the debate over the future of farming in the years during and immediately after World War II. Sensing that permanent agriculture was part of a longer-expressed desire for "equity for agriculture," Bromfield wrote: "Eventually, out of grim economic necessity, the level of our agriculture will be raised and we shall have lower costs for consumers and higher profits for the farmer arising out of higher and efficient production." While devoted to the idea that farming was a "special" segment of the economy endowed with psychic benefits, and while they held out for at least partial self-sufficiency on the farm, Faulkner, Bromfield, and most members of the permanent agriculture movement subscribed to a commercial interpretation of farming, and their new faith in ecological agriculture was not a "philosophy of despair." In other words, permanent agriculture was about making money as well as being ecologically healthy and economically sensible. It was, in essence, an idea based on superabundance. Farmers were going to make everyone wealthy for the long term, so went the ideology, by combining American technological and marketing expertise with the permanent, ecological tenets of permanency on the land, creating in turn a "greater pride and satisfaction in farming along with greater material returns." For Edward Faulkner, his humbly inspired plan had disclosed "that the world is not yet the burned-out cinder some writers have suggested in their fear of Malthusian certainties for the future."[52]

The idea that the new ecological farming would produce health benefits as well as good crops and environmental benefits formed a fourth general benefit claimed by "organics" advocates in the permanent agriculture movement. Edward Faulkner boldly proclaimed in 1943 that "agronomists as well as nutritionists are aware that lands which have been exhausted of their essential nutrients produce foodstuffs which are deficient in the end-products required by human beings." Faulkner, Bromfield, Rodale, and others actively promoted the link between ecologically "healthy" soil and human health and nutrition, a notion imported from the likes of Sir Albert Howard and author Erhenfield Pfieffer. Faulkner proclaimed that his trash farming system would serve as "groundline health insurance" and would provide "abounding health through a rich soil, restored to produce boundless nutrition." Faulkner also asserted that encouraging "natural health" for the land was a proactive alternative to American agriculture's increasing dependence on chemical prescriptions for ex post facto soil problems. Louis Bromfield supported Faulkner's claims, noting that "at Malabar we know that we have a remarkably low rate of sickness and infections among plants, animals and people." He also claimed that due to his program of ecological agriculture and livestock management, outbreaks of mastitis and Bang's disease were anomalies in his cattle population. Friends of the Land, the main organized group promoting the permanent agriculture idea, also attempted to legitimize the health claims of permanent agriculture adherents by sponsoring the conference "Soil, Food and Health: 'You Are What You Eat,'" which again linked ecological farming with the health of the general population.[53]

The champions of permanent, ecological agriculture also joined their cause to the greater concern for postwar peace and prosperity. During the years surrounding World War II, the proponents of permanent agriculture proclaimed a fifth general benefit—that, as the new farming regime brought abundance, so it would create the conditions necessary for a peaceful world. Walter C. Lowdermilk, a diplomat for the SCS, summed up the mentality of those working for permanent agriculture in 1945 when he wrote that "this war will not be ended by the mere cessation of hostilities. Great world problems will have to be solved, and deep wounds will have to be healed by many years of united effort. Otherwise the end of the war will only prove to be a pause before a new and more horrible holocaust." While particularly fearing for the future of the Levant, Lowdermilk expressed the concerns of many Americans for the future of the entire world. Some looked to the solidification of United Nations' rule under a world constitution, and other groups put forth technological solutions to the threats facing humanity; Lowdermilk and the permanent agriculture cadre were convinced that "this partnership of land and farmer is the rock foundation of our civilization; if either member of this partnership weakens or fails, the whole structure of civilization built upon it likewise weakened and fails. Nations rise or fall upon their food supply, and hence ultimately upon the condition of their land."[54]

Edward Faulkner advised that permanent agriculture would be successful for those willing to "wait patiently to work their way to soil conditions such as have now developed in this tiny plot of mine." If patient, "they could relax their fear tensions and look forward with confidence to a completely balanced future so far as the productivity of their land is concerned." Ward Shepard described permanent agriculture, as initiated in soil conservation districts, as a path to "democratic social action," while others, such as Bennett and Bromfield, envisioned permanent agriculture as a tool for building a balanced economy.[55]

But the promised societal benefits of permanent agriculture went beyond the farmstead and extended across national borders. "Well-fed, secure people are not readily persuaded to take up arms" was the message preached by Hugh Bennett in the years during and immediately after the war. Erosion and unproductive land caused hunger and poverty, which in turn created civil strife, reasoned Bennett. People turned over their freedom for food, and lack of productive land and abundant food and fiber was sure to produce "discontented people, disturbers of the peace, given to uprisings, and breeders of war." Bennett illustrated his point by reminding listeners that Germany and Japan had both gone to war to find resources, especially land, to feed burgeoning, industrialized nations. He also suggested frequently that neglect of the soil led to national decline. Hence, to Bennett, good soil was the "hub on which the wheels of industry turn," essential in ensuring "a prosperous agriculture [as] the nation's foundation." Agriculture contributed not only food and fiber but also economic sustenance to schools, churches, communities, businesses, and homes, not to mention serving as a weapon in the "defense from attack by treacherous enemies."[56]

Bennett, Lowdermilk, and other advocates of permanent agriculture felt certain that the process of building the new farming would bring prosperity and therefore world peace. Indeed, Bennett's SCS support group Friends of the Land actively promoted the idealistic and technical ideas of permanent agriculture around the world, particularly in Latin America and other underdeveloped nations, thus inserting the permanent agriculture idea (albeit quietly) into the postwar struggle between capitalism and communism. Bennett was the most vocal apostle of the idea that permanent agriculture would restore peace and prosperity to a world crippled by bloodshed and angst regarding the future. He posited a very near future in which every acre of land would be restored in such a fashion as to produce crops permanently in "millions of communities throughout the world." In the new era of abundance and harmony, planned, permanent, ecological agriculture would be the main solution to the problems confronting humanity, including "famine, food distribution and human nutrition."[57]

CHAPTER THREE

The Public Life of
Permanent Agriculture

The permanent agriculture concept offered a comprehensive worldview, a promise of material abundance and the salvation of culture and civilization. The permanent agriculture idea was important because it centered on a very basic aspect of human survival—the food system. Yet permanent agriculture emerged during an era when the number of small farms in America declined. How relevant and how useful was permanent agriculture for American farmers? Did it spark debate and change? Were the movement's ideas disseminated into intellectual, agricultural, industrial, and popular culture circles? Or was the permanent agriculture concept only an exercise in rhetoric, fuzzy science, and vague utopianism?

In the movement's brief and vigorous history, purveyors of the ideology of permanent agriculture communicated their ideas to a national audience, sparking an intense debate and resistance within the scientific and agricultural communities. The movement was co-opted and watered down by traditional elements of agriculture, and it suffered a relative decline for a number of reasons. Still, the permanent agriculture idea persisted both in the academy and in various subcultures through the 1950s, lending itself both tangibly and mythologically to a later ideology of societal permanence known as *sustainable agriculture.*

COMMUNICATION OF THE IDEA

As various notions of planned, permanent, and ecologically oriented agriculture coalesced in the late 1930s and early 1940s, advocates of the new farming recognized the necessity for publicizing their ideas. Rexford Tugwell, Morris L. Cooke, and many others in the permanent agriculture movement had entered public discourse during the Progressive Era, when reformers used publicity tools to educate the public about societal problems. Individuals and organizations of the permanent agriculture milieu set about public education with great zeal, especially the conservation group Friends of the Land, founded in 1940 to support the work of Hugh Bennett's cadre at the Soil Conservation Service. Emerging from the soil crisis of the 1930s, the permanent agriculture concept became attached to the national campaign for conservation education in the period, to the battle against fascism, and later to the cold war. Proselytizing by "erosion apostles" such as Louis Bromfield and Hugh Bennett brought national attention to the permanent agriculture movement, especially with the added attention resulting from the controversial ideas of Edward Faulkner. By 1947, the general ideas of permanent agriculture had permeated society, and the term itself appeared frequently in agricultural journals and trade pamphlets.

The communication of the permanent agriculture concept emerged in the soil jeremiads that appeared following the societal and ecological crises of the 1930s. The quest for a planned, permanent agriculture seemed quite sensible to ordinary farmers and citizens witnessing events like the dust bowl and the dismal agricultural economy. For agricultural theorists such as Henry Wallace, secretary of agriculture (1933–41) and later Vice President (1941–45), the soil crisis offered an opportunity to present the new ethic of interdependent living before large audiences. Wallace was particularly convinced that Pare Lorentz's films (The River and The Plow That Broke the Plains), financed by the USDA in the late 1930s, employed an ideal medium to popularize the idea of soil permanence. Writing to Morris Cooke in November 1939, agricultural reformer Russell Lord indicated that Wallace had "come to see conservation as something of Mr. James's 'moral equivalent' and was supportive of Lorentz's idea of shooting 'The Grapes of Wrath' outdoors, and make it better." Lord continued his discussion of the film's purpose, writing, "I guess we shall show both soil and human displacement, and the beginnings of stabilized soil and greater human security."[1]

This new version of John Steinbeck's classic tale was never made, though one filmmaker did attempt to document the abuse of the land and proposals for a new system of permanent agriculture. Director Robert Flaherty, well known for his previous work, including Nanook of the North, released his USDA-sponsored film The Land in 1941. A critical flop, the film quickly disappeared from public view, in spite of support from the permanent agriculture cadre. Flaherty's film, which embodied the general attempt to publicize past abuses of the soil, promoted all the key concepts of planned and permanent agriculture: support for planning, interdependent living, and ecologically oriented conservation of the soil.[2]

Building permanent agriculture required far more than a few films and staid USDA pamphlets. The new agriculture demanded an inculcation of values that incorporated a new blend of conservation and ecological thought. Aldo Leopold elaborated on the notion of imparting values, writing that "the evolution of the land ethic is an intellectual as well as an emotional process. Conservation is paved with good intentions which prove to be futile, or even dangerous, because they are devoid of critical understanding either of land, or of economic land use." Hugh Bennett echoed

Leopold, informing the permanent agriculture cadre that building a permanent agriculture was a "major national objective." Bennett admonished his audience that "this conservation-needs concept must become a habit, from our youth onward, and part of our culture, sunk deeply into our physiological make-up. Herein lies the challenge for thought and a call to action for every Friend of the Land." Leopold asserted that "many products of land-abuse can be identified as such, and can be discriminated against, given the conviction that it is worth the trouble." He was especially concerned with teaching ecological conservation to the youth, as were Bennett and company. Bennett wanted the new agricultural-ecological ethic to be incorporated at all levels of education and in American business culture so that people would have the "incentive" and "training" to "look at the landscape around them and wonder what was happening."[3]

By focusing on education in what Leopold called the "land ethic," proponents of agricultural permanence were part of a larger conservation education crusade in the 1940s. The overwhelming concern of those who supported this crusade was that "much of today's conservation problem grew out of the fact that people in this expanding nation never really learned the relationship between their daily lives and the natural resources of the earth." This faith in the uplifting abilities of education sparked a conservation campaign in the National Education Association and other bodies, a campaign to teach conservation as "basic to American life, that each generation recognize its obligation to future generations." Bennett, with his typical sense of urgency, stated in 1941, "It is high time to introduce into our schools courses which deal with the soil as a resource basic to continuing national welfare—as something to be preserved."[4]

As the conservation education message permeated all levels of society, the ideology of permanent agriculture also began to reach a broader audience. As a defined ideological program, the concept of permanent agriculture found its most lucid advocate in an organization designed initially to augment and support the work and message of Hugh Bennett and the SCS. "Knowing that whole regions of our country, once incredibly rich, were on the verge of becoming deserts," wrote Louis Bromfield, "these men [and actually a few women]—forestry experts, industrialists, doctors, government officials, writers, bankers, professors, farmers—resolved to educate the American people to the danger." The group Bromfield described was the conservation organization Friends of the Land, whose organizational life in many ways reflects the historical events of the permanent agriculture concept. For Friends of the Land, the main question confronting conservationists was: "How can a people who seem for the past four centuries to have been doing the wrong things to their land . . . turn in their tracks, change their minds, their basic designs of ground line culture, their implements, their ways?"[5]

The desire for a new conservation organization that would serve as a private auxiliary to the SCS had been kicked around in USDA and agricultural conservation camps in the late 1930s. The genesis of Friends of the Land was a letter from Hugh Bennett to Morris Cooke in 1938 in which Bennett singled out Cooke as the likely leader of "a group of thinking people having the interest of the nation at heart as the nucleus of a national organization." The idea for this new conservation group was partially influenced by the Society for the Holy Earth, a similar effort to promote stewardship that was founded by Liberty Hyde Bailey in 1917. Friends of the Land served as the main font of publicity for permanent agriculture; its history also contributes to a greater understanding of American environmental history, dramatically illustrating the transition from Progressive Era, "wise-use" conservation ideas and values to the new recognition of ecological interdependence. Historians often cite the life experience of Aldo Leopold (himself a prominent member of Friends of the Land) as representative of this shift in values from human-centered "use" of resources to a more holistic or biocentric approach. Historians might also cite Friends of the Land as an example of this transition into the age of ecology. The history of the group also shows the enduring importance of effective publicity in the shaping of a new idea within the public mind-set, as well as the centrality of agricultural issues in the development of an environmental ethic in the United States.[6]

Friends of the Land's formal organizational meeting occurred on March 22–23, 1940, with about sixty individuals attending at the Wardman Park Hotel in Washington, D.C. Working with Henry A. Wallace, Hugh Bennett, Rexford Tugwell, and several others, agricultural journalist Russell Lord and New Dealer Morris Cooke, the group's first president, began to define the group's mission and to build the membership roster. The initial charter proposed that the organization serve as a font of information on conservation, promote regional and local conservation associations, prepare a magazine for the general public, support and reward conservation work and research, influence legislation, promote youth conservation education, integrate with like-minded organizations, and hold periodic conferences on soil and water conservation. Founders of Friends of the Land wanted to be the locus of conservation information, hoping that in the end their efforts would "possess a strong continuity of purpose to reconcile the ways of Man to Nature and make this a green and permanent land."[7]

Although conceived by reformers and left-leaning social critics to augment the New Deal, the group quickly expanded beyond those sentiments in an attempt to offer "a wider, patriotic appeal to the business community in particular." In 1940, the group sent out hundreds of membership appeals to prominent industrialists and farm leaders, government officials, publishers, doctors, professionals, academics, and conservationists. The goal was to form the nucleus of a national organization that would eventually expand to form regional and local chapters. While the war presented an opportunity to appeal to the conservation-minded, Friends of the Land experienced some initial organizational problems, including lack of money and limited public interest because of more pressing concerns associated with war mobilization. In early 1941, the group shifted its headquarters to Columbus, Ohio, with its secretary, Russell Lord, firmly in charge as editor of the *Land*.[8]

To promote such ideas as societal interdependence and the quest for ecological permanence, Friends of the Land first had to attract interest and build membership ranks and financial support. By employing some key personalities and by attaching its ideas and work to the war crisis, Friends of the Land successfully garnered national attention in its fledgling stage from 1940 to 1942. Using an approach often associated with selling war bonds, Friends of the Land received publicity and memberships when it sent Bennett, Bromfield, and other celebrity orators across the nation on what one observer labeled a "Flying Conservation Circus." These disciples of permanent agriculture preached their gospel in person and on radio and newsreel to conservation districts; farm, civic, and business groups; schools and universities; garden clubs; and sundry other audiences. The svelte Bromfield, who earned the moniker "Sinatra of the Soil," asserted his life was divided between "night clubs and manure piles." He stated that after the first promotional tour in the spring of 1941, "scores of converts to conservation were made. . . . several dozen returned home to become evangelists, some nearly fanatics. They went back to their own communities to rouse interest in conservation programs. The Friends were besieged with requests for speakers."[9]

In addition to the mercurial activity of Bennett, Bromfield, Russell Lord, Kate Lord, and others, the Friends received publicity and editorial support from a number of national media outlets, including the *New York Herald-Tribune*, the *New York Times*, the *New Yorker, Harper's*, and *Reader's Digest*. Along with this national attention, the group and its journal benefited from contributions from the likes of E. B. White, John Dos Passos, Henry A. Wallace, Sir Albert Howard, Rachel Carson, Aldo Leopold, Paul Sears, and many other nationally recognized authors, politicians, and social critics.[10]

Judging from the volume of speeches, articles, books, and other propaganda, there is no question that the idea of building a permanent agriculture was widely disseminated. As historian David Wright has suggested, it is difficult for present-day Americans to comprehend that in the 1930s and 1940s agricultural leaders and commentators were national personalities. Individuals preaching the permanent agriculture concept, including Bennett and Bromfield, had a national audience and a following that extended beyond the farm community. Bromfield wrote books to "lure readers who never had any interest in agriculture or whose interest had been dulled or killed by pamphlets."[11]

Friends of the Land, particularly its journal the *Land*, served as a unifying force and a forum for internal dialogue between pedestrian conservationists in the organization and committed advocates of permanent agriculture. The gospel of the new farming also reached the public via articles in a vast range of journals and popular periodicals, through pamphleteering, public testimonials and appearances, conferences, thought pieces, poetry, conservation camps, monographs and conference proceedings, radio appearances, and other methods. Bromfield, Bennett, Cooke, and others traversed the land during the war and afterward, from Atlanta to Memphis, rural Pennsylvania, Texas, and Des Moines. They offered sermons on the canons of the movement—planning, permanence, ecology, abundance, and rural-urban balance. According to local legend, Mount Jeez, a prominent hill at Bromfield's Malabar Farm, where up to eight thousand people once attended a conservation field day, was so christened as a humorous tribute to Bromfield's messianic drive.[12]

The prophets of the permanent agriculture religion preferred education over coercion for converting the heathen American public to the virtues of understanding the "complex interrelationships of social and economic forces with the physical." Schools became the battleground against waste of the soil. Hugh Bennett wanted his idea to reach every level of the educational structure, from "kindergarten grade to post-graduate work in our colleges." He wished to challenge Americans to view their material goods and then "trace their sources to the soil; relate the everyday life of the pupil to the land he depends on."[13]

The permanent agriculture camp was well aware of the value of publicity. In 1945, when Friends of the Land and the Grange cosponsored a conservation field day in Maryland, the *Land* reported that "either Bromfield or Bennett would have been enough to draw a crowd, but we had them both, plus the proper mixture of state conservationists and, quite unnecessarily, a couple of eminent state politicians, including the governor. The whole affair kicked up a lot of interest." The Friends sponsored weekend country seminars, "conservation laboratories" for teachers, veteran or granger "short courses" and seminars on conservation, radio programs, and conservation clubs. The *Land* printed advice from educators, scientists, farmers, and small-plot/garden theorists, requiring only that somewhere in the educational process one had to employ "the good earth as a textbook," with the purpose of that text being the promotion of the new conservation-ecological ethic as "a way of life."[14]

The core group of permanent agriculture educators worked to show

how the new system of food and fiber production would contribute to the building of a peaceful and prosperous postwar world. Key voices in the movement, like Bennett and Bromfield, rose on behalf of the new farming in the agricultural and national press as the war approached its end. Bennett and others envisioned the integration of the permanent agriculture idea into a proposed program to create jobs. Bromfield worried that government policies would produce a postwar food shortage. The permanent agriculture group also feared that the high production demanded by the war would lead to another epoch of ecological devastation, as had the "great plow up" of 1917–18.[15]

As the now-recognized "father of soil conservation," Hugh Bennett challenged farmers and landowners in Athens, Georgia, to follow the precepts of permanent agriculture in the quest for high production and profit: "This is a great country—a land of unmeasurable opportunity. Let's fight this war through for civilization and for our lives and for our kind of government. Taking care of the land—husbanding and cherishing it and fighting for it—will keep us free and permanent and great." Another commentator, Vernon G. Carter, asked farmers to be wary of another "plow-up" type adventure, cautioning his readers that "man does not live by bread alone, but certain it is that he cannot live without bread." Educator Otis W. Freeman summed up the sense of both anxiety and opportunity at the end of World War II in the permanent agriculture camp, noting that "outstanding problems of conservation must be solved in the postwar America if our country is to retain its social standards and national rank."[16]

In the attempt to communicate the values of permanent agriculture, advocates of the new farming enjoyed particular success in the months following the release of Edward Faulkner's *Plowman's Folly* in 1943. Faulkner's book rocked the agricultural community and gained national attention even amid the monumental events of World War II. Faulkner's diatribes against the moldboard plow, drainage tiles, agricultural chemicals, and the agricultural establishment touched on many raw nerves throughout the land.

His harangues also appealed to farmers worried about a potential postwar depression, the influence of science and technology, and the decline of rural life. *Plowman's Folly* quickly sold fifty thousand copies and went into a second printing. Commentators of all stripes debated the Faulkner concept in major national outlets such as *Time* and the *New Republic,* and the *Land* devoted several issues almost solely to the Faulkner controversy. Henry Ford, Henry A. Wallace, Hugh Bennett, Sir Albert Howard, and many other prominent agricultural and national figures discussed Faulkner's ideas and in varying degrees accepted much of his system of permanent agriculture. Russell Lord later claimed that

Faulkner's revelations had "resounded around the world with a vigor and intensity worthy of such a subject as the atomic bomb." Louis Bromfield claimed that Faulkner's book "aroused so much interest and controversy" because "it exploited and defended the principle upon which all the New Agriculture is based—the thesis that what is natural in agriculture is always more desirable and sound than what is unnatural."[17]

Faulkner claimed to have taken a seventy-five-hundred-mile tour to talk with scores of agricultural college researchers, farmers, and agribusiness persons in the months following the release of *Plowman's Folly*, and he also claimed to have received tens of thousands of supportive letters. The attention given to Faulkner's ideas from roughly 1943 to 1947 was tremendous. Henry A. Wallace supported many of Faulkner's concepts, but felt that the trash mulch concept would prove impractical because of the corn borer problem that would be created with the stubble mulch system. Nonetheless, Wallace asked Henry Ford to send an engineer to assist Faulkner with the design of a tillage implement. Ford replied that the Ford Ferguson tractor had attachments that would work the ground as prescribed by Faulkner.

Faulkner's ability to draw attention to himself and his arguments exemplifies the communication skills of the permanent agriculture camp. Faulkner, Bromfield, Bennett, Tugwell, and others were effective partisans for the cause. Even during the war crisis, the general ideas of permanent agriculture unquestionably reached millions of people. Furthermore, events like the controversy over Faulkner's ideas and the postwar debate over agricultural issues led to more recognition for the movement. Friends of the Land enjoyed a modicum of success, with its membership roster climbing from the initial sixty members to nearly ten thousand members in 1947. Although they were a loosely affiliated coalition, adherents had some initial success in promoting the concepts of societal longevity, ecological interdependence, and the utopian possibilities of the new farming. Permanent agriculture's many precepts circulated through the late 1940s, reaching Americans of all stripes with their infectious promises of health, wealth, and prosperity. Evidence of the persuasiveness of the permanent agriculture ideology and how individuals brewed their own mix of science and mysticism was demonstrated in a 1951 letter to President Harry S. Truman from Henry B. Miller, one of the Miller Brothers, "Breeders of Pedigreed Seed Oats." Writing in passionate if disjointed prose, Miller sprinkled his letter with the essential ideas that resounded in the public life of permanent agriculture. He told the president that "after a life time of hard work in factual research, seeking the key to soil conservation and its related problems," he had found "the universal key" to understanding the complex interrelationships between conservation and the "indispensable existance [*sic*]" of "plants, animals, and the microscopic forms of life." Miller told the president with all seriousness about "the immensity of power, strength and health" of nature-designed agriculture that was "permitted to perform with true entity in true unity."[18]

RESISTANCE AND CO-OPTION

As Miller's letter and numerous other similar farmer-conversion testimonials indicate, the holistic notions of the permanent agriculture camp had been widely disseminated by the early 1950s. With the *Land* earning critical acclaim and Edward Faulkner's ideas being debated nationally, the concept of permanent agriculture became a subject of national scrutiny in the 1940s. While Faulkner's and similar diatribes against past soil abuses were generally supported, the scientific, political, and social claims of permanent agriculture were harshly attacked, particularly by agricultural scientists and members of the USDA–agricultural college–Farm Bureau–"agribusiness" nexus. Although naysayers proclaimed permanent ecological agriculture to be pseudoscientific and laden with unrealistic utopian social expectations, the actual term *permanent agriculture* became favored in the agricultural establishment. In essence, the idea of permanent ecological agriculture was co-opted and watered down by the USDA and companies and institutions selling their goods and ideas to the nation's farmers, contributing to the virtual demise of the permanent agriculture idea by the mid-1950s.

Although the ideas generated by the likes of Edward Faulkner and Louis Bromfield engendered much support from farmers, conservationists, and nonfarm commentators (as had Hugh Bennett's work at the SCS) agricultural scientists offered quick, emotional, and vitriolic rejoinders to the many canons of permanent agriculture, especially the efficacy of what by then had been labeled "organic" farming. When *Plowman's Folly* appeared in the summer of 1943, the excitement and publicity it created caused great consternation among America's professional agricultural community, which (as it is now) was centered in the USDA and the land-grant colleges. Surprisingly, the first resistance to Faulkner—and hence to the entire philosophy of organic, ecological agriculture—came from some members of the USDA's SCS, itself a major font of permanent agriculture ideology through its leader, Hugh Bennett.

William Albrect, professor of soils at the University of Missouri, also led a strong attack on almost all the tenets of *Plowman's Folly*, including Faulkner's diatribe against the plow and his promotion of a chemical-free agriculture. Albrect, who would later become a convert of sorts to ecological agriculture, found that "the most sensational feature of the work is the nonchalance with which he sweeps aside the accumulation of years *critic of Faulkner's* of scientific research and farmer experience while staking his reputation on meager personal experience with a few crops grown in a backyard garden." Albrect asserted that Faulkner's focus on the plow neglected other factors in soil mismanagement. Albrect dismissed Faulkner's concern about severed capillary connections (a theory abandoned by soil scientists thirty years prior to *Plowman's Folly*), noting that plants establish their roots deep in the soil, and that factors such as soil temperature and subsoil moisture were more important than having a moist, "trashy" subsoil.

Albrect and others attacked the idea that nature was a superior model for establishing soil fertility, citing the poor, acidic soils of the forest as a prime example of how nature did not always know how to produce the best soils. Albrect also attacked other aspects of Faulkner's "seat of the pants" observations, including his association of "Faulknerized" soil with increased wildlife populations and reduced problems with pests, weeds, and diseases. For Albrect, the author of *Plowman's Folly* offered "many pseudo-scientific claims centered in water and temperature" that would "not stand against the facts of science nor the judgment of experienced farmers." In their attack on Faulkner in 1943, Albrect and SCS scientists noted that his ideas were by no means new and that the obvious influence on Faulkner, Sir Albert Howard, had also been discredited by the agricultural science profession. Initially the attacks centered on Faulkner's willingness to base his system on assumptions and observations, but they also featured some emotional diatribes. One soil scientist from Iowa suggested that if Faulkner's ideas on tile drainage had been implemented, American civilization never would have crossed the Mississippi. Another milder critic lamented that if Faulknerism was accepted, the cherished symbol of the plow might have to be removed from numerous official seals and banners, including that of the Future Farmers of America.[19]

University of Wisconsin soil scientist Emil Truog joined Albrect and the USDA scientists in dismissing Faulkner, Bromfield, and most of the agronomic tenets of permanent ecological agriculture. Writing in the July 1944 issue of *Harper's*, Truog first acknowledged that while too much plowing was bad, especially on hills, Faulkner had drawn far too many insights from his tomato patch to be taken seriously. Truog rejected the idea that the interruption of capillarity was a violation of nature's laws, noting instead that most crops had deep roots and relied on subsurface rather than surface moisture. In fact, asserted the professor, dry surface soil served as insulation for subsurface moisture. Truog defended the plow as necessary to pulverize a seedbed, to rejuvenate the soil by "alternation," and to create a deep soil layer necessary for plants.

As for the "model of nature," Truog suggested that agriculture in fact was a defiance of nature and that nature itself represented an ambivalent model for building soil fertility. Because the annual harvest removed fertility from nature, he noted, humans had to artificially replace nourishing elements in the soil, and Faulkner's simplistic tillage system would not suffice. As for plants, whether they received their food from raw organic mass or from a fifty-pound bag of calcium nitrate did not matter. Truog also rejected the "myth" that Asian peasant "organic" farmers had better soils, citing the malnutrition and prevalent state of famine in that part of the world.

Truog rejected Faulkner's faith in a nonchemical future of abundance, asserting that "absolutely no evidence exists to the effect that the judicious use of mineral fertilizers is at all injurious to soils, or tends to produce crops that are unsatisfactory for animals or food for man." Truog represented a number of agricultural scientists of his day in his faith that the miracle chemicals being produced in scientific laboratories offered a burgeoning world population insurance against winter kill, drought, poor crop quality, excessive seed costs, soil erosion, and low yields. In his vision, like that of others long before him, agricultural science, not the musings of verbose and speculative soil philosophers, offered the true vision of permanent agriculture. For Truog and the like-minded, ecologically inspired permanent agriculture did not recognize that establishing a long-term productive agriculture required a battle against nature, not a nebulous, arbitrarily dissolvable partnership as proposed by Faulkner enthusiasts.[20]

Resistance to the permanent agriculture ideal included attacks on Louis Bromfield, Rexford Tugwell, Russell Lord, and other promoters of the new farming. Agricultural functionary Paul Appleby derided Bromfield's status as an agricultural commentator during the war, and others saw in Tugwell and Lord the embodiment of coercive USDA social engineering. By the end of World War II, the influence of the New Deal social scientists was on the wane, and some of the attacks on permanent agriculture were particularly nasty. In a letter to the *Nation*, Clarence Armstrong called the ideas of Faulkner, Lord, and cadre "ridiculous." Armstrong charged that the idea of permanent ecological agriculture "ignores entirely the whole purpose of the soil, which is to raise crops." Again, agriculture was a defiance, not an emulation, of nature—an industry based on extraction of resources from the soil. Armstrong scolded the permanent agriculture ideal, stating: "We cannot have our cake and eat it. We cannot put everything that grows on the soil back into it and still raise enough food to feed the people of the country."[21]

Lord, Faulkner, and others anticipated these attacks and were quick to fire back at critics. Responding to Armstrong, Russell Lord suggested that he had probably not read Faulkner's book, noting that Armstrong's views were "quite in line with the soil-mining tradition." While observing that many of his opponents were honest people working hard for farmers, Faulkner also alleged that "powerful interests have built up enormous business supplying these aids [manufactured farm chemicals] to farmers, and they will not see their investments made worthless without a struggle." Faulkner believed that "a few among the higher officials know that approval of a completely organic agriculture would doom their business." He also noted resistance from land-grant and extension service experts and actual farmers who were "jittery" at "the prospect of having none of the accustomed chemicals" despite "the fact that most of the world gets along nicely without using commercial fertilizers." Although no methodical studies could support their assertions, the proponents of organic-type farming claimed that they could produce yields nearly equal to those produced by chemical farming, with greatly reduced production costs.[22]

At the same time that resistance grew against the major ideas of ecologically inspired permanent agriculture, particularly the concept of "organics," the general idea that America should work toward "permanent agriculture" remained a goal for nearly all the actors in agriculture until 1950. Indeed, even as the ideology of permanent agriculture spread across the land, opponents and luke warm supporters co-opted the term *permanent agriculture*, while at the same time diminishing and disregarding many of the major ideas of the new farming. While championing a rhetorical form of *permanent agriculture*, the very institutions that Edward Faulkner, Paul Sears, and others had attacked came to promote themselves as frontline warriors for conservation and a long-term agriculture. But for Faulkner and Sears, permanent agriculture was far more than conservation, requiring an ecological worldview that required reverence for life and respect for nature. Furthermore, the permanent agriculture concept envisioned a society of planned abundance, with corresponding desires for social equity, the perpetuation of rural culture, and a sense of belonging and humility in a complex, interdependent world.

While some agricultural scientists were busy rejecting Faulknerism, politicians, agricultural college researchers, USDA officials, farm leaders, and agricultural manufacturers embraced the rhetorical goal of a permanent agriculture. Some of these Johnny-come-latelies hoped to make a great deal of money by marketing machines that would effect a Faulkner-like system on the farmer's fields, and others sought to promote themselves as stalwarts for conservation and the American farmer. Judging by the literature, advertisements, and monographs that appeared at the end of World War II, the permanent agriculture idea had evolved from moral crusade to business imperative. Ford, John Deere, J. I. Case, and International Harvester all illustrated the ways in which their products would help build a permanent agriculture. By the late 1940s, the USDA and agribusiness concerns bandied the phrase *permanent agriculture* in their slogans and advertisements, with little or no adherence to the original social and ecological concerns of the authors of the permanent agriculture ideal. Goodyear Corporation supported soil conservation awards, and small firms like Golden Annual Clover advertised their product as "A New Legume for Soil Building." Yet while these firms, as well as the land-grant agricultural colleges, promoted soil conservation for permanent agriculture, the holistic concerns expressed by Faulkner, Tugwell, Bennett, and others were neglected or dismissed by realists such as agricultural economist John D. Black. In 1948, Black praised soil conservation efforts, but in the spirit of Gifford Pinchot, he noted that in the land program the guide had to be "balancing of present uses and income from the land against future uses and income."[23] Thus professors, politicians, and individuals in the USDA and business responded by embracing the new terminology of permanence and abundance, as well as a few of the ideas of Faulkner, Bromfield, and company, while at the same time glossing over the holistic and grandiose intentions of the original authors of the permanent agriculture ideal.

In essence, permanent agriculture lost its edge as opponents co-opted its terms but not its concepts. Thus, when Goodyear enjoined farmers in a pamphlet, "Let's practice permanent agriculture," the company obviously viewed selling its tires—not a commitment to biological diversity, ecological health, and social equity—as the key to permanent agriculture. Jonathan Forman, president of Friends of the Land in 1952, summed up the frustrations of the early disciples of a new, ecological agriculture when, in a defense of organic farming, he said, "We need, indeed, to define our terms, for these are questions of grave consequence and the arguments pro and con are now being circulated in print to hundreds of millions of people."[24]

Forman might well have referred to an important document in this co-option process, *Grass: The Yearbook of Agriculture, 1948*, whose lead section was "A Permanent Agriculture." In the opening essay, P. V. Cardon defined permanent agriculture as "an agriculture that is stable and secure for farm and farmer, consistent in prices and earnings; an agriculture that can satisfy indefinitely all our needs of food, fiber, and shelter in keeping with the living standards we set. Everybody has a stake in a permanent agriculture." While Rexford Tugwell might have embraced this statement in 1939, and Edward Faulkner would have agreed with it in 1943, by 1947 the concept of permanent agriculture had lost much of its holistic, reformist, and comprehensive impulses and was quickly becoming divorced from many of its original tenets. While the resistance to Faulkner and "organics" damaged the fabric of permanent agriculture, and the co-option of the term loosened its weave, several other factors led to the demise of the permanent agriculture idea in the 1950s.[25]

ECLIPSE

Despite successes in communicating the idea of permanent agriculture, the acceptance of these concepts began to dissipate by the mid-1950s. Certainly the movement suffered from the often outlandish claims of advocates, as well as from co-option and the attacks of opponents. But the falling momentum of permanent agriculture also resulted from the changing structure and definition of American agriculture during the period, from divisions in the conservation camp, and finally from divisions within the guiding force of ecology.

"When I look back now, the vague and visionary idea I had in returning seems ludicrous and pathetic," wrote Louis Bromfield the year prior to his death in 1956, describing the financial and social failure of Malabar Farm. Bromfield, Hugh Bennett, and many of the old idealists in the permanent agriculture movement died in the 1950s, and so did their vision of an interdependent, cooperative society based on permanent agriculture. Americans were growing far more cynical when assessing the utopian possibilities of the future technological state. The idealism, the bold social engineering, and dreams of an agrarian-chemurgic horizon were replaced by a more pragmatic public determination to participate in the postwar epoch of corporations, consumption, and suburban living. With the crises of the 1930s and 1940s behind them, Americans of the 1950s looked apprehensively at visionaries and agrarian iconoclasts like Louis Bromfield and Edward Faulkner. The communitarian, interdependent, reformist universe of the interwar years shifted to the postwar age of atomization, "individuation," and the "bigger is better" mentality.[26]

Permanent agriculture, with its focus on a long-term plan for an ecologically based husbandry and its reliance on technique as much as technology, directly challenged some of the dominant cultural currents of the day. American agriculture underwent drastic changes from the 1930s through the 1950s. The "get big or get out" mentality triumphed over the desire for a nation of small, self-reliant farmers who supported small towns and industry. Fewer and larger farms were the trend in postwar America, with farmers expanding horizontally via mechanization, debt expansion, hybridized seeds, and chemical pesticides, herbicides, and fertilizers.

Many farmers, industrialists, educators, and government officials demanded an agriculture that was more businesslike, decentralized, and less reliant on government. This vision of a technologically and chemically intensive farming base, so contrary to the permanent agriculture ideal, emerged in part from the call for high production to help fight the cold war. Obvious side effects included a decline in soil fertility and more soil erosion problems. Farm policy after World War II, while in theory devoted to planning for permanence, frequently vacillated due to the contentious debates and shifting political winds in agriculture from roughly 1944 to 1954. This changing structure and definition of American agriculture effectively altered the status of the permanent agriculture movement from that of a vocal minority to that of a silent clique.

The relative decline of the agrarian ideal in the immediate postwar years illustrated how dominant notions about agriculture changed. Louis Bromfield's desire for a neo-Jeffersonian, self-reliant small farmer appeared quite dated in the postwar world. Farmers of the 1940s and 1950s were far less concerned with ecological issues and with working together for total soil conservation and chemical-free farming than the farmers of a decade earlier. While farm income rebounded strongly during World War II, many competitors and "marginal" farmers left the farm during the war; hence farmers were less receptive to permanent agriculture's advocacy of keeping people on the land. Instead of worrying about his farm's role in the delicate biological web, the average farmer of 1945 or 1955 was far more concerned with such issues as prices, price supports, exports, the next farm bill, loan rates, and acquiring more land, more technology, and more scientific knowledge to assist him in his work. Although the idea of the "farmer as businessman" was long in developing, the concept achieved priority status in the years following World War II.

True D. Morse, president of Doane Agricultural College, offered telling testimony that farming was now a hard-edged business rather than a lifestyle choice. Morse asked GIs and war workers in 1944: "Should I gamble on a life of drudgery for Mary, and possibly, the college education of the children, to buy a farm now?" Still, as noted in *Fortune* that same year, "People who evidently know little about farming are agitating for a great postwar back-to-the-land movement for veterans, . . . [ignoring] the tragedy after World War I." These statements are indicative of the confused, often bitter, and extraordinarily complex agricultural situation in America in the decade after the war.[27]

Most farmers remained certain that the future of American farming would be based on the expanded use of labor-reducing machinery, genetic breeding, and manufactured agricultural chemicals, not the holistic trash mulch culture of Edward Faulkner. After World War II, American farmers wholeheartedly embraced science, technology, and horizontal expansion. Among the major technologies revolutionizing postwar agriculture were machines like the cotton picker; enhanced marketing and transportation systems; the expansive use of artificial insemination; and the development of synthetic growth hormones, sulfa drugs and antibiotics, and numerous commercial fertilizers, herbicides, fungicides, and pesticides, such as the family of chemicals related to DDT.[28]

For example, production of manufactured fertilizer skyrocketed from 800,000 tons in 1946–47 to 17 million tons in 1947–48. Even with land retirement and conservation controls, agricultural production continued to expand. In the late 1940s through the 1950s, the major questions of agriculture often were decided by short-term vacillations between price supports and controls and by income guarantees for farmers. Instead of adhering to Hugh Bennett's vision of a planned, permanent agriculture and embracing the lofty promises of social harmony offered by Rexford Tugwell and Paul Sears, American agriculture became further integrated into a vast technological and marketing system, ever more dependent on capital, agribusiness, and experts in the agricultural colleges. Louis Bromfield's thoughtful dialogues on the small farmer suddenly seemed out of place to a new generation of agriculturists driven by Ezra Taft Benson's famed admonition for farmers to "get big or get out." Farmers in the 1950s also apparently became far less interested in long-term soil-building programs, especially when prices were good during the Korean War years.[29]

Unquestionably, international events also shortened the public life of permanent agriculture, which required increased expertise to implement. It also needed an atmosphere of cooperation, moral purpose, and devotion to the often vague and long-to-realize concepts entailed in the new farming. With the war creating record demands and profits, farmers naturally wanted to maintain those conditions. Despite recurrent surplus problems, high production continued to be both the boon and the bane of American farming in the postwar years. A major reason for the enthronement of this high-production regime, in addition to science and technology, was the demand created by the cold war, wherein food served as an implicit strategic weapon.

During World War II, high production obviously stood out as both a moral imperative and a financial incentive. Farmers concerned over postwar surpluses found that postwar famine in Europe and Asia, and the need for food as a strategic tool, meant that high production would continue to receive federal support. Arthur C. Bunce, an agricultural economist at Iowa State College, acknowledged that high production in wartime had led to the sacrifice of the soil. After the war, with Europe and Asia desperate for food and with the ideological battle against communism being fought in both minds and stomachs, agricultural leaders such as Secretary of Agriculture Claude G. Wickard could report that future export opportunities might help preserve the rebuilt agricultural economy. According to Edward Faulkner, the prevailing attitude in postwar America made it hard for farmers to "resist a chance to take extra income from the land." As a speech by Assistant Secretary of Agriculture Clarence J. McCormick in late 1950 shows, the immediate concern for American agriculture in the postwar years was national security, not a utopian brand of permanent agriculture. McCormick told USDA bureaucrats that "the world today is a battleground upon which two ideas—democracy and communism—are fighting for survival. It is our particular job to help American agriculture to a position where it will be able and ready to do its full part in meeting any threat against the security of our nation." McCormick and his USDA cadre also linked high American agricultural production to the ongoing efforts of the United Nations' Food and Agriculture Organization.[30]

As the need for high production shifted attention from the concept of permanent agriculture, the new farming also suffered from the contentious, confusing, and highly politicized debate over farm policy. As agricultural leaders mulled over such issues as price supports, income stabilization, and crop insurance, bolder visions of social engineering at the USDA were out the window after the war's end. Although Hugh Bennett remained in public service even after age seventy and until his death in 1953, his bold prognostications and those of his associates began to fall on deaf ears as actual (as opposed to rhetorical) support for agricultural conservation waned after the war. A telling example of the bitter debates over agriculture in the late 1940s and early 1950s was the controversy over the so-called Brannan Plan. In a letter to Allan B. Kline, president of the American Farm Bureau, Secretary of Agriculture Charles F. Brannan wrote, "I had some faint hopes for a while that [during] the Korean situation, you might find reason for redirecting your own energies and those of your immediate staff away from the vicious personal attack you have leveled against me and the Department of Agriculture and the things that must be done by, for and with the American farmers in the months to come."[31]

Part of the decline of the agricultural conservation idea, and hence part of permanent agriculture's demise, was the dissipation of governmental support and leadership. Saving the soil remained a key rhetorical objective, but the sense of urgency sparked by the soil crisis of the 1930s had passed. One reason was that conservation issues were divided among a number of federal agencies, defying attempts at a consolidated policy for saving the nation's land and waters. Another problem was a lack of federal support and leadership. In 1947, Acting Secretary of Agriculture N. E. Dodd documented the erosion of federal support in a letter to President Truman regarding the proposed Agricultural Appropriation Act of 1948. Dodd wrote: "The people of this country have demonstrated time and again that they want to encourage conservation of the soil, the basic source of our life and wealth. Yet this act will reduce the public effort in soil conservation, in disregard of a congressional promise on the statute books, in spite of the drain placed on our soil resources by extremely heavy production in recent years, and in the face of needs indicated by this year's disastrous mid-western floods."[32]

To his credit, President Truman shared some of permanent agriculture's vision, asserting in 1952 that "there is no greater domestic problem in America than soil conservation and improving our land. . . . the speed with which conservation farming is adopted, and the degree to which it is maintained, will play a key part in determining how well we and our children eat in the years ahead." Despite Truman's rhetorical tribute to conservation, Hugh Bennett's expensive plan for permanent agriculture, partially funded at best, came under strong attack from the rising Republican Party. Leaders in agricultural conservation complained that federal support for conservation was insufficient, while GOP leaders, including Milton Eisenhower, complained that New Deal–era conservation programs were wasting taxpayers' money. As the conservation impulse began to unravel with Republican ascendancy in the early 1950s, the vision of an ecological agriculture also fell prey to a public weary, it was supposed, of big and coercive New Deal–style government programs. "Oratorical tributes" to conservation appeared everywhere in the period, while a renewed form of soil mining was "successful in skimming the cream of our soil resources," according to one report in 1951. Increasingly, Congress and the farming public led the push toward voluntary and decentralized (read piecemeal and unenforceable) conservation programs. Gone was the comprehensive dream of a permanent, planned, ecological agriculture supporting a holistic, healthy, peaceable population. The land was still a mere commodity, and agriculture a matter of slicing "a big job into little pieces."[33]

Yet the demise of permanent agriculture resulted from several factors besides federal inaction and the intransigence of the GOP. In the early 1950s, memories of the dust bowl were receding, and a confident citizenry preoccupied with domestic consumption and the cold war had little time for a nebulous soil crisis. Furthermore, the cloak of the nation's conservation community frayed into "the multicolored strands of which the fabric of conservation is woven." Simmering divisions developed between Pinchotian "wise-use" conservationists and, as one commentator noted, "those who love living creatures and the beauties of nature," with agriculture generally falling on the side of the former category. Noted conservationist Alexander F. Skutch reported in 1954 on differing interpretations of "conservation" that were increasingly apparent in American life. Historian Bernard Devoto offered a sharper attack, noting in August 1952 that the GOP leadership, poised to win the presidential election that fall, planned to appoint business and industrial leaders to the major conservation posts in the federal government. Devoto also reported that during a recent reorganization of the SCS, the nation's twenty-five hundred conservation districts were not even consulted. He also lamented that the SCS reorganization was "an aggrandizement of the land-grant colleges and the extension service at the sacrifice of conservation values." Bennett-era idealists and technicians were leaving the

SCS in droves, reported Devoto, and the "SCS is half flux and half chaos." The Friends of the Land reflected the decline in the conservation ethos, slipping from a peak of ten thousand members in 1947 to below seven thousand in 1954, when the group effectively disbanded.[34]

PERSISTENT INFLUENCES

While the permanent agriculture concept failed to take hold as a major social movement, the new farming did influence the theory, practice, and policy of agriculture in many ways from the mid-1930s through the mid-1950s. The movement fostered an increased public awareness of ecological principles and helped spawn further agricultural-ecological endeavors both within the agricultural establishment and in the subculture of organic farming. The movement highlighted abuses of the soil, ecological considerations, and the need for vigilant soil conservation. Apparently a large segment of the farming public got the message. By 1942, seven years after the birth of the SCS, 2 million farmers in forty-two states had set up 793 conservation districts covering 463 million acres of land. Hugh Bennett, Louis Bromfield, Paul Sears, and others of the permanent agriculture cadre deserve credit for enlightening the public on soil conservation issues, for spreading new ideas about farming, and for nourishing a long-dormant stewardship ethos among the public. For example, Edward Faulkner was unquestionably the greatest communicator in American agricultural history. Permanent agriculture helped keep the issues of soil and water conservation in the public spotlight during the war years and influenced federal legislation to support work toward permanent agriculture.

The permanent agriculture episode helps explain the shift from conservation to environmentalism. Permanent agriculture was an idea conceived by individuals born in the Progressive Era, when conservation was generally viewed as the managing of resources for human use and a task to be pursued mainly by extractive technocrats, symbolized by a Gifford Pinchot or Herbert Hoover. Despite, or perhaps because of, their solid indoctrination in conservation values, members of the permanent agriculture cadre were susceptible to nascent ecological ideas that dictated a far more complex set of values than did mainstream conservation, including interdependence and a heightened reverence for all life-forms. Although Aldo Leopold, himself a preacher of permanent agriculture, is often cited as a John the Baptist figure in the rise of environmentalism, Leopold's ideas were standard concepts in the call for the new ecological farming, emanating from a variety of sources. As a central activity in American life, agriculture provided an outlet for ecological thought, with the result that ecological ideals—the basis of postwar environmentalism— escaped the confines of academia and wildlife management. No one can know how many people who adopted an environmental ethic were influenced by a discussion of *Plowman's Folly,* an article by Louis Bromfield, or an appearance by an influential speaker such as Hugh Bennett.

The history of the Friends of the Land illustrates the association between agriculture and ecology. The organization was founded by old guard conservationists but was transformed by ecologists like Paul Sears into a font of holistic ecological thought. In 1951 Russell Lord wrote that the group's founders had possessed only a vague concept of ecology in 1940. From that limited focus on ecology, the Friends evolved into an ecological think tank, fostering conferences and publishing books on such topics as "Soil, Water and Health" and giving valuable space in the *Land* to ecological writers such as Sears and the young Rachel Carson.[35]

In addition to promoting agricultural conservation and spreading a growing gospel of ecology, permanent agriculture forged other lingering influences. Certainly, many of the most active proponents in the permanent agriculture camp did not die or fade from the scene. During the 1960s and 1970s, Paul Sears wrote several books designed for ordinary readers that could be described as "popular ecology." Indeed, the concerns over soil depletion that launched permanent agriculture reappeared in the mid-1950s, prompting new soil jeremiads such as Vernon Gill Carter and Tom Dale's book *Topsoil and Civilization* (1955).[36]

By the late 1950s, the agricultural establishment began to pursue many of the central ideas of permanent agriculture, such as enhanced soil conservation research and the need to teach ecological principles. The main difference was that institutions of the agricultural establishment left out the comprehensive program of permanent agriculture that emphasized social equity as well as the utopian ideals of the movement. Soil conservation, said SCS official Robert M. Salter, "had come to mean efficient abundant production."[37]

Still, a few members of the USDA–agricultural college complex maintained the original intent of ecological agriculture ideas, especially organic farming. William Albrect, once an opponent of Edward Faulkner, numbered himself among a small group in the agricultural establishment that supported the holistic, ecological concept of agriculture in the 1950s and early 1960s, before issues such as pesticide poisoning were debated by the public at large. Albrect, while dissociating himself from the organic farming camp, told *Farm Quarterly* upon his retirement in 1960 that his main concern had been that American agriculture was "producing bulk and sacrificing quality." The highly regarded Albrect stated: "All I am doing is defending the biology of the plant and animal against being overwhelmed by the industrial concept." Clearly, the permanent agriculture idea had resounding influences, as Albrect recounted his philosophy of agriculture in terms Edward Faulkner could have sympathized with in 1942, including viewing pests and plant disease as the symptoms, not the causes, of a failed crop; citing the need for nature appreciation among farmers; accepting Sir Albert Howard's linkage between healthy soil and healthy people, plants, and animals; requiring beginning logic for agricultural college students; and criticizing the "chemical empiricism" then overwhelming American farming. Albrect joined a few others such as chemist Lewis Herber in breathing fresh life into ecological agriculture. In 1962, he wrote of his fear that Americans had replaced their "natural system" of diversified agriculture, having "congregated into congested polluted cities which require monoculture and chemicalized forms of agriculture." By the early 1960s, in part thanks to the movement for permanent agriculture, young members of 4-H were learning that "the farmer, but more importantly, those who seek to modify and regulate his behavior, must understand that man is an integral part of nature, suspended in its equilibrium and subject to its laws."[38]

Strands of the permanent agriculture movement were also woven into the underground culture of organic farming in the late 1950s and early 1960s. In 1954, Scott Nearing, the aging socialist agitator and back-to-the-lander, and his wife, Helen, published the fabled tract *Living the Good Life*. The book and the Nearings themselves achieved virtual cult status in the following years. Scott and Helen Nearing practiced a simplistic lifestyle based on vegetarianism, vigorous physical and intellectual work, and tilling the soil according to the principles of ecological agriculture established in the prior decades. As a well-known leftist agitator, Nearing drew attention to his lifestyle and to agricultural ecology over the years as he mixed political and social messages with testimonials for ecological farming, health food, and "appropriate" technology and diatribes against the city. The Nearings were among a small, nontraditional group of farmers, gardeners, Svengalis, and theorists, mainly acting outside of the academy and establishment agriculture, that helped sustain ecological agriculture in its lean years, before Rachel Carson's monumental *Silent Spring* (1962) ignited latent concerns about what was now called the "environment," and spark new interest in creating a long-term, ecologically oriented food production system.[39]

Born and sustained in crisis, nurtured by a planning ethos, and animated by ecological ideals, the permanent agriculture movement enjoyed a relatively brief time in the sun, historically speaking. As an ideology, permanent agriculture was loosely assembled but widely communicated, especially from the late 1930s until briefly after World War II, when other concerns decoupled agricultural permanence and ecological awareness. The permanent agriculture episode illustrates how Americans in the crisis years of the 1930s and 1940s looked to broad solutions to society's problems, solutions that emphasized concepts such as interdependence, social harmony, prosperity, and longevity. Permanent agriculture also gave witness to the rapid and deep infusion of ecological ideas into the world of old-line conservation. Finally, the permanent agriculture movement provided, both mythologically and in a tangential sense, a useful history for post-1960 proponents of ecological agriculture to use for their own conceptions of an agriculture devoted to something larger than the bottom line and next fall's target price.

PART II: SUSTAINABLE AGRICULTURE, 1960–85

In the years following 1960, lingering concerns about agriculture's role in the environment reemerged within a reconfigured context of new societal concerns and deepening ecological knowledge. Some observers feared a Malthusian crisis, while others, such as Rachel Carson, illustrated the dangerous side effects of agricultural technology. By the late 1960s, agricultural commentators, farmers, and environmentalists leveled renewed criticism at the agricultural establishment (the nexus of farm and commodity groups, "agribusiness," the USDA, experiment stations, the extension service, and the land-grant colleges and universities) regarding the misguided technological advances in agriculture. Holding up the social and ecological failures of green revolution technology as the ultimate example of scientific hubris, critics from both within and outside the "system" began to offer a new vision of agriculture generally known as sustainable agriculture. This movement mirrored the concerns, the techniques, and the public life of the permanent agriculture movement that preceded it. Ecology and ecological metaphors permeated both the permanent and sustainable agriculture movements, and thus we refer to *sustainable ecological agriculture.*

Proponents of the various ideologies of sustainable agriculture modeled the "new farming" on chemical-free "organic" techniques and what they perceived as the scientific and ethical imperatives provided by ecological theory. Part and parcel of the overall environmental movement, the new farming embraced the "holistic" flavor of the late 1960s and early 1970s and was partially affiliated with counterculture communalism and visions of agrarian revival. But sustainable ecological agriculture also emerged from contemporary concerns for human survival in a world defined by an apparent sense of geographic and technological limitations. In addition to its association with the quality-of-life issues of the environmental movement and millennial agrarianism, the new farming also embraced societal planning, ethical or social ecology, a redirection of the establishment's research and planning, and the inculcation of a new stewardship ethic. By the late 1970s, several systems of ecological agriculture had appeared on the Amer-

ican scene—schemes laced with the well-developed tenets of organic farming and stewardship yet fleshed out with new concepts such as agroecology,
appropriate technology, renewable energy, and the double-edged sword of
biotechnology. Sustainable agriculture promised to contribute to the growth
of a healthy and ecologically diverse environment, to economic balance and
long-term prosperity, and to the salvation of civilization and culture from
Malthusian crisis and spiritual decline.

Like the crusaders in the permanent agriculture movement before
them, the founders and disciples of the sustainable agriculture ideal first
defined themselves and the movement through apocalyptic jeremiads
warning of impending ecological crisis. Leaders in the sustainable agriculture movement promoted their ideas by linking ecological farming to
the burgeoning environmental movement of the 1970s and 1980s, the
energy crisis of the 1970s, and the rural economic crisis of the 1980s. Individuals and groups promoting the sustainable ideal, such as biologist
Wes Jackson and "soft technologists" at the New Alchemy Institute,
enjoyed success in communicating the expansive concepts of the new
farming as alternative agriculture became an organized force with supporting constituencies and institutions.

Often castigated by the proponents of sustainable agriculture, supporters of the agricultural establishment, including agricultural scientists,
farm chemical manufacturers, and agricultural economists, offered a
strong initial resistance to the new farming. Even while most components
of the agricultural establishment resisted the challenge offered by ecological agriculture, some individuals found the sustainable agriculture camp's
arguments persuasive. By the time *sustainability* became a household word
in the 1980s, the USDA and land-grant schools had begun to participate in
research and discussion of sustainable agriculture methods. Even the manufacturers of farm chemicals began to embrace the rhetoric of sustainability and ecological stewardship by the late 1980s. As the agricultural
establishment adopted the terminology of sustainable agriculture, many of
the original canons of the new farming, such as the desire for a chemical-
free agriculture and devotion to smaller-scale farming, were abandoned or
watered down in the establishment version of sustainable agriculture.

While many of the original goals of sustainable ecological agriculture dissipated as the movement was co-opted and adopted by traditional agricultural forces, the alternative agriculture movement
profoundly influenced how Americans perceived farming, food, and
fiber; sparked drastic changes in farming practices that reduced soil erosion and environmental pollution; and reshaped the policy guidelines of
American agriculture. The history of sustainable agriculture highlights
the centrality of agricultural issues in the rise of environmentalism in the
United States and illustrates the problems and promises inherent in
adopting ecological agriculture.

CHAPTER FOUR

Soil and the Crisis of Humanity

In the years after 1960, a more educated and informed generation of Americans increasingly desired environmental amenities, such as wilderness areas and national parks, as well as healthier food, water, and air. The ever-present threat of nuclear contamination, coupled with other concerns about pollution, urban and suburban ugliness, lack of wilderness and protected areas, species decline, and limited resources, helped launch an environmental movement in the 1960s. Although farmers were rarely categorized as environmental activists, agricultural issues were fundamental to the rise of environmentalism in the United States.[1]

A prevailing sense of crisis animated the environmental movement, from the outcries over Rachel Carson's *Silent Spring* to the reaction to the oil spill at Santa Barbara and toxic pollution at Love Canal. Agriculture also suffered from a series of crises beginning in the 1960s that tied the development of sustainable ecological agriculture to the broader human and environmental crises of the period. With dramatic increases in population, especially in less developed nations, the world appeared to be facing a Malthusian crisis. Furthermore, the national battle against soil erosion still had not halted the loss of topsoil, and the nation's farmers and rural citizens faced economic decline and environmental degradation.

Agriculture's role in the overall biological environment appeared in stark form with the publication of *Silent Spring* in 1962. Farming was intricately tied to the pollution crisis of the 1960s and widening concerns over groundwater contamination and the presence of chemical residues in the food supply. Agriculture's part in the ecological crisis of the 1960s and 1970s was well documented by various critics examining the fallout of green revolution technology and chemical-based, mechanized agriculture in the United States. The principal establishment proponents of technological and industrialized agriculture—the USDA and the land-grant schools—sustained vitriolic attacks by antiestablishment farmers, scientific outsiders, and ecological thinkers. By singling out the role of the USDA–land-grant nexus in promoting an unhealthy farming system, proponents of sustainable ecological agriculture highlighted the centrality of agriculture in the environmental crisis and set the stage for imagining a new system of farming based on ecological diversity, appropriate technology, and societal permanence.

AGRICULTURE AND THE HUMAN FUTURE

When John F. Kennedy won the presidency in 1960, American agriculture rightfully envisioned itself as the envy of the world. America's soil had helped win wars and feed the vanquished. Yet President Kennedy's secretary of agriculture, Orville L. Freeman, had inherited a gargantuan surplus production problem from the Eisenhower administration. High demand associated with World War II had meant rising prices for American farmers, reaching 123 percent of parity by 1946. During the war, acreage under cultivation increased by 5 percent, yet advances in science and technology increased yields from America's farms by 11 percent. After the war, when prices began to decline, farmers disagreed on the proper course for public policy partly because no single approach could serve all farmers well. For their part, consumers favored reduced price supports to lower the cost of food. Congress wrestled with choices between high levels of fixed price supports or a return to prewar policies of flexible price supports linked to production control requirements. Despite foreign food aid, federal purchase of surplus commodities used in school lunch programs, and land retirement under the Eisenhower-era Soil Bank program, the surplus problem persisted. Critics charged that federal programs merely encouraged the farmers to remain on their course of excess production. Although the Korean War temporarily lifted farm prices, surplus production continued, contributing to a 23 percent decline in commodity prices from 1951 to 1956.[2]

In 1954, Congress passed flexible price supports yet limited the USDA's ability to curtail production. Eisenhower's secretary of agriculture, Ezra Taft Benson, employed cold war fears as he advocated increased crop production and attempted to dismantle New Deal farm programs restricting production. During the late 1950s and 1960s, large-scale farmers, the Farm Bureau, and Republicans generally favored reducing government intervention in agriculture, while other farmers, the National Farmers' Union, and many Democratic politicians advocated firm price supports. Yet the farm vote dwindled, and federal agricultural policy became complicated by the demands of urban constituencies. For example, the food stamp program became a major political issue by 1974, when 17.1 million Americans enrolled, and $5.4 billion of a total $7.7 USDA budget paid for mainly urban-oriented relief programs.[3]

During the 1972 campaign, President Nixon's secretary of agriculture, Earl Butz, bought up surplus corn, increased land set-asides (thus reducing production), and raised price supports to historically high levels. Yet Republicans had every intention of ending price supports and selling off federal stocks of commodities. In 1972, Butz repeated the idea "get big or get out," as the administration sought to boost commodity exports to raise prices. Farm income rose quickly during the 1970s, with land values following, in Iowa rising from $419 per acre in 1970 to $2,066 by 1980. Many farmers borrowed against rising land values to upgrade equipment or expand their production acreage during these boom years. Yet by the late 1970s, rising inflation and interest rates started to take a toll on farmers. Disenchanted with the federal government's failure to provide support after pushing increased production in the 1973 farm bill, Great Plains wheat growers founded the American Agriculture Movement. In 1978, three thousand farmers drove tractors to Washington to lobby Congress, which increased price supports by 11 percent and halted Farmers Home Administration foreclosures. The troubles of the 1970s turned into a larger crisis during the 1980s.[4]

While farmers and farm policy makers fought over price supports and subsidies, more fundamental problems, such as world overpopulation and hunger, promised to extract great demands from American agriculture in the near future. Lester Brown, an agricultural researcher for the USDA, wrote in 1963 of the tremendous importance of American agriculture within the world community. Brown expressed his belief that a burgeoning world population and a decline in available productive land would force America's farmers to heighten their use of resource-demanding green revolution technologies pioneered by Norman Borlaug and the Rockefeller Foundation. Like hydrogen bombs and helicopter armies, food and hunger became part of America's cold war arsenal. In addition to confronting a potential Malthusian crisis, Brown thought American farmers had to revive efforts to hold the soil, protect the nation's waters, and confront the continued severe decline in small-scale farming and rural life.[5]

For those agriculturists, researchers, and observers with an ecological worldview, the threat of a hungry planet seemed to be the prevailing environmental problem facing agriculture and humanity. Overpopulation and soil degradation were obviously not entirely new concerns, but threats of a Malthusian crisis burgeoned in the 1960s. Fairfield Osborn, a holdover from the permanent agriculture era, often expressed his fears that agricultural production could no longer match population growth. As Osborn wrote in 1962, "The results of population pressures are not merely physical, such as the daily crisis of starvation facing hundreds of millions of people; they generate as well a host of other undesirable conditions in human life affecting not only happiness and conduct of the individual, but also involving the basic questions of economics, religion, forms of government, and finally, the ultimate dilemma of war and peace." Throughout the 1960s and 1970s, works such as Paul Ehrlich's book *The Population Bomb* (1968) and Garrett Hardin's essay "The Tragedy of the Commons" (1968) reaffirmed Osborn's thesis that agriculture might be exhausted by leaps in world population and in stress on land, fuel, water, and other resources.[6]

FARMING, POLLUTION, AND HEALTH

The perceived threat stemming from overpopulation was partially relieved in the 1960s and 1970s by the success of mechanical, chemical, and genetic technologies championed by the American agricultural establishment. In spite of ever-increasing numbers of people to feed, ongoing topsoil loss, and the encroachment of suburbia, America's farmers continued to produce record yields and enjoy profitable years in the 1960s. Although the problem of feeding the world seemed solvable and profitable, establishment agriculture endured an increasingly trenchant series of criticisms during the 1960s and 1970s.

Attacks on the misguided leadership and ecologically devastating teachings of the agricultural establishment were not new. Unlike the permanent agriculture advocates of the 1930s, however, critics during the 1970s found that their arguments were more acceptable to a new generation of Americans concerned with preventive environmental health. Concerns about agriculture's role in pollution served as the locus of attacks on the agricultural establishment, representing the results of misguided science and technology leading American agriculture into ruin. William Albrect spoke to the pollution problem in 1961 when he wrote, "We must characterize man, at this stage, as the main biological liability, not only for himself, but to the populations supporting him. He is the contamination of the environment."[7]

Rachel Carson's analysis of the ecological effects of chemical use in agriculture proved an essential catalyst for a wider environmental awakening. The furor over *Silent Spring* (1962) rocked the agricultural establishment and the federal government and ushered agriculture into the age of ecology. Questions over pesticide contamination of food and the safety of DDT-related "biocides" had appeared several years prior to the publication of Carson's book. Yet Carson's well-reasoned, meticulously researched arguments forced the American public to seriously consider the wide environmental effects of mechanized, chemically intensive production-oriented agriculture. Stewart Udall, secretary of the interior throughout the Johnson administration, recalled the impact of *Silent Spring*: "The crystallization of thinking that took place in the 60s was to a substantial degree encouraged and pushed on by Racheal [sic] Carson's book. . . . I talked to my scientists about the time the book came out. They felt that in the main she was on target and that we ought to come down on the side of that argument." Udall mentioned that "agricultural interests generally pooh-poohed the book," but that he and the scientists in the Department of the Interior, after first understanding the book in terms of the food chain, "began to see . . . that man himself was going to be ultimately endangered and imperiled."[8]

As Linda J. Lear, Thomas R. Dunlap, and other historians have documented, the public response to *Silent Spring* overwhelmed the federal government, especially the USDA. Carson reserved her strongest indictments for the Agricultural Research Service (ARS) for its wholesale advocacy of chemicals without regard to biological control and ecological considerations. Fighting the agricultural chemical industry, antagonistic agricultural scientists, and some of her own faulty findings, Carson succeeded in making the public more cautious regarding the agricultural technology promoted by the agricultural research and production establishment. She created an uproar in traditional agricultural circles, ensuring that farming would never be the same again. *Silent Spring* taught farmers about the impact of their chemicals on the food chain, and urban dwellers started to express heightened concerns over the safety of their food and water supply.[9]

The linkage between farming, pollution, and health extended beyond the furor over *Silent Spring*, continuing throughout the 1960s and 1970s. As Carson's fellow "politico-scientist" Barry Commoner noted, agriculture's environmental problems were "more than DDT." Commoner recognized that agricultural pollution was symptomatic of a culture that wasted its resources with little regard for the future. For Commoner, the problem could not be "glossed over." America's agricultural pollution problem (for example, groundwater contamination by nitrates) "represented a failure on the part of modern chemical technology to predict a vital consequence of a massive intervention into nature." Commoner noted that for a million years humans had "survived and proliferated on the earth by fitting unobtrusively into a life-sustaining environment." Sadly, humans of a technological age had wrecked this "elaborate network of mutual relationships." Despite American agriculture's effort to create factories on the farm, Commoner asked his readers to understand that "agriculture remains a part of the larger, over-all system of life which occupies a thin layer on the surface of the earth—the biosphere." In their appropriately titled book *Technology: The God That Failed*, Dorothy Slusser and Gerald Slusser echoed the findings of Carson, Commoner, and others when noting that agricultural practices, "more than most of man's other activities," had "disturbed the ecological balance of nature." The Slussers cited the negative effect of chemical fertilizers and biocides on the natural bacterial content of the soil and upon the earthworm population as prime examples of how agriculturists both knowingly and unwittingly degraded the environment.[10]

TECHNOLOGY MISGUIDED

Carson's and Commoner's analyses of agricultural pollution and environmental contamination pointed to a larger questioning of the role of technology in American life. Alan I. Marcus and Howard P. Segal have noted that technology, traditionally viewed by many Americans as "a social benison, pristine in every way," by the 1960s seemed "a villain, a destroyer of communitarianism." While the debate over technological advance became a key question for intellectuals, the public at large seemed to realize that technology—good, bad, or ambivalent—was now a "driving force behind modern life." Advanced agricultural technology, formerly enshrined as the ultimate representation of American efficiency and production, became the focus of a debate that became central to the rise of sustainable agriculture.[11]

Critics of establishment-fostered agricultural technology first associated the endless technological advance on the American farm with an overall critique of Western scientific hubris, anthropocentrism, and ecological blindness. Commoner summed up the general mood of the period in 1971 when he noted, "The environmental crisis is somber evidence of an insidious fraud hidden in the vaunted productivity and wealth of modern technology-based society. This wealth has been gained by rapid short-term exploitation of the environmental system, but it has blindly accumulated a debt to nature." Commoner attributed the misguided technological advance in America to what he labeled "reductionism"— the tendency to design technology to solve "singular, separate problems and fail to take into account the inevitable 'side-effects' that arise because, in nature, no part is isolated from the whole ecological fabric." Thus, "the reason for the ecological failure of technology" was that, "unlike the automobile, the ecosystem cannot be divided into manageable parts." Commoner suggested that "in the popular image the technologist is often seen as a modern wizard, a kind of scientific sorcerer. It now appears he is less sorcerer than sorcerer's apprentice."[12]

Commoner found many like-minded critics of technology in general, but he also found fellow critics of agricultural technology. One problem, as viewed within an ecological framework, was that agricultural technology worked all too well, but at the same time it led toward "the failure of success." Pesticides killed bugs, but they also affected the biological web outside of agriculture. Huge tractors allowed one person to replace the labor of ten or twenty others, but they also contributed to the decline of rural life and soil compaction. Yet, reasoned supporters of the ancien régime, America's farms provided the most abundant and inexpensive food supply in the history of modern civilization. The spread of American agricultural know-how appeared to be the lodestar that would lead humanity out of a potential Malthusian crisis.

Despite optimistic assessments by export-oriented commodity groups, agricultural scientists, the USDA, and agribusiness, and a Nobel Peace Prize for Norman Borlaug, the green revolution technology came under persistent and effective attack both abroad and at home. Critics of the agricultural establishment lashed out at the ecological and economic folly involved with extensive use of genetic, chemical, and mechanical technology in less developed countries. These critics, many of whom became "founders" of sustainable, ecological agriculture, also castigated the industrialization of America's farms.

John Todd, a marine biologist and in 1969 a cofounder of an alternative-technology enclave centered in Massachusetts, was among the more effective critics of the green revolution. Todd and William O. McLarney called their research center the New Alchemy Institute and began a long quest for a sustainable and ecological agriculture. Todd's attacks on the green revolution were representative of other indictments of misguided technology. He described it as "the agricultural equivalent of the *Titanic*, only this time there are several billion passengers." Writing in 1971, the scientist asserted that "the Green Revolution has not been shaped by an ecological ethic and its keenest enthusiasts are usually manufacturers of chemicals and agricultural implements backed by government officials."[13]

Todd's attacks on the green revolution were supported by voluminous evidence that the program's hybrid seeds, expensive chemical and mechanical technologies, and monoculture farming had disrupted economies and ecologies worldwide. For example, Filipino farmers found Borlaug's "miracle rice" strain IR-8 expensive, distasteful to consumers, and lacking resistance to pests and drought. Borlaug's "miracle" dwarf wheat varieties, developed to assist Mexico, were too low in gluten content to be made into bread. This solution also overlooked the fact that corn and beans, not bread, constitute the staples of the Mexican diet. Thus, in the ecologist's view, the green revolution miracle of Mexican wheat production was a triumph only of monoculture agriculture, was affordable only to elites, and was devoted primarily to producing livestock feed for the export market, not to feeding hungry Mexicans. To critics of the green revolution, misguided technology forced on developing nations by the American agricultural and foreign policy establishment was a form of cultural imperialism that disrupted rural social patterns and made poorer nations even more dependent on energy for irrigation and machines and on capital for seeds and chemicals. Furthermore, green revolution mono-culture polluted rural environments, and the technological solutions offered by the Norman Borlaugs of the world threatened to produce pes-ticide-resistant insects and fungicide-resistant crop diseases.[14]

Although the green revolution still has its apologists and supporters, throughout the 1970s the attack on this misguided technology continued unabated. One commentator wrote in 1972 that "many agriculturists think the Green Revolution will overcome the earth's biological limita-tion. It is an extremely dangerous attitude, an illusion that leads to a slowdown in the efforts to save man and his environment through eco-logical planning."[15]

That same year, Barry Commoner noted that American agricultural "experts" had failed to understand that "introduction of a new technol-ogy into developing countries is always an *ecological* operation." Com-moner and others offered numerous examples of green revolution folly, from mice infestations in Malaysia resulting from pesticide contamination deaths of the feline population to parasitic outbreaks in human popula-tions resulting from large irrigation projects. Susan DeMarco and Susan Sechler, in their trenchant study *The Fields Have Turned Brown* (1975), noted that "there is an increasing concern around the world about the dangers of a chemically dependent agricultural system." Robert Steffen, an organic farmer and popular ecologist from Nebraska, in a letter to a United States Agency for International Development (USAID) official in 1972, noted, "The 'shining success' of this technology even in the devel-oped countries is now beginning to fade for various reasons. The realiza-tion that even our resource and energy stores are not limitless is giving reason to pause. So the Green Revolution is no longer quite so green when one comes to the realization that our technology can't really help them."[16]

As Steffen's statement indicates, and as many others were quick to point out in their attacks on misguided agricultural technology, America was far from immune to the ill effects of industrial agriculture. Richard Merrill, a critic of the agricultural establishment, offered this indictment of traditional agricultural science and technology in 1975: "We brag of being a nation where food is relatively cheap and agriculture efficient, yet ignore the fact that most measures of food processing and farm efficiency fail to take into account the endangerment of such valuable resources as soil fertility, water, wildlife, public health and a viable rural economy." Steffen, who also served for decades as farm director at Boys Town in Omaha, Nebraska, pointed to other ecological failures or "hidden costs" of modern agriculture, such as the demise of grass and legume rotations, the decline of vital bee populations, and the pollution created by concen-trated lot feeding of livestock. Steffen, a man with daily ties to the soil, thought the American farmer had "become a misfit in his own environment." Wes Jackson, whose concept of ecological agriculture would draw much attention in the 1980s, compared modern till agriculture to a "global disease" that, if unchecked, would "wilt" the human race "like any other crop." Throughout the 1970s, critics of misguided technology gnashed their teeth loudly over the social and environmental consequences of large-scale farming, agricultural mechanization, and the genetic and chemical "victory" over nature. By the late 1970s and early 1980s, critics of American agricultural technology could draw upon voluminous supporting evidence, including American farmers' reliance on expensive, imported energy supplies, as well as lingering problems with heavy silting, salinization, groundwater depletion and contamination, the appearance of chemical-resistant strains of pests and fungi, the decline of small farms, and the increasing domination of the food industry by corporate conglomerates, to demonstrate where American agriculture had gone wrong.[17]

If American agricultural technology appeared headed toward adverse ecological ends, then by implication someone or something guided this "bull in a china shop" system of farming. While individuals such as Wendell Berry suggested that cultural traits—including a "crisis of the spirit," lack of stewardship, obsessive greed, and a disregard of nature—constituted the roots of the ecological crisis in agriculture, nearly all the ecological critics of the American farm and food system targeted the agricultural establishment as the source of misguided technological advance. In books, speeches, and protests throughout the 1970s and 1980s, farmers, scientists, ecologists, writers, and others seeking to promote an ecological vision of agriculture singled out various elements, institutions, and individuals responsible for the soil and human crises that threatened America in this period. These attacks on the agricultural establishment made conditions ripe for an organized movement in sustainable ecological agriculture.

Just as Ralph Borsodi charged the land-grant–USDA complex with "treason" and "rape of the land" in the 1930s and 1940s, the critics of the agricultural establishment in the 1970s and 1980s threw a great number of slings and arrows at agribusiness, the land-grant schools, the USDA, and a "Farm Bureau mentality" that supported larger, wealthier farmers at the expense of their less fortunate or less "efficient" comrades in agriculture. Farmers concerned with the perennial question of why wheat prices were always low yet bread expensive also questioned the environmental and social fallout of misguided agricultural technology and the unchecked path toward concentration in American agriculture. While worries over the negative consequences of food-processing conglomerates, corporate farms, contract farming, agricultural chemicals, and governmental policy were core concerns in the attack on misguided technology, the land-grant colleges appeared to critics as the most conspicuous villains in the faulty apparatus of American agriculture.

Why single out the tyranny of the land-grant schools, formerly viewed almost universally as fonts of agricultural efficiency, rural uplift, and American expertise? Nearly every person associated with the entire crop production establishment graduated from or is affiliated with the land-grant college system. Schools such as Iowa State, Kansas State, the University of California–Davis, and many others enjoyed large budgets, bureaucratic power, and institutional prestige in postwar America. The green revolution at first appeared to be another affirmation that the research complex was guided by wise and ingenious scientists working in the service of humanity. In their pervasive attack on misguided technology, however, observers making an ecological and social cost-benefit analysis of the land-grant schools found the institution itself to be a main source of the central problems of American farming. Two representative attacks deserve attention for their potent and well-received arguments: Jim Hightower's *Hard Tomatoes, Hard Times* (1973) and Wendell Berry's *The Unsettling of America: Culture and Agriculture* (1977). While Hightower's book did not deal with environmental issues, both of these tracts are canonical in sustainable agriculture circles, and they detail the sundry problems leading to the perceived ecological, economic, and cultural crisis confronting American farming in the 1970s.

Hightower, formerly the elected state commissioner of agriculture in Texas, was a founder of the Agribusiness Accountability Project (a non-profit research group) in the early 1970s. He steered a research project on the USDA–land-grant–extension service–experiment station complex. *Hard Tomatoes, Hard Times* documented the focus of establishment agriculture on wealthy farmers and "corporate structures" at the expense of small-scale farms and rural communities. Most unsavory, in Hightower's opinion, were the linkages between academia, government, and industry. In the Nixon era, Secretary of Agriculture Earl Butz epitomized the inbred state of contemporary agriculture. Butz, the top federal agricultural official and a hard-core disciple of megamachine export-oriented farming, was also a former professor at Purdue University and served as a board member of several corporations, such as agribusiness giant Ralston-Purina. In Hightower's opinion, men like Butz divorced agricultural production from the maintenance of an economically and environmentally healthy rural America. Land-grant products like Butz had slavishly labored for the demands of implement and chemical manufacturers, the Farm Bureau, and prosperous farmers, while ignoring the demise of rural American civilization under the onslaught of exorbitant land prices, high debt, foreign competition, and technological unemployment. Consumers also suffered as they confronted fewer choices in the food market, higher prices, and less healthy and tasteful food. The land suffered as well when farmers, bureaucrats, and scientists continually attempted to outwit nature in the battle for high production. Hightower called for a public information campaign regarding the misguided technology affecting American agriculture, legislative and academic reform, an end to racial discrimination in USDA programs, and an eventual restructuring of the entire national farming system.[18]

A fundamental concern of Hightower and the Agribusiness Accountability Project was the increased tendency toward vertical integration of the food system, contract farming, and large corporate farms. Hightower and others thought that the "economy of scale" mentality in agriculture neglected issues such as environmental pollution and soil stewardship, energy consumption, and the value of rural culture and smaller-scale independent "family" farmers. Hightower's concerns about the failures of establishment science and technology were echoed by another central figure in the history of ecological agriculture, the Kentucky farmer, essayist, poet, and teacher Wendell Berry.

Berry's *Unsettling of America* stands as one of the most lucid contemplations on the meaning of agriculture in American life. Berry, whom Edward Abbey labeled "our contemporary Isaiah," offered some of the more reasoned and deeply penetrating blows at the misguided technological development of American agriculture. Like Hightower, Berry assailed the research establishment's blatant disregard for ecological considerations and the health and value of rural culture. Berry suggested that many problems had led to the ecological crisis in agriculture, including the American preoccupation with specialization that he labeled "the disease of the modern character." For him, the main "hazard of the specialist system is that it produces specialists—people who are elaborately and expensively trained *to do one thing*." He cautioned against "inventors, manufacturers, and salesmen of devices who have no concern for the possible effect of those devices."[19]

Attacking "farm boys" who had turned into calculating agricultural economists, scientists, and bureaucrats, Berry viewed the onset of industrial, chemical, mechanized, corporate agriculture as the successful outcome of a generation of agricultural research from individuals, such as famed Iowa State University agricultural economist Earl O. Heady, who had rationally redefined the farm as a mere mechanical component in the larger "input-processing" and "food-processing" industrial machine. For Berry, one could expect agricultural chemical and implement manufacturers to stop nowhere in the pursuit of industrial agriculture, but for educators and public servants to embrace the "too many farmers" doctrine represented an ultimate betrayal of small farmers, rural communities, and the social and ecological constitution of the nation. Berry wrote:

"If the farmer sells his foodstuff to 'agribusiness' at a narrow profit and buys it back ready-to-serve from 'agribusiness' to its great profit, then the cash flow has at that point deftly inserted its tail into its mouth, a wonder of sorts has been accomplished, and a reverent 'Golly!' is heard from certain agricultural economists."[20]

Berry, Hightower, and other critics of the agricultural establishment attacked imprudent policies and the values that gave rise to misguided technology. Beyond the quest for efficiency and profits, a sense of hubris and human dominance over nature's limitations drove the misdirected technology of American agriculture. Scientist and visionary agricultural theorist Wes Jackson saw a more clearly defined threat—the field of molecular biology. Since the discovery of DNA in 1953 and the increased science budgets following the *Sputnik* controversy of the late 1950s, molecular biology had been a favored child in the research establishment. Just as the attacks on green revolution technology had begun to infiltrate traditional agriculture circles and the public consciousness, fantastic claims in the field of biotechnology offered yet another technological miracle to avert potential Malthusian crises. Yet as with other cutting-edge agricultural technologies, the molecular biologists showed little interest in the ecological and social ramifications of their findings. This "single vision focus," as Jackson called it, was symptomatic of the failed vision of technology offered by the agricultural establishment.

Critiques of misguided agricultural technology suggested the time had come to bring change to agriculture and society at large. For those individuals and groups with an ecological vision of agriculture, the "faulty technology" of postwar America had to be replaced. Barry Commoner asked Americans to take lessons from nature, which taught people that "nothing can survive on this planet unless it is a cooperative part of a larger, global whole. . . . Human beings have broken outside of the circle of life." Commoner was not alone in his belief that "present productive technologies need to be redesigned as closely as possible to ecological requirements." A new type of agriculture and society had to be built. But a new, ecological agriculture had to have more than revamped technology and social criticism at its heart; it required animation from the domain of ethics, practical research initiatives, and sweeping changes in the structure and practice of agriculture. As the threats of overpopulation, pollution, and misguided technology illustrated, the stakes of building a sustainable ecological agriculture seemed nothing less than human survival.[21]

CHAPTER FIVE

Ecological Inspiration for Agriculture

In many ways, the sustainable agriculture phase of the ecological agriculture movement reflected the earlier quest for a permanent agricultural system. In the 1930s and 1940s, the crisis of the soil appeared to threaten American civilization. In the 1960s and 1970s, a wider and deeper ecological crisis of the land appeared to threaten the very survival of humanity. At both times, critics cited misguided technology as a major obstacle to building a new, ecologically oriented husbandry, and they looked to ecology as a scientific and ethical guide for piecing together the new farming.

As in the 1930s, the proponents of sustainable agriculture used ecology in several ways. First, the new agriculture employed ecology to create ① new environmental ethics. Many of those interested in ecological farming thought that agricultural sustainability required a cultural change entailing a new devotion to ecological stewardship and responsibility. Second, ② ecology informed a revived holistic perspective on environmental problems. During the 1960s and 1970s, it became increasingly clear that chemical and toxic pollution affected not only immediate environments but also living systems far away from the point sources of pollution. The pervasive effects of chemicals revealed the interconnected nature of living systems. The new holistic ideal, derived partly from ecological notions, argued that agriculture had to be refashioned in order to promote better health for all life but especially for human life, and to find less disruptive technologies that would preserve the planet's overall ecological community. Calls for new sorts of holistic farming systems arose from many corners, especially from the counterculture ranks of organic farmers and back-to-the-land communalists, as well as some alternative scientists. Third, ecology informed technique. We discuss four of the most important models for ecological agriculture, namely, agroecology, organic farming, permaculture, and perennial polyculture. While most proponents of ecological agriculture in the 1960s and 1970s came from outside the ranks of establishment agriculture, an increasing number of voices within the agricultural establishment also suggested that agriculture might benefit from "green thinking" and "soft technology."

While ecological agriculture in the 1960s and 1970s offered several distinct methods for the new farming, promoters of the new holism in agriculture sought to create a long-term farming system that would support a world faced with hunger, pollution, and other ecological, economic, and technological threats. Advocates of a sustainable and ecological agriculture emphasized the limitations of technology and the need for planning to prevent disaster. While for many a certain spirituality or stewardship ethic animated the sustainable ideal, the roots of alternative farming techniques ultimately drew nourishment from the science of ecology.[1]

HOLISTIC VIEWS OF AGROENVIRONMENTAL PROBLEMS

In the 1930s and 1940s, permanent agriculture emanated partly from conceptions of nature's balance, from ecologically inspired holistic conceptions of nature utilized by figures such as Lewis Mumford, Rexford Tugwell, and Paul Sears, and from a broad contextual view of environmental problems. Even though the permanent agriculture concept enjoyed some successes, the movement's decline mirrored the dissipation of its guiding force—a holistic style of ecology that looked at environments as complex and interactive units. For people like Paul Sears, ecology examined a natural world largely characterized by balance. It is important to realize that ecologists like Sears did not believe in a perfect balance. Evolutionary concepts relied upon the notion of change and precluded attachment to climax states that remained unchanged. For Sears and others, the balance of nature was a useful metaphor that helped explain the myriad interrelationships in nature, especially to a wider public. The popular metaphor of balance persisted until the mid-1970s when ecology shifted toward a worldview incorporating change and emphasizing random events.[2]

With the full development of quantitative, or "economic," ecology in the 1950s, holistic views espoused by ecologists, including Sears, appeared outdated. Quantitative ecologists focused on energy flows in nature and statistical models that benefited from advances in theory and computing technology. Charles Elton, a zoologist at Cambridge University, laid the groundwork for this economic brand of ecology in 1927 with the publication of *Animal Ecology*. His work emphasized the idea of food chains and food webs, the roles of producers and consumers, and the niche concept. Arthur Tansley's ecosystem concept, Chancey Juday's work on Lake Mendota's energy budget in 1940, and Raymond Lindeman's work on trophic levels completed the basic conceptualization and working tools of "the New Ecology, an energy-economic model of the environment." A bioeconomics paradigm ruled during the 1950s as a generation of mathematically minded ecologists, including G. Evelyn

Hutchinson, Robert MacArthur, and Howard Odum, brought ecology closer to other "hard sciences." At the same moment that reductionistic approaches were perceived as more legitimate, however, understanding the interrelationships within an ecosystem required some attempt to build understanding of larger wholes. Significantly, scientists developed systems approaches in several fields at this time, and ecologists borrowed their techniques. For ecologists, systems studies promised to help make sense of the complex interrelationships in nature previously examined piece by piece. The International Biological Program (IBP) of the 1960s provided $50 million to eighteen hundred American scientists to study biomes in the United States, advancing ecosystem studies. Ironically, while the IBP grassland biome project sought to study the entire system, its methods and scientific questions were reductionistic and concentrated on particular components.[3]

Holistic and reductionist conceptions existed side by side in a complex relationship, although most mainstream scientists remained suspicious of any hints of organicist thought. For example, Lindeman's work of the early 1940s on the energy flow through the trophic levels of Cedar Bog Lake is cited as a foundation of the economic style of ecology. Yet ecologist Frank Golley also cites it as "important in maintaining a holistic point of view." The ecosystem concept in particular could be used in several ways, depending on one's point of view or philosophical commitments. Those sharing a managerial ethos saw tools of manipulation within economic ecology, not just for exploitation and production but also for healing damaged landscapes. Those predisposed to organicist understandings tended to see in the ecosystem concept a confirmation of the interdependence of nature. In agriculture, the land-grant institutions used reductionist approaches to expand production and push progress, while organic and sustainable advocates saw farms as whole systems tied not only to a living landscape but also to the human rural community.[4]

While scientists debated the finer details of methodologies for investigating the complexities of field and forest, holistic conceptions of nature expanded, becoming strongly embedded in colloquial understanding and parlance. Popular notions of nature's balance reemerged in the early to mid-1960s, together with shifts in ethical views of human relationships with nature, animated by a new and seemingly more complex set of crises to confront. Many proponents of the new agriculture reclaimed ecology's status as a scientific and ethical guide in the 1960s, making it central to the development of environmental ethics and sustainable agriculture.

Significantly, proponents of new agriculture borrowed the concept of the interdependent ecosystem to derive their approach to problem solving as well as their environmental ethic. If an ecosystem was composed of mutually dependent elements, then pesticide use in all probability affected other parts of the system and must be understood and accounted for. It is significant that advocates of alternative agriculture rejected the view of agriculture as a simple system of inputs and products, preferring a view of the land as a complex organism, a dynamic whole. Not satisfied with a prescription such as simply adding more nitrogen, new agriculture advocates looked at the entire system, for example, devising manure and cover crop systems to rebuild soil fertility. This vision of an interdependent, living world implied the need for an ethic that valued biodiversity. Books like Paul Errington's *Of Men and Marshes* and Aldo Leopold's *A Sand County Almanac* found receptive audiences.

STANLEY A. CAIN

The reemergence of a holistic style of ecology employed in thinking about complex problems can be seen in the career of ecologist Stanley A. Cain. Trained as a traditional field ecologist in the 1920s, Cain went on to embrace the quantitative, technical revolution in ecology in the 1930s and 1940s. He served a term as president of the Ecological Society of America and was the assistant secretary of the interior for fish, wildlife and parks in the Department of the Interior during the Johnson administration. In his many speeches and pronouncements from that post, Cain reflected how many people looked to ecology as a scientific and ethical guide in the 1960s.

Referring to the multifaceted environmental crisis readily apparent in the mid-1960s, Cain suggested, "We do not have to endure the Apocalyptic revolution by the Four Horsemen: War, Conquest, Famine and Death. We do not have to do this any more than we have to live by gathering the wild fruits of the field like our forebearers." He advocated population control and ecological training for engineers, resource managers, medical personnel, biologists and agricultural researchers. Although not opposed to the advances in biochemistry, genetics, and "hard science," he did assert that "our concentrated attention to physical technology with quick, profitable pay-offs has worked—up to a point—but we are now appreciating that the relative neglect of systems of nature, especially the vastly more complicated systems of biology and culture, have given us the urgent critical problems of our time." Cain was convinced that "ecology—or perhaps better, the ecological way of looking at nature—is beginning to provide the means of synthesizing the sciences and finding out how nature really works."[5]

Injecting contemporary concerns with the older notion that ecology could serve as a guide for scientific and ethical conduct, Cain noted in 1966, "We have historically proceeded as though the facts of nature and the raw materials of our economy were discrete entities and not parts of complex, interacting systems. Doing things this way, we have had book-keeping on the benefits, but generally not on the costs of our procedures. We have mined each mineral, cut each tree, farmed each acre, and used each body of water as though there would be no significant effects on any part of the environment. In doing so we have bought economic progress out of nature's capital." For Cain, ecology represented an avenue leading away from environmental catastrophe. He noted that "the ascendancy of ecology . . . in recent years seems to be due to certain very human concerns," which included rising population, nuclear bombs and nuclear waste, pollution threats, and general concerns over preserving natural beauty. For Cain and other ecological prognosticators, America could not afford to abandon ecological investigations in the all-out pursuit of "hard science." Ecology would guide humanity to better cooperation with nature, would help overcome the "compartmentalization" of science and culture, and would serve as a "cognitive, appropriate, and moral" guide for the human ecosystem. Importantly, Cain recognized that this new enthusiasm for ecology as a holistic ethical and scientific guide was tempered by the fact that "the environment cannot be completely analyzed, and that diverse analytical data cannot at present be synthesized back into anything like the ecosystem as a whole." To his credit, Cain realized the limitations of science and human understanding.[6]

Cain's concept of ecology and his notion of a holistic foundation for science and ethics found significant support in the ecological community. In a special issue on ecology in 1964, the journal *Bioscience* printed several testimonials to the reemergence of holistic, ethical, and political forms of ecology in the period. Among the contributors was a pioneer from the earlier period of holistic ecology, Paul B. Sears, who wrote, "By its very nature, ecology affords a continuing critique of man's operation within the ecosystem. The application of other sciences is particulate, specialized, based on the solution of individual problems with little if any attention to side effects and practically uncontrolled by any thought of the larger whole." Another contributor suggested, "Most of the problems facing man's ability to live happily and survive on this planet are largely concerns with environment, which is closely allied to his renewable resources. His ability to obtain enough food, clear water, and clean air along with his needs for leisure, recreation, and aesthetics involve sound ecological understanding and action."[7]

The reemergence of ecology as a scientific and ethical guide influenced an environmental awakening and fostered new visions of building a holistic society devoted to long-term survivability. Sears, who by the early 1960s was Emeritus Professor of Biology at Yale University, thought Bertrand Russell had correctly perceived the essence of the modern dilemma when he posed the question "Will men be able to survive the changes in environment that our own skill has brought about?" Sears contended that coping "with our environmental problems will demand effort, not only on the local and state level, but also on the regional, national and international level. Modern man must be helped to see the whole wood as well as the single tree, the well-being of all, rather than that of one street or town or state. This is one world, in which we share our inheritance and our future." Writer Osborn Segerberg noted that "the goal of the biological community is to achieve both stability within its physical setting and maximum ability to adjust to whatever changes may take place." Social critic Charles Reich spoke to the main concern of the maturing new holism in his 1970 environmentalist classic, *The Greening of America*, stating that "the great question of our times is how to live in and with a technological society; what mind and what way of life can preserve man's humanity and his very existence against the domination of the forces he has created?"[8]

The environmental ethic of the 1960s and early 1970s appealed to many groups, from ordinary citizens worried about clean air and water to dreamers determined to rebuild America's cities on ecological principles. Attached to this movement was the realization that agriculture had to be redirected to "the soft path" of ecologically conscious technology. While individuals like ecologists Stanley Cain and Paul Sears hoped to incorporate ecological ideals into the academy, industry, and government, they also joined with others seeking to blend ecological holism into mainstream thought by creating a new ethic and a new technological foundation for American farming. In 1970, Charles Reich claimed that "America is dealing death, not only to other lands and other people, but to its own people" in the form of pollution and mismanagement of natural resources. He asserted, "There is a revolution coming. It will not be like revolutions of the past. It will originate with the individual and with culture, and it will change the political structure only as a final act." For Reich and others thinking in terms of human survival, peace, and ecological harmony, one method of changing the "machine rationality of the corporate state" was to replace the "mindless" technology of the past with the "small is beautiful" technology of the future. A holistic ecological revolution in America had to encompass all segments of society and also had to appeal to the public consciousness. For advocates of this new way of thinking, one area for immediate action lay in a revitalization of the American land. The nation's food production machine powerfully symbolized the misguided ethic and technology of the past. From diffuse roots rose what may be labeled the "counterculture" agriculture of the 1960s and 1970s, a loosely affiliated group that would make significant contributions to the conception of sustainable agriculture.[9]

THE ETHICS OF COUNTERCULTURE AGRICULTURE

While the science and ethic of ecology reemerged within the ranks of ecologists in universities and the government, those working outside of the agricultural establishment were the first to effectively link agriculture to the new holism of the period. Part of the drive for a new ecological agriculture came from disaffected, back-to-the-landers who practiced the fundamentals of organic farming on farms, on individual plots, and sometimes on communes. Scott and Helen Nearing, intellectuals who fled the city during the Great Depression, epitomized the countercultural roots of sustainable ecological agriculture. The Nearings' *Living the Good Life*, first published in 1954, was reissued in 1970 and became a best-seller. Thousands of ecologically conscious young people, disillusioned with politics and the Vietnam War, either read about or personally descended upon the Nearings' New England farmstead to study their organic farming techniques and simple lifestyle. As stated in *Current Biography* in 1971, "The society that rejected Scott Nearing as a political heretic a half century ago has come begging at his door for ecological wisdom."[10]

The Nearings, who derived their income from lectures, writing, and maple sugar production, were advocates of biodynamic farming, a system of organic farming originally devised in the 1920s. They espoused simple, nonconsumptive living, vigorous physical and mental exertion, and the use of composts, natural fertilizers, and pest fighters in their greenhouse and gardens. But the Nearings represented much more than advocacy of organic farming—their lifestyle and ideas represented the new holistic conception of life in that period. Other manifestations of this new holism included the publication of such journals as the *Futurist*, *Future's Conditional*, the *Vegan*, and *Natural Living*, which advocated organic farming and gardening, health food, and the use of "appropriate" technology. Scott and Helen Nearing also represented an alternative lifestyle devoted to independence, ecological health, and opposition to industrial and corporate capitalism.[11]

In farms, in reclusive communes (such as the anarchist Cold Mountain Farm in New Jersey or the Benton Farm near Frankfort, Kansas), at self-styled experiment stations, and in garden plots in cities across America, a new breed of agrarians sought to promote an ecologically aware husbandry. If the Nearings were prophets of the new farming, canonical texts included *The Whole Earth Catalog* (1970), E. F. Schumacher's soft technology guide *Small Is Beautiful* (1973), and the works of philosopher-technologist R. Buckminster Fuller, father of the geodesic dome.

John Todd, an academic biologist turned counterculture agriculture pioneer, is particularly representative of the blend of ecological training and counterculture ideology in sustainable ecological agriculture. After reading an essay by Paul Ehrlich during the Woodstock summer of 1969, Todd left the confines of university life with his wife, Nancy Todd, and fellow scientist William O. McLarney to found the New Alchemy Institute in 1970. Located at Falmouth, Massachusetts, the institute worked as an adhesive that bonded agriculture to holistic ecology. The goal of the New Alchemists, or "Alchies," as they quickly came to be called, was to build a place "where individuals will learn good stewardship of the earth as they assist us in the development of new world skill and technologies."[12]

Work at the New Alchemy Institute commenced with a seriousness founded in fears that America was "a society whose technology tends to be more and more centralized, increasingly impersonal, and remote from the control and comprehension of its ultimate users." For John Todd and the cadre of the New Alchemy Institute, the goal of ecological survival would be reached through the application of "small and innocuous" technology that was an "autonomous, human-scale, low energy, low pollution alternative to 'supertechnology.'" Throughout the 1970s, the New Alchemists worked on projects devoted to solar energy, microcomputer application, aquaculture, composting, and small, high-yield gardens. They pioneered the "biosphere concept" as well, building several self-contained, self-sufficient "Arks." "They will be needed," wrote Todd, "if mankind is to avoid famine and hardship and manage to shift to modes of living which restore or rekindle our bonds with nature." The New Alchemists successfully drew attention to themselves, prompting one writer to describe them as visionaries "dedicated to the principles of an earlier age when science, art and philosophy were regarded as parts of a unified whole; the people who tend the farm are musicians, philosophers, feminists, craftsmen and trained scientists."[13]

As sustainable agriculture emerged in the 1970s and 1980s, the public's conception of "organic" thinking never shook off a perceived association with health food fanaticism and hippie communalism that seemed to follow the Nearings and other New Age sorts like the New Alchemists. Any new form of ecological agriculture seemed a challenge to traditional American agriculture and to established culture as well. The new holism also confronted the cultural maladies that many thought fostered racism, imperialism, and ecological devastation. Yet the ecological challenge posed to America and to traditional American agriculture also emerged from farmers in middle America and from consumer demands for safer, healthier food.

As the farm manager of the expansive fields at Boys Town in Omaha, Nebraska, farmer Robert Steffen was a fascinating example of a college-trained production agriculturist who linked agriculture and the new holism from the 1960s through the 1980s. Steffen was a follower of the biodynamic school of organic farming, an environmental activist, and a regular contributor to J. I. Rodale's *Organic Farming* magazine in the early 1970s. A photo in the *Omaha Sunday World-Herald* in 1975 showed a gapped-tooth Steffen with a pitchfork and a farmer cap, ever the image of a Midwestern farmer. Despite this hayseed look, Steffen held some rather unconventional views for a production farmer. Rejecting his college teachers, he managed the two-thousand-plus acres of farmland at Boys Town for over three decades on a totally organic regime, completely avoiding chemicals and making extensive use of composts, green manures, and crop rotations.

Steffen also concerned himself with suburban encroachment, agricultural pollution, and other environmental issues, describing his agricultural philosophy as "a form of land use designed to produce optimum yields for crops and livestock of the highest nutritional values free from anything detrimental to health and impairing future productivity." He contended that "the organic farmer is telling the technologist 'enough,' there must be a way that will be better for me as well as all of society." In 1970 he suggested that "agriculture is deeply involved with the religion of production and the god of efficiency, which of course are the basic tenets of any successful industry. Until we realize that more is not always better and that quality is not always something that inevitably follows quantity we will never solve the current environmental problems." For Steffen, farmers, researchers, and agribusiness needed to realize that "man's survival still depends on this thin layer of soil." Yet his ideas were sufficiently outside of the mainstream to encounter resistance. Steffen was eventually dismissed as farm director at Boys Town because of his continuing advocacy of organic farming techniques.[14]

In 1978, sustainable agriculture advocate Garth Youngberg suggested that many people in alternative agriculture shared the view that "conventional agriculture is destructive of both human and natural resources and is therefore destined to destroy itself as well as the larger population." Youngberg detailed the rise of organic farming from its counterculture roots to its growing intrusion into traditional agricultural circles during the 1970s. Although relatively unorganized and anarchistic by nature, those seeking a unification of ecology and agriculture in the 1970s could point to a growing number of organic producers' associations with links to large food processors and distributors, to the burgeoning supply business for organic farmers, and to the formation of such groups as the International Federation of Organic Agriculture Movements in 1972 as signatory of the successful infiltration of the new holism into American agriculture. Proponents of the new holism in agriculture could also gain inspiration from an improving academic reception to organic farming research and from heightened consumer demand for "organic" food. Clearly, ecological agriculture was moving from the status of countercultural oddity toward aspiring challenger to traditional agriculture by the middle to late 1970s.[15]

SHIFTS WITHIN THE ESTABLISHMENT

Minority elements within the much-castigated agricultural establishment also adopted some aspects of a holistic conception of agriculture. Ecological thought had made inroads in land-grant colleges, and ecological investigations by academic researchers in fields such as botany and entomology had given ecology legitimacy as a scientific discipline in the United States. The biological and ethical implications of ecological ideas that gave rise to the ecophilosophical musings of Aldo Leopold and Paul Sears did not die a total death within academic ranks in the 1950s and early 1960s. Revealed in the writings of some USDA and agricultural college personnel, the ecological vision of life simmered quietly within establishment agriculture. Other parts of the permanent agriculture movement, such as the agenda for planning, can also be seen in the 1970s.[16]

In a role that could be compared with Rexford Tugwell's place in the permanent agriculture movement, Orville L. Freeman (secretary of agriculture, 1961–69) contributed to an intellectual foundation for the sustainable ideal. Freeman was liberal in some ways yet far more of an "establishment man" in the American agricultural scheme than the collectivist Tugwell. Although confronting a different set of crises, Freeman and the New Dealer shared the view that agriculture operated as a vital part in an interdependent economy, and that any solution to the problems in agriculture had to come from comprehensive planning and not the politicized, sentimental, single-issue approach that dominated agricultural policy making.

Faced with huge crop surpluses, an agricultural pollution problem, declining rural communities, and growing demands for safe food, Freeman advocated several "visionary" policies in the 1960s. His agricultural program remained embroiled in the debates over prices, subsidies, and surpluses that characterized farm policy, but under him the USDA also worked toward some ecological ends under the guise of the Great Society. In 1967, Freeman told the National Association of Soil and Water Conservation Districts in Cincinnati, "We are a nation bedazzled by technology, and addicted to crash programs. But there are no instant ecologies or instant forests. And so, in the final analysis, we must devote much more attention in the future to assessing each new technological development for its ultimate impact." He noted that pollution had been fostered by traditional agriculture, yet he remained convinced that the environmental problems of agriculture could be best solved by traditional agricultural researchers and leaders.[17]

Freeman envisioned the USDA as the vanguard in the fight against "galloping suburbanism and creeping pollution." He also worked to increase the food stamp and other entitlement programs, and to supply land use planning advice and support to the inner city as well as the suburbs. Freeman wished to improve life in the city and country, part of his quest for "rural-urban balance," and supported a proposal for rural "opportunity homesteads," designed to provide resettlement and vocational training for impoverished urban families. In his speeches throughout the 1960s, he spoke on issues such as "total environmental management," "quality of life," and the need to "smell the flowers" via federally sponsored beautification programs. Freeman sought to guide suburban development in an aesthetically pleasing and ecologically healthy fashion, and he organized numerous task forces or gave speeches on agricultural pollution, wildlife and recreational opportunities in the countryside, biological pest control, soil conservation, and retirement of millions of acres of highly erodible or ecologically important lands. While part of Freeman's ecological idealism unquestionably stemmed from efforts to reduce crop surpluses and allay public fears of pollution, he claimed that his efforts were also aimed toward promoting preventive health, attacking poverty, and asserting the nonutilitarian principle that humanity must not forget "the 'inner prosperity' of the human spirit."[18]

Freeman's holistic vision represented a minority faction within the agricultural establishment that found useful elements in the new holism during the 1960s and 1970s. Indeed, the new holism had infected certain elements within the very bastion of the agricultural establishment's misguided technological apparatus—the land-grant colleges and universities.

Roger Mitchell, an agronomist and vice president of the College of Agriculture at Kansas State University, gave witness to the permeation of the ecological ideal into the agricultural establishment in a speech to the American Society of Agronomy in Los Angeles in 1977. Mitchell spoke of new ideas entering agricultural science in the period, stating that "the mid-1970s have been a time of broader vision, reevaluation, and renewed emphasis on the global condition. . . . A global view calls for a conscious concern that technology be viewed in proper perspective." While opposed to the view that the green revolution was a total failure, Mitchell believed that agricultural scientists had to operate in the context of the "total culture" and not remain aloof from larger problems. Continuing in this vein, this establishment functionary admitted almost sheepishly that he had "been captured" by the "small is beautiful" syndrome. "Yes, I do believe," stated Mitchell, "that E. F. Schumacher's ideas about appropriate technology are very germane. . . . we will make the greatest contribution by using care to adapt to the culture in which we work."[19]

Another rogue in the agricultural establishment, Iowa State University agricultural engineer Wesley F. Buchele, in a paper originally presented at a meeting of the Social Concerns Committee of the American Society of Agricultural Engineers at the University of California–Davis in 1975, expressed ideas that would have been acceptable to the most visionary holistic agriculturalists. Buchele called for interdisciplinary agricultural research focused on solving the interrelated ecological, economic, and cultural ills of American farming and food production. He also demanded a multifaceted program to promote a new stewardship ethic among farmers and the general public, governmental support for small-scale farmers and small farms, and small-scale, ecologically cognizant technology.[20]

THE ETHIC OF SUSTAINABILITY

Ecologists and other scientists and environmentalists, in addition to agriculturists and commentators of all stripes, sought to integrate the holistic principles of agriculture into the American farm and food system for many years, even decades prior to the 1970s. Yet with the scale of the environmental problems in agriculture looming so large in the 1970s, and with general support from a burgeoning environmental ethos, holistic ecological ideals infiltrated the domain of American farming and agricultural research more deeply in that crucial decade. Ecological agriculture emerged from its counterculture shadow in the 1970s somewhat as it had in the 1930s and 1940s by attaching the new farming concepts to the greater cause of human survival. As the link between agriculture and the new holism of the period solidified, a new term entered the American lexicon: *sustainable agriculture*.

Sustainable agriculture, as a definable ideology, emerged in the middle to late 1970s. But as the proponents of sustainable agriculture recognized, "ecology" alone was not a cure-all for America's agricultural and environmental problems. Sustainable agriculture blended ecological concerns with a new sense of human limitation, a renewed push for planning, and a call for a revived stewardship ethic. The term *sustainability* first appeared in the environmental movement in 1972, and the word increasingly appeared in environmental literature during the 1970s before becoming an established part of the lexicon in the 1980s and 1990s. As the energy crisis of the 1970s exacerbated a growing sense of environmental doom, individuals throughout society called for Americans to recognize that the resources of the world were finite.[21]

Lester Brown, a preeminent expert on food and hunger issues and a key figure in the inception of sustainability, led the drive to make Americans aware of the physical and technological limitations facing a very small and hungry world. Brown, originally trained as an agricultural scientist at Rutgers University in the 1950s, wrote in 1978 that "the need to adapt human life simultaneously to the carrying capacity of the earth's biological systems and the [use] of renewable energy sources will require a new social ethic. The essence of this new ethic is the accommodation of human numbers and aspirations to earth's resources and capacities." For Brown, "the deterioration of biological systems is not a peripheral issue of concern only to environmentalists. Our economic system depends on the earth's biological systems. Anything that threatens the vitality of these biological systems threatens the global economy. Any deterioration in their systems represents a deterioration of the human prospect."[22]

Brown's call for sustainabilty and recognition of limits represents the overall desire to avoid environmental catastrophe in the late 1970s. Political observers have noted that President Jimmy Carter suffered further damage to his public image when, in his fireside "sweater" chats, he called his nation's citizens to battle against the energy and environmental crises. Carter commissioned the much-publicized *Global 2000 Report to the President of the United States* (1980), whose dour summary indicated that obstacles to "sustaining the possibility of a decent life for human beings" were "enormous and close upon us." This apocalyptic observation resounded from other sources as well in the late 1970s, as a number of jeremiads warned Americans of a global ecological crisis that was particularly threatening to agriculture. As Lester Brown, the *Global 2000 Report*, and sundry other studies from the period show, the world appeared to face a deluge of environmental problems ranging from a lack of arable land and overpopulation and desertification to overreliance on ecologically damaging agricultural chemicals and the genetic vulnerability of hybrid crop strains. The ongoing erosion problem, exacerbated by the export-driven plow-up of farmland in the 1970s, also drew an extraordinary amount of attention in the national press.[23]

Lester Brown and many other observers of agricultural and environmental trends noted in the late 1970s and early 1980s that the era of cheap energy and technologically inspired production increases appeared near its end. The need for food continually expanded as the human population grew, yet the amount of arable land declined as more acres succumbed to erosion, infertility, desertification, and nonagricultural use. Problems in the world agricultural situation would only increase the ecological demands placed on American soil. Brown and other social scientists and academics, government officials, and corporate representatives agreed that family planning and food planning were essential to survival. Significantly, the sustainable ideal reshaped the concept of planning from "growth at all costs" to variations of "zero growth" and "sustainable development." Planning a sustainable future demanded attention to resource inventories and limitations; human health and happiness; the need for biodiversity, wilderness, and open recreation spaces; and the reorientation of human values from a "technological world view" to an "ecological world view."[24]

Advocates of sustainable agriculture thought a general solution required more than a holistic ecological conception of farming, a sense of limitations, and advocacy of planning. A long-term ecological agriculture demanded a revival of the stewardship ethic among farmers and the general public. Cultural change had to occur if the ideas of sustainable ecological agriculture would ever come to fruition. People had to recognize that the continuation of the status quo in American farming would eventually lead to ruined land, economic blight, and societal decline. The sustainable ethic challenged Americans to redefine success outside of the traditional standards of material consumption and economic growth. In essence, the argument went, Americans needed to abandon their long-held devotion to an endless quantity of goods and services for a better long-term, sustainable quality of life for citizens present and future.

E. F. Schumacher, the British guru of sustainability, suggested that "the foundations of peace cannot be laid by universal prosperity in the modern sense, because such prosperity, if attainable at all, is attainable only by cultivating such drives of human nature as greed and envy, which destroys intelligence, happiness, serenity, and thereby the peacefulness of man." Bill Mollison, the Australian promoter of permaculture, claimed that sustainable societies of peasants and pygmies emphasized "duties and responsibilities to nature equal to those of people to people." For Mollison and Schumacher, sustainability meant far more than maintaining the supply of food; it also meant a right to an independent livelihood, a right to live free of debt, and a duty to be socially and environmentally responsible. Wes Jackson and Wendell Berry also suggested that the basis of the new farming would be not only technical but also cultural and spiritual, since technical efforts alone had failed to effect any true permanence on American farms.[25]

Berry's words deserve attention because they were among the most widely noted in the rise of sustainable ecological agriculture. Speaking of the cultural changes necessary to build a holistic, enduring agriculture, the Kentucky farmer and poet wrote, "The great question that hovers over this issue, one that we have dealt with mainly with indifference, is the question of what people are *for*. . . . Is the obsolescence of human beings now our social goal? One would conclude so from our attitude toward work, especially the long-term preservation of the land." For Berry, the excessive mechanization of agriculture and industry had led to rural decline, urban squalor, and suburban ignorance regarding the sources of food and fiber. In a society geared primarily to comfort and leisure, he could hardly find it surprising that America was rife with "permanent unemployment and welfare dependency." He did see a way out of the nation's cultural and agricultural dilemmas. If a new stewardship ethic, a true work ethic, could be instilled in the citizenry, then Americans could begin the "inescapably necessary work of restoring and caring for our farms, forests, and rural towns and communities—work that we have not been able to pay people to do for forty years and that, thanks to our forty year 'solution to the farm problem,' few people any longer know how to do."[26]

During the late 1970s and early 1980s, agriculture and the new holism became linked under the rubric of sustainability, an ideology that also encouraged adherence to such ideas as material limitation, long-range societal planning, and deep cultural change. Clearly, building a sustainable ecological agriculture could only result from cooperation among an educated citizenry, one that had to stop focusing solely on short-term reward instead of long-term economic and ecological stability.

As the term *sustainable agriculture* gained wider usage in the early 1980s, advocates of the new farming started to reach beyond discussion of agriculture and the new holism and the ringing of ecological alarm bells. Recommendations for "limitation" and "cultural change" needed to be augmented by some sort of definable program for sustainable ecological agriculture. The Rodale Institute, funded by the Rodale Press, commissioned a study of America's farms and food supply labeled the Cornucopia Project. The summary of that group's report, *Empty Breadbasket* (1981), described the major problems facing the sustainability of the food supply, including the aforementioned agricultural pollution, suburban sprawl and rural decline, soil erosion and soil debility, high energy costs, concentrated livestock facilities, and the ecological problems presented by monocultural, chemically dependent agriculture.

Empty Breadbasket called for drastic changes in the American farm and food system. Among other suggestions, it recommended rediversification of American farms, decentralization of feedlots (which would cut pollution as well as transportation and grain-drying costs), abandonment and/or reform of the irrigation system of the Great Plains, biological control of pests, a shift from hybrid monoculture to locally based varieties and diversified crop patterns, use of renewable farm energy sources, recycling of all agricultural wastes, and governmental support for more farmers regardless of gender or race. The Cornucopia Project also prescribed local distribution and marketing of food; an educational campaign against junk food and tobacco; establishment of a Department of Food to encourage local production of food for cities; creation of urban gardens, greenhouses, and aquaculture centers; experimentation with new crops and crop uses; and a sounder ecological management of the country's farms, forests, and fisheries. *Empty Breadbasket* challenged its readers to recognize that farmland was a "national trust," of equal importance to all citizens. America's future, according to the study, depended on finding solutions to the difficulties of providing safe, affordable food without destroying the precious resource of land.[27]

As the Cornucopia Project indicates, by 1980 theories of the new agriculture were indelibly merged with holistic ecological thinking and the ideals of sustainability. The time had now arrived for the design and implementation of new farming systems and greater public awareness of the benefits of sustainable ecological agriculture. In other words, the new farming had to be removed from books and speeches; it was time to place it in the scientific laboratory and, more importantly, in the farmer's field and on the consumer's table.

THE MODELS AND THE METHODS OF
SUSTAINABLE AGRICULTURE

The advocates of sustainable ecological agriculture used ecology in a third way: to inform technique. Imbued with the new holism of the environmental movement, scientists, theorists, and farmers began to offer some definitive models and methods for sustainable agriculture. In many ways sustainable agriculture represented a leap of faith for many farmers and researchers, as technical, financial, and psychological barriers faced the new converts to ecological farming. It seemed easy to criticize past mistakes in agricultural technology and to single out the cultural maladies leading to the environmental, social, and economic crises of farming and rural life. But as the followers of more than one social movement have discovered, it was far easier to proclaim the dawning of a bold new age than to carry out its actualization.[28]

By the mid-1980s, four distinct varieties of sustainable agriculture had formed. *Agroecology*, a term favored by scientists in the sustainable agriculture camp, describes an approach that promoters believed possessed firm foundations in empirical science. *Organic farming* denotes methods that sought to avoid synthetic herbicides, pesticides, and fertilizers. These models emerged over several decades before gaining national recognition in the 1970s and 1980s. *Permaculture* refers to agriculture that emphasizes small-scale technology and the individual farm as a self-sufficient unit. *Perennial polyculture* combines stewardship and organic-type farming with scientific plant breeding aimed at producing a mixed-crop polyculture requiring little, if any, tillage. While other varieties of the sustainable ideal also emerged on the American agricultural scene during the 1970s and 1980s, these particular systems thoroughly incorporated holistic viewpoints and a sense of respect for nature. Also embedded in these systems was the notion that a renewal of rural society and a general ethical revival were required for a truly sustainable agriculture to take hold on the American landscape.

Agroecology

Agroecology represented a scientific response to the perceived shortcomings of agriculture as practiced and preached by the agricultural establishment and mainstream farmers. From the view of the agroecological wing of sustainable agriculture, modern farming seemed to be a victim of its own successes. For example, agroecologists noted that hybridization, monoculture, and massive chemical application had led to a reliance on genetically vulnerable, biologically uniform plants that had most of their natural pest and disease resistance bred out of them. For agroecologists, the task for researchers and agriculturists of the future was to model agriculture upon the example of natural ecosystems. In other words, American farms had to become more self-sufficient, self-regulating, energy-efficient, ecologically diverse, and biologically complex entities.

Agroecology, as a self-aware concept, emerged in the late 1970s and early 1980s in various academic and scientific circles. In essence, agroecology was a new name for the much older field of applied ecology. Phytopathologist J. Artie Browning presaged the agroecological ideal in a 1974 paper on biological (as opposed to chemical) pest management. Browning wrote: "A sound pest management system must be based on natural or biological means of pest management, especially the use of resistance and the encouragement of antagonisms as our first line of defense." Second, stated the scientist, biological pest control could not always count on one gene or other type of resistance to work. "Finally," he wrote, "we must study natural eco-systems from which knowledge can be gained that is readily applicable to agro-ecosystems."[29]

For the agroecological branch of sustainable agriculture, farming was "not just about producing food, but is increasingly about conserving elements of a natural (if albeit, planned) environment on behalf of society." Because agroecosystems covered 30 percent of the earth's landscape, agroecologists thought that agricultural scientists had to look at the model of natural ecosystems and then provide information to agriculturists on how to achieve high yields without manufactured "inputs." Agroecologists envisioned their role in building sustainable agriculture as advisers on topics such as how to get crops to mimic ecological succession, nutrient recycling, finding rotations that would enhance decomposition of organic material and contribute to an active soil community, or establishing natural methods to fight pests and diseases.[30]

Although they hailed from the scientific branch of the new farming, agroecologists nonetheless envisioned themselves as "outsiders," seeking to use the science and ethic of ecology to overthrow the old agricultural regime and install sustainabilty. Stephen D. Gliesman, later head of the Agroecology Program at the University of California at Santa Cruz, helped define the scope of agroecology in his essay "An Agroecological Approach to Sustainable Agriculture" (1984). Gliesman stated that agroecology was based "on the premise that the short-term mainly economic focus of food production must be directed to long-term management systems—systems based on cycles and interactions found in natural systems. The term agroecology is new, yet its practice is as old as cultivation itself. Past civilizations often modeled their farms after the natural environment."[31]

Miguel Altieri, a research scientist in the Division of Biological Control, University of California–Berkeley, also envisioned agroecology as a scientific and ethical guide for sustainable agriculture. In his testament *Agroecology: The Scientific Basis of Alternative Agriculture* (1983), Altieri suggested a multitude of applications that would stem from the development of agroecology as a discipline. In Altieri's view, the agroecologist would be a true interdisciplinarian, drawing from diverse sources, empirical evidence, and subjective observation to give the farmer advice on cropping, rotations, row spacing, soil nutrients, integrated pest management, energy and resource conservation, environmental quality, public health, and "equitable development." Furthermore, in his opinion, agroecologists needed to present an alternative to the "Western capitalist view of agricultural development." In contradistinction to the generalized research of the land-grant colleges and the experiment stations, the agroecologist must proffer "holistic" plans and "site-specific" techniques for a sustainable and ecological agriculture.[32]

Prototype agroecologists such as Gliesman and Altieri recognized that agriculture represented a major human encroachment into natural ecosystems. By combining the knowledge provided by conventional agricultural science with the study of traditional, premodern, and organic farming systems, agroecology could help solve the monumental environmental and social problems of agriculture. Drawing upon a long history of research, Altieri suggested, agroecologists would create a "scientific basis" for sustainable ecological agriculture. "In agriculture," he and fellow author Helen Vukasin wrote, "the appropriate level of organization to be studied and managed is the agroecosystem and the corresponding discipline is agroecology. All that ecologists study—such as the distribution, abundance, and interactions between organisms and within their physical environment, succession, and the flows of energy and materials—are important for the understanding of agroecosystems."[33]

Serving as proselytizers of holism at a time of social and scientific atomization, agroecologists blended fields such as meteorology, entomology, and the social sciences into a new formula for farmers to ensure long-term production without the ill effects of a chemically based monoculture. Agroecologists recognized that modern agricultural science and technology had captured the productive potential of nature. Agroecology sought to harmonize the productive efforts of agriculture with the maintenance of ecological diversity, environmental health, and long-term fertility of the land.

In the early stage of the new discipline in the 1980s, the ideology of agroecology appeared all-encompassing. Describing this broad-reaching approach, Altieri noted that "agroecologists study ecosystems long affected by people where experimentation is frequently impossible. Furthermore, people and their social systems are as important to agroecology as are ecological systems themselves." Thus agroecology encompassed both concerns over the best techniques for a plot of land and concerns over issues such as politicizing and unifying small-scale farmers. It also concerned itself with public education for consumers regarding the benefits of ecological agriculture. Agroecologists thought that their knowledge would be especially useful for farmers in the three- to five-year transition stage to an ecological agriculture regime. For agroecologists such as Altieri, "the requirements to develop a sustainable agriculture clearly are not only biological or technical, but also social, economic, political, and illustrative."[34]

Organic Farming

While agroecology began to define itself in the 1980s as an academic discipline supportive of sustainable agriculture, adherents of various systems of organic farming could rightfully claim that the development of "organics" over several decades provided appropriate models and methods for sustainable, ecological agriculture. Like the agroecologists, the organic farming element of sustainable ecological agriculture operated under the conviction that the new farming would correct mistakes of the past. Organic farming advocates in the 1970s and 1980s saw their models and methods of ecological agriculture as survival tools "in a resource-limited world with an increasingly fragile environment" overwhelmed by ecologically disruptive forms of agriculture. Sustainable organic farmers sought to enhance "natural systems" rather than replace them with the chemically supported monocultures of contemporary agriculture.[35]

Significantly, organic farming advocates believed their systems incorporated a higher form of technology than that offered by the "single enterprise agriculture" of the machinelike research and production establishment. Sustainable organic agriculture involved a complex system involving "crop and animal co-existence with naturally occurring flora and fauna" founded upon more "intricate biological relationships than are found in conventional systems." In essence, organic farming employs a production system that "avoids or largely excludes the use of syntheti- cally compounded fertilizer, pesticides, growth regulators, and livestock feed additives." The code of "organics" prescribed the use of "naturally occurring chemicals" such as green and animal manures. Employing a broad definition of ecology, the ideology of sustainable organic farming expanded the definition of ecological agriculture to include far more than composting strategies and the use of earthworms. The organic approach also factored in support for small "family" farms and a dedication to reshaping the distribution and consumption of food in America.[36]

The Rodale Press and the affiliated Rodale Research Center and Institute of Emmaus, Pennsylvania, have been central institutions in the proliferation of organic farming and ecological agriculture since the 1940s. Robert Rodale, the son of Rodale Press founder J. I. Rodale, also assisted in the solidification of sustainable agriculture as an ideology until his tragic death in the 1980s. Just as Edward Faulkner demanded soil restoration as well as soil conservation in the 1940s and 1950s, Robert Rodale called for sustainable agriculture to expand beyond the limits of "sustainability" and to call itself regenerative agriculture. Notwithstand- ing Rodale's semantic challenge, in essence his ideas were quite similar to those of others promoting the idea of sustainable ecological agriculture in the 1970s and 1980s.

Rodale thought that the ecological crisis facing agriculture and humanity could be avoided with the wholesale adoption of organic farm- ing techniques. Through the publication of books and magazines and the sponsorship of research, the publisher-agriculturist tried to convince farmers and a wider public that "with the aid of advanced technologies, we will be able to combine resources from the air, water and soil into regenerative systems that will build continuously and will be the basis of ever greater security and health." Rodale and fellow travelers in the organic movement relied on a long legacy of research, observation, and practice to assist their construction of a sustainable and ecological agri- culture that "first looks at building a quality environment without people, then it looks to see if there is a place for people."[37]

Although organic farming had developed several schools of thought using the innovations of Sir Albert Howard, Rudolph Steiner, J. I. Rodale, and Edward Faulkner, two organic farming models illustrate the ideas and techniques of organiculture in the 1970s and 1980s. One model, *bio- dynamic farming,* is an older version of organic agriculture that has per- sisted to the present day and represents several major ideas of the overall organic movement. Another model, the *ridge-till method* advocated by organic farmer Dick Thompson of Boone, Iowa, highlights how many farmers pursued sustainable ecological agriculture in the 1970s and 1980s. While many original ridge-tillers went organic, nonorganic farmers later adopted this and similar methods.

Biodynamic agriculture, founded in Europe by prolific author Rudolph Steiner in the 1920s, continued to enjoy intellectual support and popular implementation in organic farming and health food and vegetarian circles in the United States since the 1930s. Adherents of the biodynamic method perceived organic farming as a sane alternative to the technologically misguided industrial agriculture being practiced in America during the 1970s and 1980s. To them, agriculture appeared hazardous because of its monoculture techniques and the destructive forces of large-scale machines and manufactured agricultural chemicals.

To counter the perils of modern industrial farming, the proponents of biodynamic farming asked agriculturists and consumers to "look at agriculture in its totality as a whole" and at the individual farm as an "organism." According to the spiritual and scientific philosophy of biodynamic agriculture, the farmer had to show "concern for the farm organism, for the cosmic environment of growth, and for the application of dynamic measures." Biodynamicists combined traditional restoration procedures, such as the use of soil-building crop rotations and legume plantings, with applications of organic-based "natural" sprays composed of various herbal or mineral preparations. Biodynamic agriculture stressed the necessity of diversified farm operations, total recycling of crop wastes and manure, and the establishment of a decentralized agricultural system characterized by marketing techniques such as farmers' markets, roadside stands, and wholesaling relatively unprocessed, "healthy" food.

By treating the farm as a living organism and by sparing the microfauna of the soil a dousing with poisonous chemicals, for example, biodynamic agriculture purportedly could produce crops and livestock less susceptible to stress and endowed with greater abilities to withstand the chaos of nature. Described as a "Goethian approach to agriculture," the biodynamic model provided for biological and natural pest and disease control (via the herbal sprays), extensive use of crop rotations, soil-building crops and composts, and the production and marketing of increasingly popular "organic" food.[38]

The search for examples of non-Western sources for sustainability was a significant feature of sustainable agriculture in organic farming manifestos during the 1970s and 1980s. Just as Edward Faulkner could cite F. H. King's observations of Asian peasant farming as a form of permanent agriculture, so, too, could organiculturists draw upon numerous examples of "natural farming" around the world. The canon of texts that emerged in the organic movement included Masanobu Fukuoka's book *The One Straw Revolution*. A Japanese microbiologist trained in the World

War II era, Fukuoka later abandoned his academic post in order to work on restoring an old farm plot near his home village. Fukuoka's system employed terraces, the extensive use of rice and barley straw as a mulch, and a perennial ground cover of white clover. Onto this mixture he planted rice and other small grains without any tillage equipment save for a planting stick, employing no chemical fertilizers or biocides, and producing without any need to cultivate for weeds. Fukuoka experienced high yields on his land in the 1960s and 1970s as he and numerous other pioneers of organic agriculture gained worldwide fame by successfully integrating holistic ecology into the realm of agriculture.[39]

While the case of Masanobu Fukuoka and the experience offered by the biodynamic school and other organic farming schools provided many lessons for America's organic farmers, proof of economic viability was necessary if sustainable ecological agriculture was to take hold in American agriculture and in the public imagination. Organic models and techniques had to go beyond organic gardening, health food fanatics, and experimental pronouncements, and find their way into production agriculture. One example of the infiltration of organic ideas onto mainstream farms is provided by the case of Iowa farmer Dick Thompson.

Thompson, who earned a master of science degree in animal husbandry at Iowa State University, began farming in the 1960s as a conventional corn grower, borrowing heavily each year to pay for expensive seed and applications of inorganic fertilizer, pesticides, herbicides, and fungicides. Thompson found it increasingly difficult to pay for the cost of production, even with the increased yields resulting from his conventional chemical-based farm system. He also noticed that his cattle always seemed to be sick, thus requiring expensive antibiotics that further tapped his bank accounts. During the late 1960s, Dick and Sharon Thompson looked at their farming life partly from a religious or spiritual perspective, realizing that while they were busy building an earthly kingdom of land and equipment, they also had embarked on the treadmill of industrialized agriculture where "enough was never enough, and quick was never quick enough." Thompson abandoned monoculture and chemicals "cold turkey," switching to a five-year mixed rotation of corn, soybeans, oats, and hay. Like other commercial farmers embracing organic farming methodologies during this period, he also found motivation for this change in the growing environmental and consumer safety movements, in concerns for the health of his family and community, and from his awareness that the average Iowa farm in the 1970s and early 1980s experienced an eight- to ten-ton topsoil loss per acre per year, twice the acceptable standard set by soil scientists.[40]

Thompson's system utilized several organic methods, including cover crops, crop diversity, and extensive applications of green and animal manures. Always experimenting, he found particular success with what he described as a "ridge-till" system. Using a 1965 Buffalo Till planter, Thompson built ridges in a field during the June cultivation of the previous year's corn crop. As these twelve-inch-wide ridges were built, buried foxtail seeds would come to the surface, germinate, and then die out as they were smothered by the corn. Any remaining foxtail had an allelopathic (growth-inhibiting) effect on broadleaf weeds. In the following spring planting, Thompson's planter apparatus would scrape any remaining weeds (that had held the topsoil over the winter) from the top two inches of soil while it planted soybeans. This system utilized fast-growing varieties of soybeans with thick canopy shade and high pod clearance to further assist in nonchemical weed control. With careful cultivation, soybeans planted in this manner could, according to Thompson, nearly equal the average yield of conventional growers, with substantial reductions in cost thanks to avoiding the use of chemicals. Using organic and ridge-till methods, Thompson found he could survive economically, even with increased tillage costs.

Thompson's method extended beyond the field to the livestock pen. Using common sense and ecological insight, Thompson resolved to produce healthier animals at a lower cost than he had using established techniques. In his hog lot, he spread lime in sleeping hutches to raise the pH level and control abscesses in his sows. He also "immunized" gestating sows by exposing them to manure from the farrowing pens. Instead of inoculating his animals with antibiotics, Thompson fed them beneficial "pro-biotic" bacteria. He picked medium-frame hogs with large lung capacities, thinking that this type of animal best survived the effects of cold weather. He also weaned his hogs a couple of weeks later than conventional agriculturists and chased his hogs out of their bedding area early in the morning, so they would "develop good toilet habits."[41]

Thompson was one of many farmers who found they could "go organic" and survive economically. After initial resistance from bankers and the local agricultural college, Thompson watched as the ideas of organic farming spread quickly during the late 1970s and 1980s. He also found that, along with economic success and intellectual recognition, his farm enjoyed greater populations of wildlife, reduced wind and water erosion, more organic matter in the soil, more earthworms (and presumably other microfauna), faster seed emergence, higher quality grain, and healthier livestock with a superior feed-to-meat ratio than achieved by most conventional livestock producers.[42]

Dick Thompson's case represents the ingenuity and experimental verve required to practice a relatively sustainable, ecologically oriented type of husbandry. He made many mistakes in switching to the new system but saved himself economically by diversifying and becoming more self-sufficient, with his wife in charge of a large garden for home consumption and local sale. Thompson became an active member of the boards of the Institute for Alternative Agriculture and the Regenerative Agriculture Association. He also promoted the ideas of sustainable ecological agriculture for a number of years as a cofounder of the Practical Farmers of Iowa (PFI), one of the nation's most vocal and successful organizations promoting the practical benefits of agricultural techniques that also fulfilled many central imperatives of ecological agriculture. The PFI disseminated cost-saving techniques, many of them from organic traditions, to mainstream farmers. Thompson, who publicly challenged the idea that organic farmers were granola-crunching dreamers, also realized that what he attempted was part of a cultural shift to holistic thought and ecological ethics.

Thompson, as well as followers of the biodynamic school, joined thousands of other farmers and "intentional community" homesteaders in the 1970s and 1980s who were pursuing organic forms of sustainable agriculture. Organic farmers helped popularize many techniques and ideas that epitomize sustainable ecological agriculture, including a commitment to farming without chemicals and increasing the diversity of crops for both ecological and financial reasons. Organic farmers in the 1970s and 1980s could be found discussing the role of earthworms in agriculture, planting shelter belts to prevent wind erosion and increase wildlife numbers, and practicing strip-cropping to increase biodiversity and reduce water erosion. The organic farming community emphasized the need to escape monoculture and increase market options and home self-sufficiency by diversifying into aquaculture, raising "exotic" animals such as Vietnamese potbellied pigs, growing biomass fuel, planting fruit orchards, and finally switching to various types of nontraditional crops for seed oil and other markets linked to the "alternative use" movement.[43]

Both the practitioners of biodynamic farming and the thousands of converted organic farmers like Dick Thompson sought to bring the ideas of sustainable ecological agriculture into the mainstream of American farming. In doing so, they found an increasingly receptive food-consuming public and a grudgingly less hostile research establishment. As one account from the mid-1980s noted, "From Virginia to Oregon, tens of thousands of farmers have reduced their costs and increased their profits by replacing conventional industrialized farming techniques with sophisticated organic ones. They are not, however, the backyard gardeners usually associated with back-to-the-land organic movements. They include some of the biggest farms, some of the largest users of petrochemical pesticides and fertilizers." Like Thompson, many farmers shifted from conventional to organic techniques out of personal ecological concerns as well as a desire to ensure profitability. Farmers switching to the organic route "cold turkey" usually experienced about a 40 percent drop in yields the first year and then within three years recovered to 80 to 90 percent of preconversion yields. While success depended on a number of factors, including crop type, climate, and the resources of a given farmer, those switching to organic methods often found they made more money even with reduced yields because they had lower costs for chemicals and energy and received higher prices for their organically produced products. As its practices spread during the 1970s and 1980s, organic farming became more mainstream, more organized and self-defined, more successful, and a major contributor to the ideas of sustainable agriculture.[44]

Permaculture

If agroecologists presented themselves as scientific advisers for ecological farmers, and if organic farmers served as the frontline fighters for sustainable ecological agriculture, then practitioners of other schools in the new farming could claim they presented more far-reaching and visionary models and methods for agricultural sustainability. One such branch in the sustainable agriculture movement is the concept of permaculture. Introduced by Australian Bill Mollison in the 1960s, permaculture represents a strain of ecological agriculture devoted to "organic" principles and to designing and testing self-sufficient farmstead and village models, replete with appropriate "soft" technology models and techniques of sustainable agriculture.

"Permaculture (permanent agriculture) is the conscious design and maintenance of agriculturally productive ecosystems which have the diversity, stability, and the resilience of natural ecosystems," wrote Mollison in 1988. He envisioned permaculture as "the harmonious integration of landscape and people, providing their food, energy, shelter, and other material and non-material needs in a systematic way." Rooted in the Taoist notion of "necessitous use," in past prophets of land stewardship, and in the ideas of technologist R. Buckminster Fuller, permaculture sought to create a world of small-scale, self-sustaining villages with ecological agriculture at their center.[45]

Permaculture emphasized high-yielding, small-plot, and greenhouse agriculture and aquaculture ponds, as well as forage agriculture, forest agriculture, and the development of individual and "village" self-sufficiency and on-site alternative energy sources. Any permaculture model had to be based on the conditions of the bioregion in which it was designed and had to comply with ecological guidelines regarding energy cycles, food webs, biological and ecological diversity, and a tendency toward ecological stability with the highest possible yield. For the permaculturist, finding the appropriate model and techniques for sustainable agriculture would result from an understanding of science and a willingness to observe, deduce, cooperate with society at large, and care for the earth. Like others in sustainable agriculture, Mollison insisted that any change in agricultural models and methods had to be accompanied by a corresponding shift in ethics. People had to give up the idea of accumulating wealth beyond one's needs, especially in the acquisition and use of land and the propagation of large families. For Mollison, "the only ethical decision is to take responsibility for our own existence and that of our children." Without permaculture, he reasoned, there would be "no possibility of a stable social order."[46]

Employing some of the same rationales and techniques as Mollison, the scientists and technicians at the New Alchemy Institute pioneered the use of soft technology applied to ecological agriculture. According to cofounder John Todd, the "core of the effort" at New Alchemy was to build "an ecologically derived approach to the intensive culture of foods—systems that are independent of food and fuel shortages, systems that can be adopted to many climates throughout the world, even urban areas." Devotees of the Renaissance chemist Giordano Bruno, who saw science as "a sacred discourse with nature," the New Alchemists conceived of their efforts as an alternative to the ecologically vulnerable and unhealthy system of establishment agriculture and the "doomwatch" of 1970s environmentalism.

"We aren't anti-science or anti-technology," claimed Todd. "I think it's essential to *save* science and technology—but it can and must be done on a human scale." As an 1975 article in *The Sciences* suggested about the New Alchemy Institute, "the electronics, the microcomputers, attest that this place is far from a Luddite-like rejection of technological innovation." The New Alchemist contribution to sustainable ecological agriculture centered on building family- and village-level permaculture models and techniques that employed small-scale but practical, durable, and inexpensive technologies.[47]

The New Alchemist permaculture model featured high-yield plots and greenhouse food crops; traditional organic farming techniques such as biological pest management, multiple cropping, and companion planting for allelopathic and nitrogen-fixing effects; use of experimental crops such as Jerusalem artichokes, amaranth, and sunflowers; composting; extensive planting of nitrogen-rich cover crops such as clover; and use of hedges to prevent wind erosion. In geodesic domes, greenhouses, and "mini-arks," New Alchemy researchers sought to refine and understand ecological relationships between plants, animals, and humans in order to design self-sustaining systems for small groups and communities.

One method of permaculture-style sustainable agriculture practiced at New Alchemy was the "solar tube." In fifty-five-gallon plastic barrels, New Alchemy scientists raised a fast-growing (three-month), high-protein, tasty species of African tilapia fish, using the fishes' waste as food for shellfish on the bottom of the tanks and as fertilizer for garden plots. The New Alchemist version of ecological agriculture also used old-fashioned guard dogs for livestock manipulation and predator control, and varieties of geese, chickens, and ducks that were not particular eaters. Solar energy and windmills with Dacron sails were among the alternative energy sources explored at the institute. "By weaving together the elements of micro-climate, annual and perennial plants, water and soil management, and human needs," the New Alchemists claimed, the permaculturist forms an energy-efficient, low maintenance, high-yielding, and intricately inter-connected system."[48]

Perennial Polyculture

Like the founders of the New Alchemy Institute, Wes Jackson abandoned a university job to pursue his own vision of building a sustainable and ecological agriculture at the Land Institute in Salina, Kansas. Trained as a biologist and geneticist in the 1960s, Jackson left a faculty position in California and returned to his native state to form his own research and training facility in 1976, dedicating it to "sustainable alternatives in agriculture, energy, waste management, and shelter." Starting with a meager piece of land, a sparse annual budget of less than fifteen thousand dollars, and a handful of students, Jackson sculpted his ecological model of agriculture with tools provided by history, classical biology, modern genetics, personal observation, and a classic Kansan mixture of entrepreneurship and evangelical mission.

Just as John Todd and cadre were inspired to redirect their lives after reading an essay by Paul Ehrlich, so did Wes Jackson and his wife, Dana, become imbued with a sense of mission in a world desperate for answers to the sprawling environmental crisis in the 1970s. Dana's interests lay in the social side of alternative agriculture, such as women's issues and marketing strategies, as well as in organic gardening techniques. Wes remained fascinated with the scientific issues of ecology and plant genetics. He discerned that inbreeding between agribusiness and the academy would never allow the construction of a truly permanent and ecologically oriented agriculture. Thus he left his position as departmental chair for a less certain future as the founder of the Land Institute. After years of ruminating over ideas from his personal and literary mentors—ranging from his major professor Ben Smith and the 1920s and 1930s work of Russian geneticist N. I. Vavilov to the poems of Homer and Wendell Berry—Jackson's mission crystallized when he was on a field trip with students to the Konza Prairie, a native tallgrass preserve near Manhattan, Kansas.

Observing the self-sustaining biodiversity of the prairie, Jackson noted,

"From the point of view of the ecologist, the prairie is doing everything right." He contrasted chemical-dependent American industrial agriculture with the prairie: "Like the wheat field, the prairie is a sprawling factory for turning sunlight into fiber, starch, fat and protein: but while the prairie relies on today's sunlight, the wheat field lives on mummified sunlight in the form of fertilizers and pesticides derived from oil and gas. The prairie lives on income, the wheat field on capital." For Jackson, a proper model for sustainable agriculture derived from nature's model of self-renewal, modified by human needs and appropriate technology. Although he often referred to sustainable agriculture, by 1985 Jackson also began to use the term *ecosystem agriculture.* Wes Jackson's brand of theory and practice utilized the major elements of sustainable ecological agriculture.[49]

Calling their system *perennial polyculture,* Jackson and researchers at the Land Institute embarked on a program to design systems and techniques of agriculture that emulated the prairie. The idea was revolutionary: Jackson aimed to reduce or eliminate row crop monoculture and supplant modern American farming with a mixed-crop polyculture of perennials free of both tillage and the need for chemicals.

The idea of a mixed polyculture had been employed previously. Native Americans, in their traditional corn, bean, and squash polycultures, employed annual plants in a self-fertilizing and highly sustainable agricultural system. What Wes Jackson proposed to accomplish over time was to combine old Indian techniques with a sense of stewardship and genetic breeding to produce a sustainable perennial polyculture of seed-bearing herbaceous crops. The problem with modeling agriculture after the prairie, Jackson quickly realized, was that for evolutionary reasons the plants of the prairie produced far more root structure and leafy material than edible seed. Thus the mission of the Land Institute was refined to one of breeding new strains of prairie grasses with seed yields matching those of traditional small-grain agriculture.

Jackson and fellow supporters of perennial polyculture attempted to use seed selection and crossbreeding to produce composite polycultures of grass, legume, and seed crops. Choosing strains, crosses, and hybrids not just for qualities of yield but also for desired agronomic effect (such as nitrogen-fixing or pest-resistant qualities), Jackson and disciples sought to identify and breed for human use crops such as Maximillian sunflower, Illinois bundleflower, eastern gama grass, bee balm, lespedeza, winebark, white snakeroot, crosses between milo and Johnson grass, and wild forms of rye. Jackson's work has been augmented by researchers worldwide, including the discovery of high-producing mutant strains of eastern gama grass. Inherent in Jackson's vision of perennial polyculture is the codevelopment of food, feed, and industrial uses of alternative crops. Researchers supporting the polyculture idea have devised healthy, allegedly palatable dishes such as "gamma grass flakes" and multigrain "prairie rolls."

Also inherent in the philosophy of Wes Jackson and others devoted to perennial polyculture was an ecological vision of agriculture and the human future. Perennial polyculture researchers look for ecological relationships between plants, animals, microbes, genes, and people and claim that polyculture eventually might bring about a high-yielding, soil-saving, energy-efficient, and chemical-free farming system. But advocates also recognize that cultural changes are necessary for the implementation of sustainable agriculture. Jackson has been one of the most vehement opponents of establishment agriculture; he has often lashed out at the misguided technology of the land-grant colleges and at the increased power and prestige of molecular biology, which he perceives as an ecologically dysfunctional discipline.

Even though Wes Jackson recognized that all human activity represents an intervention into nature, like others in ecological agriculture, he asked that humans respect the productive power and internal maintenance systems of nature when building an agriculture for the future. In their quest to understand and develop "nature's model" of farming, Jackson and cohort represent the general vision of ecological agriculture during the 1970s and 1980s. They also have advocated the reintroduction of horsepower onto American farms as an ecologically and economically viable option and have sought to develop solar and other alternative energy strategies for the farmstead.[50]

The work of Wes Jackson and the perennial polyculturists also represents the broader, holistic notions of ecological agriculture in expressing the desire for saving humanity from ecological ruin and promoting the revival of rural culture. While Jackson and others often lambasted the notion that the "family farmer" had any inherent virtue, he did claim that his vision of ecological agriculture was a "moral system" that embraced an "ethic of sustainability." In the work of perennial polyculture, in Land Institute projects such as the model solar-powered Sunshine Farm, and in the recent small community redevelopment project at Matfield Green, Kansas, Jackson illustrated the notion that the various strands of ecological agriculture are united by a devotion to ecology and nature as a guide, and in the need to redirect American agriculture toward environmental responsibility and the uplift of a faltering rural America.[51]

MEANS TO AN END

Born out of the environmental crises in agriculture and renewed holistic approaches, the sustainable agriculture movement of the 1970s and 1980s promised to lead America into a future endowed with safe, abundant food supplies and a revitalized environment. From its conceptual stages, sustainable agriculture sought to incorporate the science and ethic of ecology into agriculture. In proposing systems such as agroecology, organic farming, permaculture, and perennial polyculture, advocates of the new farming sought to reharmonize agriculture with the natural environment, creating long-term productivity and ecosystem health.

Sustainable ecological agriculture offered health benefits for both farm people and city dwellers, economic uplift for rural America, and the prospect of long-term societal and ecological harmony. These systems promised to lessen soil erosion and to build the topsoil, use ecological measures to increase fertility and fight pests and disease (as opposed to using chemical measures), help eliminate most agricultural pollution, feed the hungry with abundant, nutritive food, and replenish biodiversity in the countryside. The main differences among these systems of ecological farming were their sources of inspiration and their spiritual, scientific, and public relations orientations.[52]

Proponents of sustainable agriculture claimed that the new farming would offer better long-term economic benefits for American farmers and argued that sustainability in agriculture would promote an overall cultural devotion to rural revival and to long-term ecological accountability. Like the permanent agriculture movement before it, sustainable agriculture offered worldwide societal harmony and a chance for humanity to achieve an enduring prosperity. Because the ideology of sustainable agriculture presented a challenge to the entrenched American agricultural establishment, adherents of the new farming needed to further define the benefits of sustainable ecological agriculture and to communicate the challenge of the new systems and methods to farmers, researchers, and the general public. To become more than another speculative panacea, sustainable agriculture had to reach beyond the confines of its experimental, "alternative" status and capture the attention of farmers and consumers, as well as convert at least some portion of the agricultural establishment.[53]

CHAPTER SIX

The Public Life of Sustainable Agriculture

Since the mid-1970s, ideas of a sustainable and ecological agriculture evolved in the public arena. Like the permanent agriculture movement that began in the 1930s, the concept of sustainable agriculture first emanated from prophetic figures who issued jeremiad-like protestations regarding the impending ecological and economic crises facing farmers and the general citizenry. Sustainable agriculture successfully linked itself ideologically to the environmental and energy crises of the 1970s, as well as the farm economic crisis of the 1980s. Throughout the 1980s, the movement became more organized, self-aware, and nationally recognized. In time, sustainable agriculture began to enjoy some degree of institutional support in the form of academic and governmental recognition, research funding, and political backing.

By the late 1980s, the concept of sustainability had become a household term. It seemed as if everyone—agriculturists, politicians, businessmen, and common folk—demanded that America confront the future and adopt programs that would lead to societal permanence. By broadcasting the ideas of new farming in the 1970s and 1980s, the movement for sustainable ecological agriculture not only remodeled the structure of American farming but also helped sustain a floundering environmental ethic in the dark years of the early 1980s. The public life of sustainable agriculture highlighted the central role of agriculture in the human interaction with nature.

Because it challenged the technology, economy, and culture of established agriculture, the sustainable ecological agriculture movement sparked intense resistance in academic, government and agribusiness circles. Yet eventually the agricultural establishment, the original enemy of sustainable agriculture, co-opted many of the ideas and most of the terminology of the new farming. The process of co-option involves adopting some portion of the program in question, but doing so without a sincere desire for fundamental change, incorporating the language of the opposition for rhetorical or public relations purposes. Words and terms specific to the challenging program are redefined by the majority program, with the result that the general public fails to recognize the difference between the two.

The adoption of ecological agriculture's terminology and ideas, however, also can serve as one measure of how the movement swayed mainstream agriculture over the past twenty years. To the extent that established institutions acknowledged the program of alternative agriculture as presenting legitimate issues that needed to be addressed, the movement successfully levered public understanding toward the reformers' viewpoint. The adoption of alternative ideas by segments of mainstream institutions was partly a sincerely motivated effort to incorporate positive changes that made sense in terms of a worldview that celebrated progress and technology. But to the extent that the agricultural establishment was able to borrow the language of sustainable agriculture while continuing to use industrial approaches, the movement's agenda failed to carry along American farming. While the process of adoption and co-option increased the legitimacy of many of the ideas and techniques of sustainable agriculture, the establishment versions of sustainability focused on short-term profitability rather than long-term ecological integrity, land health, or any substantial social reform.

COMMUNICATING THE IDEA

On a warm May Day in the mid-1980s, amid the friendly and quite conservative confines of Kansas State University, a group of twenty to thirty angry, placard-bearing, bullhorn-carrying farmers attracted a crowd in front of the student union. Of the several farmers who spoke that day, Stephen Anderson ably communicated to the student audience the reason for the protest. Anderson and colleagues were on the campus of a leading land-grant university to express their belief that the land-grant schools and the overall agricultural establishment had failed the average American farmer and consumer. For these embittered farmers, "conventional" farming and research had to be recast in order to sustain the fragile economies, ecologies, and cultures of rural America. By advocating policies and technologies that had led to the decline of rural America and the physical environment, reasoned the angry farmers, agricultural college professors and researchers (usually the offspring of rural America themselves) were the ultimate traitors to the very people they were supposed to uplift.

After some additional speech making, the procession of protesters and as many as two hundred new student followers proceeded across the campus to the College of Agriculture. The farmers demanded that a particular agricultural economist, long a promoter of "industrial" agriculture (and chief mentor to Secretary of Agriculture Dan Glickman), explain his ivory-towered views to these disenfranchised agrarians. Eventually, with no professors emerging from the building to debate or reason with the crowd, the protesters ended their rally by dumping a wheelbarrow of manure in front of Waters Hall, home to the College of Agriculture.[1]

This episode illustrates some of the emotional and intellectual fervor, as well as the agrarian attitudes, expressed by parts of the sustainable agriculture movement as it developed in the 1970s and 1980s. Perhaps Robert Steffen, the organic farmer from Nebraska, best expressed the sentiment of the new farming as far back as 1971 when he noted that "hundreds of thousands of farmers know what they are doing is wrong, but they are hooked." Forecasting the upcoming battle between ecological agriculture and the traditional agricultural establishment, Steffen told the *Omaha World-Herald*, "Some people will tell you that we'll all starve if farmers give up chemical fertilizers, pesticides, etc. . . . but that's a lot of bunk." Steffen thought that ecological agriculture had to educate farmers, consumers, and policy makers about the need for cultural reappraisal and technical change in farming and food production.[2]

Communicating the ideas of ecological agriculture was as important as conceiving them. Borrowing from a long tradition of American crisis mongering and messianic visions of societal renewal, the task of communicating sustainable agriculture first fell upon self-appointed proselytizers who quickly became the icons of the movement. The primers for the movement unquestionably were Wendell Berry's works, especially the classic treatise *The Unsettling of America: Culture and Agriculture* (1977). Berry provided insightful analysis regarding the ecological foundation of sustainable agriculture and offered rhetorical ammunition against the misguided technology of the agricultural establishment. He also contributed a poet's sensibility and a sense of Christian zeal to a critique of a national culture apparently stricken by a pathological devotion to thoughtless consumption, rampant materialism, social decay, and impermanent agriculture. Berry, though considered a radical by conservatives preaching sustainable agriculture and a "puritan" by those on the left of the issue, is still cited by nearly everyone purporting to be advocates of sustainable agriculture. His books are mentioned in nearly every philosophical treatment of sustainable agriculture, and his notoriety as an essayist and poet helped attract a national spotlight onto sustainable agriculture.[3]

If Wendell Berry served as a central figure—a John the Baptist—of sustainable ecological agriculture, then Wes Jackson was another of the movement's larger-than-life preachers. Through his speeches, interviews, articles, and books and his work at the Land Institute in Salina, Kansas, Jackson emerged in the 1980s as the chief communicator in the public life of sustainable agriculture. His work in perennial polyculture came to be portrayed by the media and in intellectual and farming circles as visionary and of potentially vital importance in the future. But the lanky Midwesterner offered more than his ideas on plant breeding and ecological models for farming. Jackson also embodied the sense of mission, social responsibility, and faith in human and environmental renewal that characterized the culture of sustainable ecological agriculture. He became a central figure in the movement, at one time or another appearing in or garnering attention from nearly every important national media outlet. National Public Radio's *All Things Considered*, for example, devoted a half-hour segment to Jackson and the Land Institute in the late 1980s, and *Smithsonian* and other periodicals ran feature stories on the eloquent Kansan.

Evan Eisenberg, in a 1989 piece in the *Atlantic Monthly*, offered a classic portrait of Wes Jackson as alternative scientist, ecological steward, and communicator of sustainable, ecological agriculture. Eisenberg wrote, "From a hillock on this Kansas prairie Wes Jackson *is* watching, and what he sees, and says, and does, makes him the most radical of America's agricultural prophets." Following the lead of Wendell Berry, Jackson offered a cultural critique as well as an ecological "fix" for American farming. Farmers, as well as the monolithic agricultural establishment, were culpable for the destruction and pollution of the American land and the fracture of cultural bonds in the rural community. Shopping at a town's Walmart instead of the family-owned stores in the community, or buying out one's financially troubled neighbor constituted actions that undermined rural people.[4] Jackson, described by Eisenberg as a cross between Charles Darwin, William Jennings Bryan, and Will Rogers, pointed out that farmers used 160 pounds of nonrenewable nitrogen, phosphorus, and potash fertilizer each year for every American. Jackson also linked sustainable agriculture to the general agricultural-environmental concerns of the 1970s and 1980s, including topsoil erosion, the depletion of the Ogallala aquifer, siltation behind dams, soil compaction by large-scale equipment, and the threat of misguided science in the form of unchecked devotion to the products of molecular biology. In his work Jackson also addressed the decline of rural culture, fostering projects intended to revive the cultural wealth of rural America, as well as sustain a future food supply in an ecological fashion. His work won praise, financial support, and national recognition, causing one commentator to suggest, "If you cut out the contiguous United States and balanced it on a finger, you would be pointing at the Land Institute. The country's center of gravity is here, and you can feel it. There is a sense of poise and deliberation, something in the air that counsels against rashness." Along with Jackson's favorable press coverage in the national media, he also successfully communicated the idea of sustainable ecological agriculture as a popular speaker at the land-grant schools he has consistently assailed.[5]

Jackson effectively stated what many others were thinking: humanity had reached the age of limitation. In the 1970s and 1980s, the recognition of technological, resource, and production limitations altered the landscape of American thought. By the late 1970s, the public was aware of several agricultural-environmental crises or potential problems, including agricultural pollution, genetic narrowing, desertification, and the loss of farmland to suburban sprawl. Furthermore, the farm economic crisis of the early to mid-1980s created an atmosphere conducive to change, both within the public mind and within the ranks of established production agriculture.

Sustainable ecological agriculture drew attention as it emerged with the general public and intellectual concern over the environment. For example, in the late 1970s a topsoil scare brought the soil conservation issue back into the national spotlight for the first time since the 1930s. Although the administration of soil conservation was sometimes poorly conceived (the fabled "soil bank" program of the 1950s ensured greater use of agricultural chemicals and the overtaxation of nonidled acres), few argued that soil conservation was not a national imperative. Yet despite nearly fifty years of political support and conservation work by the Soil Conservation Service and farmers, conservation measures had failed to stop the erosion and debilitation of the American land. Studies conducted under various government directives, including the Soil and Water Resource's Conservation Act of 1977, the National Agricultural Lands Study (NALS), and the *Global 2000 Report,* all suggested that America's soil erosion problem was at an all time high, exacerbated by the export-driven "great plow-up" of the 1970s.[6]

Proponents of sustainable ecological agriculture successfully established their ideas as legitimate proposals for the problems confronting American farming and food production. Conservationist R. Neil Sampson, writing in 1981, claimed that in the age of limitation, "new realities" demanded "a new set of individual actions and collective, or public policies." Sampson warned that "the clock is running. . . . so what is needed—and soon—is enlightened action by people working to improve the world for themselves and their children." The author called for a truly sustainable agriculture that went beyond piecemeal conservation measures and environmentalist rhetoric to embrace holistic farm plans that would provide "the right of humans to a life where they can meet their basic needs and have the opportunity to achieve a high quality of life within the cost ranges they can afford."[7]

The energy crisis of the 1970s also boosted the cause of sustainable ecological agriculture. Writing in 1979, *Des Moines Register* farm editor Lauren Soth noted that "the energy crisis may turn farmers back toward crop rotations with legumes and fewer chemicals—something the environmental movement has not been able to accomplish." That same year, in a presentation to Secretary of Agriculture Bob Bergland, organic farmer Robert Steffen indicated that "the increased cost of fossil fuels has finally drawn our attention to modern farming practices and what the future holds. Farming today is an energy and capital intensive system of food production." As the energy crisis worsened in the 1970s, farmers across the country began to search for ways to cut fuel costs and develop on-farm and renewable energy sources. Farmers trying to pare energy costs could look to the developing systems and methods in the sustainable agriculture community for answers to both their energy problem and topsoil loss.[8]

While the environmental and energy crises helped the apostles of sustainable agriculture communicate their ideas to a more receptive audience, the farm economic crises of the late 1970s and early 1980s particularly assisted the cause of the new farming. Convinced during the Nixon administration that the export market would continue to burgeon, Secretary of Agriculture Earl Butz enjoined farmers to tear out their hedgerows and plant "fence row to fence row." Borrowing heavily, with overvalued land as collateral, many farmers expanded their production by using more expensive seeds and chemicals and larger equipment and by bringing more land into production. From 1970 to 1981, grain production in the United States rose 20 percent. As the export market crashed in the late 1970s following a reduction in grain sales to the Soviet Union and increased production worldwide, American farmers, small-town banks, and rural communities endured the worst economic downturn since the 1930s. The U.S. government lowered price supports in an effort to keep American grain prices competitive, and in 1979 the Federal Reserve raised the prime rate, contributing to loan rates rising from the neighborhood of 8.75 percent in 1979 to around 14.75 percent in 1983. As farmland values fell 63 percent in five years, average net farm income in Iowa fell from $17,000 in 1981 to a negative $1,900 by 1983. From 1981 to 1987, about 20 percent of Iowa agriculturists—twenty-six thousand of them—quit the farming business.[9]

Farming has long held an emotional grip on the nation's imagination, and with good reason. The products of the farm sustain life itself. If those who produce life's necessities are not safe from economic chaos and financial failure, what hope can there be for anyone in a modern economy to find a secure place, a situation of needed employment, and a dignified living? The farm economic crisis of the late 1970s and early 1980s created a general sense among Americans that someone should rescue "family farmers" from a misguided food and agricultural system. As one commentator noted in 1986, "The farm crisis of the early 80s has caused many farmers to consider how they approach their operations," seeking to cut costs at every corner and regain financial independence. Economic problems stripped many farmers of their faith in establishment agriculture and prompted them to get "back to basics." As the protesting farmers on that May Day at Kansas State illustrated, many voices within and outside of agriculture used the farm crisis to challenge the production-oriented establishment to examine the positive attributes of a sustainable and ecological agriculture. The new farming appeared to many farmers, agricultural observers, and researchers as the best avenue away from the problems confronting American farming. Because many small-scale and more "old-fashioned" farmers seemed to survive the economic crisis better than large-scale farmers, the farm crisis of the 1980s also seemed to indicate that *bigger* and *more*—key words in the establishment lexicon—did not always translate into *best*.[10]

As sustainable agriculture experienced a transition from cult status to recognized contender to the agricultural establishment, the communication strategies of the new farming became more sophisticated. The ideology of sustainable agriculture infiltrated the public sphere through its lively personalities, organized demonstration and action, and institutional and media support. Organic farming organizations in the 1970s helped set the stage for an organized communications effort for sustainable agriculture by lobbying for organic farming research, setting standards for "organic" certification, and making the public, farmers, and policy makers aware of the alleged benefits of ecological agriculture. From the 1970s into the 1990s, groups like the Practical Farmers of Iowa, the Center for Rural Affairs, the Institute for Alternative Agriculture, American Farmland Trust, and the National Family Farm Coalition promoted organic farming, ridge-till methods, sustainable rural redevelopment, and other ideas related to sustainable ecological agriculture. For example, the Practical Farmers of Iowa (PFI), founded in 1985, grew to include five hundred Iowa farmers and associate members of varied philosophies. Major elements of the organization's program include educational workshops, well-attended field days, on-farm demonstrations, and research projects. Members also lobby for legislative support for sustainable agriculture. The PFI newsletter, which contains information on techniques and reports on experimental trials, illustrates the support and "networking" functions of alternative agriculture groups, featuring poems, conference reports, a "hotline" number for those with ideas and problems, news notes, and book reviews. *New Farm* magazine, a Rodale Press publication claiming a circulation of one hundred thousand in 1987, cited the PFI as one of the most effective and well-organized groups promoting the new farming.

A secret of PFI's success, according to Gary D'Agroza of Boyden, Iowa, one of the early members of the group, was that "farmers respond best to other farmers." He stated that farmers who wish to continue in their profession would have to "figure out how to farm as economically as possible, and be as environmentally sound as possible. . . . the name of the game today is how to grow corn for $1.25 to $1.50 a bushel. There's no way to do that by using traditional inputs." Starting with the economic concerns common to most mainstream farmers, the PFI drew farmers' attention to the methods of ecological agriculture.

The PFI benefited from the recognition accorded to member Dick Thompson, whose successful ridge-till techniques garnered national attention. While other PFI founders contributed organizational skills, Thompson provided an indispensable intuitive ability to inspire people. On "field days" at his farm, Thompson stood with a bullhorn in a field of corn "strong, vibrant and oozing with the juice of life" and communicated the ideas of low-input sustainable agriculture to ordinary farmers and citizens, as well as USDA, USAID, and World Bank officials. From 1986 to 1998, the Thompson farm sponsored 263 on-farm tours that attracted 7,871 observers, as well as 300 presentations to various audiences that informed over 27,000 people in attendance. Thompson, who could "never be taken for a back to the earth guy," served as an effective communicator for sustainable agriculture. A man with the looks and all the trappings of traditional farmers, Thompson and others like him helped chemical-free agriculture shed the counterculture trappings that impaired mainstream adoption of ecological farming techniques.

Especially during the first ten years of its existence, the PFI sought to downplay the term *organic*. The organization's founders thought too much cultural baggage was associated with the term. The original provisional board intended to change American agriculture, and its members felt they could not successfully share their ideas if farmers identified the PFI as too far outside the mainstream. The PFI, they decided, should appeal to all farmers. As Sharon and Dick Thompson put it, "We are not the convictor, we just share our experiences"; their approach of not blaming or castigating other farmers for their choice of technique has paid off with wider community interest in what is happening on the Thompson farm. During the 1980s, the PFI founders hoped that most farmers would embrace the principles of low-input, sustainable agriculture, and therefore it would not become necessary to market their crops under a separate "organic" system. Perhaps they were ahead of their time, as most farmers continued to use the high-input industrial model. As organic techniques became more widespread, however, these methods became more familiar and created less distance with other farmers. During the late 1990s, many influential members of the PFI had their farms certified as organic.[11]

Dick Thompson's farm, interestingly enough, is not certified organic, largely because his use of 28 percent liquid nitrogen fertilizer is disallowed under organic standards. Yet his practices might be considered more organic than those on many farms that have been certified. This demonstrates the interchangeable nature of the numerous specific techniques that make up agricultural practice, as well as the lack of agreement on the exact components of organic production. Most significant, however, was the PFI's inclusive nature. At the same time that Thompson intended to change American agriculture, he knew that shifts occurred one farmer at a time, one field trial at a time. The PFI did not seek a litmus test for organic production but instead encouraged farmers to make a gradual transition toward a sustainable agriculture that included but was not limited to organic techniques. Organizers intended that the PFI would help develop "farming practices which will result in higher net income for *farmers*, which will be less threatening to the health of farm families, and which will more adequately protect the productive capacity of the land." This statement reveals several of the major intellectual elements of ecological agriculture since the 1930s, with its emphasis on social justice for farmers and community, a concern for sustaining the soil, and misgivings over implications for human health.[12]

Just as the publicity afforded to Dick Thompson helped launch the PFI, the attention given to the Land Institute and the New Alchemy Institute helped these organizations communicate their message of sustainable ecological agriculture. By the early 1990s, the Land Institute's research and teaching facility supported fourteen staff members plus several interns on 275 acres, with a budget exceeding $350,000 per year, as well as growing institutional ties to Kansas State University and other research institutions. Wes Jackson received substantial grants to support Land Institute research and increased support for his ideas within the land-grant schools. Furthermore, through Jackson's expansive personality and entrepreneurial talents, the institute became a focal point of the increased national coverage of sustainable, ecological agriculture. The Land Institute now issues newsletters, and a quarterly summary of research entitled the *Land Report*, and it engages in sophisticated fund-raising. The facility also sponsors tours, field day demonstrations, workshops, other publications, a model solar farm and community redevelopment project, and an annual Prairie Festival featuring local and national speakers, workshops, dances, and other festivities.[13]

Far removed from the plains of Kansas, the New Alchemists of Cape Cod also represented the successful widespread communication of sustainable ecological agriculture in the 1970s and 1980s. Like the Land Institute, the New Alchemy Institute rose from humble roots to enjoy favorable assessments in the national media, as well as the fiscal support of grant-providing institutions and governments. New Alchemy eventually offered courses, seminars, workshops, publications, and conferences in such areas as "sustainable design" and "biological agriculture." It also hosted weekly tours that brought over ten thousand people into the facility each year, including fifteen hundred schoolchildren, who marveled at features of technological ingenuity such as the self-contained "ark" ecosystem. The institute also engaged in highly professional fund-raising efforts, offered research internships, and held social events such as the annual Harvest Festival.[14]

Although the message of sustainable, ecological agriculture benefited from the pronouncements of iconic figures such as Wes Jackson and the organized efforts of innovators such as the New Alchemy Institute, in some ways these groups and individuals preached their message to already converted audiences. The ultimate communication task for supporters of the new farming was to blend the prophecies of a Wes Jackson, the innovations of alternative technology, and the work of everyday farmers and farm groups, while soliciting general political and institutional support. As the 1980s drew to a close, this institutional support slowly grew in the agriculture establishment. Divergent groups such as the National Research Council of the National Academy of Sciences, the American Farmland Trust, and the publishing giant Rodale Press offered support for sustainable agriculture. The need of governmental, academic, and agricultural research circles to respond to the criticisms posed by alternative agriculture was reflected in the establishment of organizations such as the Kerr Center for Sustainable Agriculture in Oklahoma and the Leopold Center for Sustainable Agriculture at Iowa State University, and in the founding of new publications such as the *Journal of Sustainable Agriculture*.[15]

Although the new farming movement received increased public attention and institutional support throughout the 1980s, sustainable agriculture also presented an intellectual, financial, and cultural challenge to a century-old agricultural establishment. While nominally in favor of "sustainability" and the environmental responsibilities of agriculture, many opponents within the agricultural establishment questioned the efficacy of the new farming. The public and many farmers were receptive to the ideas of sustainable ecological agriculture, but the new farming still faced a stiff challenge from the well-entrenched, well-funded, and highly productive agricultural establishment.

RESISTANCE

Just as the pronouncements of the permanent agriculture movement during the 1930s sparked resistance from the agricultural establishment, so sustainable agriculture endured attacks from the representatives of pro-

duction agriculture. Agricultural scientists, agricultural chemical manufacturers, agricultural economists, people associated with the Farm Bureau
and the USDA, land-grant officials, the agricultural press, and many ordinary farmers assailed the ideas, models, and methods of ecological agriculture from the 1960s through the 1980s.

As far back as the mid-1960s, the ecological critique of establishment
agriculture singed the nerves of some very important members of the
agricultural establishment. Wheeler McMillen, a prominent agricultural
commentator since the 1920s and longtime *Farm Journal* editor, issued the
first rejoinders to the ecological agriculture agenda in his 1965 response
to *Silent Spring* entitled *Bugs or People?* For McMillen, Rachel Carson's
dedication of her treatise to the "reverence for life" dictum of Albert
Schweitzer was a twisted irony. The true people "revering life" in the
1960s, in the eyes of McMillen, were the scientists and other agents of the
green revolution who fed the multitudes and helped effective farmers
become successful businessmen. The agricultural journalist wanted his
readers to know that in the battle of bugs or birds versus people, the only
ethical choice was to fight nature "with the best weapons" humanity
could command. "Let the insects go unchecked?" rejoined McMillen.
"They will go their relentless ways. For humankind they will produce
disease and death, poverty, hunger and discomfort."[16]

He also disdained what he viewed as the misinformed "alarmists"
who "spread the impression that the entire American landscape is being
doused with insecticides" when actually, according to McMillen, 95 percent of the nation remained free of pesticides. McMillen painted a rosy
picture of past efforts to control bugs and increase production, of the ability of the Food and Drug Administration to monitor pollution problems,
and of contemporary efforts to instruct farmers on the safer use of agricultural chemicals. For those tempted to believe the warnings of Carson
and the ecologists, McMillen asked them to first picture "a hungry child,
sick from malnutrition, staring hopelessly toward a troubled future."
This early critic of the ecological imperative in the sustainable agriculture
milieu thus attempted to contrast the "morality" of industrial agriculture
against the dreaminess of the organic farming crowd.

McMillen found support for his criticism of Carson and others who
called for an ecological reassessment of agriculture in the 1960s. Jamie L.
Whitten (Democrat-Mississippi), longtime chairman of the House Appro-
priations Subcommittee for Agriculture, echoed McMillen's diatribe in
his tract *That We May Live* (1966). Whitten asked readers to recall the
exaggerated public fright during the cranberry contamination fiasco of
1958, which had cost cranberry growers $10 million in losses. Americans
were blessed with productive farmers and competent scientists who, in
Whitten's view, were the chief source of the nation's unprecedented high

standard of living. The congressman asked urban Americans in particular to "understand somehow that *Silent Spring*, which they read so avidly, is not a balanced account of the place of pesticides in the world."[17]

Donald F. Hornig, chief science adviser to President Johnson, although active in forming an effective research response to the issues posed by Carson, also offered caution about the ecological critique of production agriculture in the 1960s. For example, an ethical critique of technology was ludicrous to Hornig, who saw technology as morally ambivalent. Referring to a distracting phrase he had noticed in an upcoming speech by the president, Hornig told presidential aide Joseph Califano: "The recurrent references to 'technology' in this draft are naive and will cause the President no end of trouble. 'Technology' means a collection of skill, methods or means. It is not to be confused with *doing*. I would like to protest strongly . . . the notion that technology brings us the pollution problem." Hornig pointed out that doomsayers had been predicting pollution catastrophes for five hundred years regarding the condition of the Thames, and England seemed to have survived nonetheless.[18]

Norman Borlaug, Nobel Peace Prize winner and father of the green revolution, did not allow the ecological critique of agricultural technology to escape unscathed. Throughout the 1970s and early 1980s, Borlaug defended the green revolution, agricultural chemicals, and hybrid seeds, attacking the "smug" view of the ecologists who, in his view, would prefer to see a world devastated by perpetual want, eternal hunger, and subsistence level "sustainability." Fearing that the green revolution was "being betrayed by the same scientists that once fostered it," Borlaug called for stepped-up research on artificial fertilizers, new agricultural chemicals, and biotechnological solutions to impending hunger problems. For the scientist Borlaug, the green revolution was a chapter in the progressive history and bright future of agricultural science.[19]

The ecological critique of agriculture endured continued attacks through the 1970s, especially during the topsoil crisis that appeared late in the decade. Under the auspices of the Soil and Water Resource Conservation Act of 1977, the USDA conducted the National Agricultural Lands Study, the first national inventory of farmlands since 1934, finding, along with the 1980 release of the *Global 2000 Report*, that soil erosion was still a national menace. While the topsoil crisis drew national attention and helped advance the sustainable agriculture movement, many members of the agricultural establishment dismissed the continuing erosion problem as a hysterical reaction fostered by reactionary environmentalists and misguided scientific assumptions.

Notable agricultural economists such as Earl O. Heady of Iowa State University, Theodore W. Schultz of the University of Chicago, and Earl R. Swanson of the University of Illinois presented the agricultural establishment's rebuttal to ecological critics regarding the topsoil crisis. In 1983, Heady and Swanson concluded "that the nation could count on continued gains in crop and livestock productivity" into the next century and thus "the need to reduce soil erosion would be lessened, since minor soil losses would be offset by technology."[20] These hopes are widely shared in the agricultural research establishment; a 1994 report sponsored by the Council for Agricultural Science and Technology (CAST) suggested that advances in productivity were important if the world hoped to leave enough landscape for nature preservation purposes.[21]

Farm journalist Lauren Soth responded to Heady and Swanson's study by noting that "continuing technological improvement and the consequent decreasing importance of land as a factory farm product can lead to complacency about resource depletion." But Heady and Swanson were supported by fabled agricultural economist Theodore W. Schultz, who crafted a response he hoped would echo James Malin's 1946 attack on the erosion hysteria created during the New Deal. Schultz maintained that because the measuring methods used in the 1977 soil survey differed from those of 1934, no accurate depiction of soil loss could be drawn. Furthermore, he suggested that soil erosion was specific to climate and site and that farmers in the 1980s practiced better soil stewardship than ever before in American history. Finally, Schultz argued that ecological critics were actually snobbish in implying that America's most efficient and productive farmers had "no perception of the value of their soil resources and . . . act as if they were indifferent to soil losses." Shultz's opinions were augmented by Julian Simon and Herman Kahn's optimistic assessment of the soil erosion problem in their 1984 response to the *Global 2000 Report* entitled *The Resourceful Earth*.[22]

As various types of ecological agriculture gained credence among a growing number of farmers during the 1970s, the agricultural establishment reacted harshly to the challenge of the new farming. Reacting to the organic farming craze of the early 1970s, Secretary of Agriculture Earl Butz stated on national television that if America wanted to try an organic farming regime, somebody had to decide "which 50 million Americans we are going to let starve or go hungry." Later in that decade, however, Bob Bergland, Jimmy Carter's secretary of agriculture, expressed interest in ecologically based agriculture when he commissioned a well-received study of nonchemical farming, and later appointed Garth Youngberg as a full-time organic farming coordinator at the USDA. Youngberg worked diligently to promote what he labeled "alternative agriculture," but because of resistance from John Block, the incoming Reagan administration agricultural secretary, and the Council for Agricultural Science and Technology, Youngberg's position at the USDA was soon eliminated, as was USDA support for the new farming.[23]

CAST, a research and opinion group formerly headquartered at Iowa State University and now located in Ames, Iowa, was established in 1972 following a meeting sponsored by the National Research Council (NRC). Its early years were shaped by the reaction against Rachel Carson's critique of pesticide use in agriculture. The pendulum of public sensitivity had swung too far for agronomist Charles Black, who as the first director of CAST used the organization to counter the environmental movement. Originally partially funded by agricultural chemical and agribusiness concerns, CAST invited the participation of agricultural economists, scientists, policy makers, commodity group representatives, and other members from scientific and academic societies. As an institution during the late 1970s and early 1980s, CAST remained supportive of the establishment view of agriculture. Although CAST and the Center for Agriculture and Rural Development (also headquartered at Iowa State) expressed sentiments about improving the environment and voiced support for a select few of the new farming ideas, these organizations nonetheless epitomized establishment resistance to sustainable ecological agriculture from the late 1970s into the 1980s. Institutions are capable of change, however, and during the 1990s CAST gained a reputation for objectivity and scholarly analysis of agricultural issues.

Following the issuance of the NRC's *Alternative Agriculture* (1989), a favorable report on the new farming, Indiana congressman Lee Hamilton, chair of the Joint Economic Research Committee, asked CAST to offer an appraisal of the report and the ideas of ecological agriculture in general. *Alternative Agriculture Scientists' Review*, CAST's response to sustainable ecological agriculture, detailed the reservations traditional agriculture held regarding the new farming. While not completely critical of the NRC report's support for some concepts of ecological farming, CAST suggested that the ecological critique of establishment agriculture would assist in "fine tuning" and "correcting unforeseen consequences" of an American production agriculture system that "has served us well . . . from a long history of solid research." CAST noted that the NRC's tentative support for ecological agriculture failed to take into account the total economic, political, and social framework under which farmers operated. Furthermore, CAST noted, in a thinly veiled reference to the sustainable agriculture camp, that "the subjective approach used in this, or any report, is fraught with the danger of being interpreted as conclusive evidence or legitimization of a movement or advocates of particular philosophies that, while mostly rooted in sound husbandry practices, have not been verified through established protocols. . . . Despite qualified statements to the contrary, the report goes on extensively in places as if alternative agriculture [is] a proven, if not exclusive, option."[24]

CAST's reactions represented the establishment's discomfort with the new agriculture, which persisted through the 1980s and into the early 1990s. Lauren Soth noted that "agribusiness and other big-farming interests have laughed at the new farm movement, labeling it unscientific and a retreat to the inefficient technologies of our great-grandfathers." CAST and other opponents of ecological farming always were quick to note that "the long-term viability of American agriculture cannot be taken for granted. . . . But without supportive macroeconomic, science, education, trade, resource, and environmental policies, the competitive advantage of agriculture can be lost at great cost to farmers and consumers at home and abroad." For CAST and the agricultural establishment, environmental concerns had to be balanced with the economic concerns of farmers, agribusiness, and consumers and "investments in human resources, science, technology, and the wise use of soil, water, and other natural endowments."[25]

Judged by the scale and seriousness of their response to the new farming, CAST and other opponents of sustainable agriculture saw a direct threat to their way of life and to the food production system they had known throughout their careers. Many of the opponents of ecologically inspired agriculture apparently did not study the ideas, methods, and systems of their nemesis in great detail. For instance, opponents insisted (contrary to the written record) that ecological agriculture stood as a neo-Luddite opposition to science and technology. By employing the term *wise use* and focusing on economic viability as sustainability, CAST and other elements of the agricultural establishment suggested that the true stewards of the American land were the farmers and scientists providing an ever-increasing bounty of inexpensive food and fiber to the world. In the eyes of CAST and the like-minded, Americans did not need to worry about agricultural-environmental problems, the decline of family farmers, or the future of the food supply, due to a "remarkable fusion of science, technology and practice." Those within establishment agriculture, especially agricultural economists but also agricultural scientists and politicians, continued to express disdain for ecological agriculture while positioning themselves as the "wise use" stewards of an optimistic future.[26]

Feeling especially threatened by the ecological agriculture agenda, the nation's farm chemical manufacturers also issued stiff rejoinders to sustainable ecological agriculture, particularly during the 1980s. In 1980, Jack Early, president of the American Agricultural Chemical Manufacturers Association, expressed concern that his industry "needed help" because it was under siege by environmentalists and an ill-advised public. Early stated that his industry was "one of the most closely, tightly regulated industries in the United States today, our products . . . regulated from cradle to grave" by the USDA, CEQ, EPA, FDA, FTC, OSHA, DOT, and other government agencies. In trade journals such as *Farm Chemicals* and via public relations, political lobbying, support of pro-chemical research, and consumer awareness campaigns, the chemical industry shot back against sustainable ecological agriculture, claiming that its efforts were vital in the effort to avoid famine and sustain America's role as the leader in the world economy. Throughout the 1980s, as alternative agriculture appeared as a more defined threat, the chemical industry fought for regulatory relief and attempted to reengineer its products, packaging, and public image in order to present itself and farmers as environmentally conscious stewards of the land and as the victims of misinformation. In turn, groups like the Chemical Producers and Distributors Association and Lyndon LaRouche's Schiller Institute attacked sustainable ecological agriculture as immoral, unscientific, and inhumane.[27]

CO-OPTION

Just as in the 1940s, when establishment agriculture dismissed the core assumptions of the permanent agriculture movement while linking itself rhetorically to conservation and the term *permanent agriculture,* the established institutions of agriculture claimed the mantle of conservation and sustainability. As the ideas of a sustainable and ecological agriculture surfaced on the American farm scene, the very agents who were attacking the ecological, technical, economic, and cultural assumptions of the new farming also attempted to present themselves as the true champions of sustainable agriculture.

This co-option of the sustainable agriculture movement happened in several ways. First, the agricultural establishment engaged in an extensive debate over the meaning of sustainable agriculture, usually divorcing the paramount concerns for ecological diversity, smaller-scale farming, and cultural change from the concept of sustainability, and replacing those original tenets with an emphasis on "resource conservation" and, most important, a devotion to "economic viability." Sustainable agriculture thus became less of an ecological imperative and opportunity for rural revival and more of an economic ideology laced with protestations of environmental concern. Second, the agricultural establishment joined the no-till/minimum-tillage revolution of the 1970s and 1980s, and agricultural chemical manufacturers engaged in an impressive publicity campaign to refashion themselves as environmental stewards. Third, sustainable agriculture in essence helped co-opt itself. Rather than remain outsiders with sparse intellectual and budgetary prestige, some advocates of sustainable ecological agriculture chose to pursue change from positions within the establishment's system.

Initial evidence of the establishment co-option of sustainable agriculture is found in the redefinition of the term *sustainable*. As the new agriculture emerged as a self-conscious movement in the 1970s and 1980s, the term *sustainable agriculture* evoked some fairly specific models and methods. In its challenge to the traditional establishment view, sustainability developed as an idea to make agriculture "ecologically sound, economically viable, socially just and humane." Ecological viability meant working to emulate "nature's model" of growth, virtual elimination of agricultural chemicals by incorporating an "organic"-style crop and livestock regime, and devotion to biological diversity and human health. Economic viability, from the original conception of sustainable, ecological agriculture, meant both the planned survival of smaller-scale "family" farmers and the production and equitable distribution of abundant, inexpensive food that took into account "hidden costs" of environmental degradation. Sustainable agriculture also emerged out of a committment to cultural change, out of the human recognition of resource and technological limitation, and from the need to phase out the unsustainable acquisitiveness and industrial age values threatening the survival of humanity.[28]

As the sustainable agriculture movement took hold in its protest, contrarian form, the agricultural establishment shifted from actively resisting the concepts of sustainable agriculture to borrowing its terminology and some of its ideas. Deftly avoiding some of the ecological and social concerns of the movement, the USDA, the land-grant schools, and agribusiness presented a watered-down version of the meaning of agricultural sustainability from the mid-1980s onward. Just as some politicians attempt to please all the people all the time, so the redefinition and co-option of sustainable ecological agriculture tried to encompass and please all segments of establishment agriculture.

In the establishment version of sustainable agriculture, the ecological and holistic notion of agriculture became subsumed under an emphasis on economic viability, although support for "improving the environment" also fit under the establishment umbrella of "sustainable agriculture." In other words, sustainable agriculture meant building a form of farming that was economically profitable and carried the side benefit of improving the environment. By co-opting the popular term *sustainable* and nodding to some of the ideas of the new farming movement, the agricultural establishment helped justify ever more research into defining and reinventing sustainable agriculture. In the eyes of many critics, the word *sustainability* was becoming more a code term for "development" than an ecological strategy for survival.

One example of sustainable agriculture's redefinition occurred in the language of federal farm legislation establishing the USDA's Low-Input Sustainable Agriculture (LISA) program in 1987. The Senate defined sustainable agriculture as a system "that, for generations to come, will not only be productive and profitable but will conserve resources, protect the environment, and enhance the health and safety of the citizenry." Agricultural economists such as Oklahoma State University's Michael R. Dicks revealed the establishment's truncated redefinition of the concept in a 1992 article, writing, "The more moderate environmental groups are defining sustainability as long-term workable solutions between agriculture and the environment. These groups seek adjustments within agricultural institutions that will enable agriculture to maintain renewable resources at the current level; avoid wastes beyond the environment's assimilative capacity, and avoid the use of non-renewable resources while maintaining production efficiency and capacity to ensure a future standard of living at least as high as the current level."[29] While the Senate and Dicks gave lip service to some of the original tenets of the new farming, their redefinition of sustainability was vague, avoided the ecological issues of soil productivity and chemical use, and deftly skirted issues of corporate centralization in agriculture. Dennis R. Keeney, director of Iowa State University's Leopold Center for Sustainable Agriculture (created in 1987), lashed out against "vague" versions of sustainability, looking instead for "the relevant concepts and terms in a manner conducive to progress in research outreach and farm practice . . . that can be tested scientifically and transferred to farmers." Large institutions remain uncomfortable with the holistic and social reform conceptions of sustainable ecological agriculture, focusing instead on relatively short-term steps to sustainability that center on the unchallenged devotion to "bottom line profitability."[30]

For some, the infiltration of the sustainable idea into mainstream institutions signified the successful adoption of new ideas into the research and policy establishment. But many critics remained less sanguine about the intentions and flexibility of the land-grant institutions. In 1988, William Lockeretz noted that "some people interested in sustainable agriculture—both within mainstream institutions and on the outside—do not view with undiluted optimism the changes that have already occurred in mainstream research, teaching, and extension. For some, the established research institutions are under some very powerful constraints, especially the constraints imposed by disciplinary boundaries and by researchers' need to publish frequently. The latter in turn may discourage long-term projects such as studies covering several cycles of a many-year rotation." Furthermore, Lockeretz noted that critics of the establishment co-option of the new farming "argued that such institutions not only have failed to grasp the spirit of sustainable agriculture, but do not even want to. The flurry of recent programs is said to be merely a way to appear to be responding to outside pressures, and perhaps also to blunt the full thrust of the movement. In this view, advancing the cause of sustainable agriculture means challenging some far-reaching economic, social or political constraints, a challenge that mainstream agricultural institutions are unlikely to make."[31]

Lockeretz and others correctly suggested that the establishment co-option of the terminology and some of the ideas of sustainable ecological agriculture allowed the establishment to choose the "least-threatening" version of ecological agriculture and to "sanitize it further to make it bureaucratically acceptable, and appropriate it as their own." With the concepts of ecological holism and social and institutional reform passed over via the co-option process, critics of the establishment feared the term *sustainable agriculture* would "degenerate into just another bureaucratized buzz word used to show that something new and exciting is going on, even though nothing really changed."[32]

Another example of the co-option of sustainable agriculture's terminology is the ongoing contest to define the meaning of "organic," as demonstrated in the fractious discussions of organic standards. In 1998, the Food and Drug Administration declared its intention to establish national organic standards and definitions of "certified organic" that would replace the various standards followed by several dozen state and private certification groups. Organic growers protested, fearing that federal standards would be watered down. Organic growers and marketers had already spent time and effort instituting their own requirements for organic production, a process complicated by the fact that growers did not agree on what specific practices should be excluded from organic production techniques. For their part, consumers wanted some assurance that they received fair value for their money. The independent certification of organic quality has become increasingly important to marketing organic foods. Organic growers and marketers lobbied Congress through late 1999, advocating their definitions for the certification system.[33]

One of the most important tools used by the mainstream agricultural establishment in the co-option of sustainable agriculture came with the no-till/minimum-tillage revolution on American farms in the 1970s and 1980s. The idea of reducing tillage and leaving a surface mulch, particularly eliminating fall plowing and the use of the deep-plowing moldboard, had been suggested and employed to a small degree since the 1930s and 1940s, especially in response to Edward Faulkner's *Plowman's Folly*, published in 1943. In the 1970s, concern over high energy costs and topsoil erosion led to a renewed emphasis on no-till and minimum-tillage research, techniques, and equipment, especially within the land-grant institutions.

Like the Faulkner system from the 1940s, the no-till/minimum-tillage systems in the 1970s and 1980s used disc plows, chisel plows, and mulching equipment to "chop up" crop and weed residues for spring planting. This surface residue would hold soil, water, and nutrients and would add organic material to the soil, while requiring less energy for seedbed preparation. New equipment such as grain drills, complex coulter and press wheel mechanisms, and hydraulic planters allowed farmers in the 1970s and 1980s to "blast" or "blow" their seed into the ground through the surface rubbish. Unlike Faulkner's system and that of subsequent organic farmers, which envisioned minimum tillage as one part of a comprehensive, chemical-free ecological agriculture, for most farmers the no-till/minimum-tillage revolution of the 1970s and 1980s remained dependent on chemical treatments for preplanting "burndowns" and preharvest weed, insect, and disease control. While no-till and minimum-tillage systems held the soil better than terraces, and in some cases were part of multicrop, biological pest control schemes, the no-till/minimum-tillage revolution did not fulfill the aim of ecologically based agriculture, despite claims of sustainability from many land-grant scientists and agricultural chemical manufacturers. Quite aside from the chemical issue, the technique required specialized equipment that kept many farmers on the technological treadmill.[34]

While land-grant researchers, farmers, and agricultural chemical and implement dealers could note that no-till/minimum-tillage saved fuel and labor costs and substantially reduced soil erosion, "conservation tillage" (as the technique is sometimes called) nevertheless required the use of agricultural chemicals, in some cases increased groundwater pollution, and never challenged the efficacy of monoculture production agriculture. No-till systems remain a mixed bag. Many farmers feel they can achieve most conservation objectives by using techniques derived from the original ridge-tillers. Depending on soil type, terrain, climate, and crop selection, these systems can cut erosion significantly compared with standard techniques. Yet they do use some herbicides to control weeds, applied in precise bands down the crop row, and like organic farmers still need to make passes with a cultivator for weed control.[35]

Agricultural equipment manufacturers such as Deere and Company actively linked their equipment and corporate image, merging reduced tillage, herbicide use, soil conservation, and sustainable agriculture into happily interchangeable ideas. In Deere's mouthpiece publication the *Furrow*, a writer glowingly reported on the developing relationship between the staunch ecological agriculturists and the establishment research complex. On the opposing page Deere advertised its line of "Land Preserver" equipment, including the Mulch Tiller, the Mulch Finisher, and the 7000 Conservation Planter. Another advertisement suggested farmers could drastically increase the number of acres they farmed under "conservation tillage." Among the successful "alternative" farmers highlighted in the *Furrow* were the Reichers family, who were "diversifying but staying with chemicals." Deere's attempt to capture the reduced-tillage market and promote the company's view of sustainable agriculture was mirrored by others in the industry, such as DMI, Inc. of Goodfield, Illinois. DMI produced "knifing" fertilizer applicators designed to "knife nutrients down into the seed zone," cutting through surface rubbish and allegedly lessening groundwater pollution. DMI also marketed a tillage tool called the "DMI Ecolo-Tiger Yield Till Tool" featuring "quad/spring parabolic shank assemblies that have patented winged Q/P Tiger-Points for an open, mellower and healthier soil."[36]

The attempt by equipment manufactures to cash in on the notions of sustainable agriculture pales before the effort of the chemical industry to assert itself as the paragon of environmental virtue while continuing to draw vast profits from sales of its products to America's farmers. In a revealing series of testimonies, leaders from the nation's top agricultural chemical manufacturers talked of their vision of sustainable agriculture in the January–February 1990 issue of the *Journal of Soil and Water Conservation*. Samuel J. Barrick, a public relations representative from Dow Chemical U.S.A., characterized his industry's definition of sustainable agriculture when he said, "We believe sustainable agriculture is a management system that maintains and enhances the ability of U.S. agriculture to meet environmental needs now and in the future." Barrick continued, stating, "It is also a farming system that uses inputs—both those available as natural resources and those purchased—in the most efficient manner possible to obtain productivity and profitability from farming while minimizing adverse effects to the environment."[37]

In 1991, *Wallaces' Farmer*, one of the nation's most respected farm magazines, quoted Mobay Corporation scientist Leroy Cobia as saying, "Industry and university weed control specialists are listening to what farmers and the general public want. We're working to help farmers improve yields by controlling weeds as well as protecting the environment." The magazine also reported on the recent formation of the Alliance for a Clean Rural Environment (ACRE), an "independent organization which collects and dispenses information to help farmers use chemicals safely," funded by Dow, Mobay, CIBA-GEIGY, Du Pont, and other chemical combines.[38]

Chemical manufacturers effectively co-opted the sustainable agriculture ideal by portraying their activities as "green." Chemical giant Du Pont started a campaign in early 1991 to recycle herbicide containers, and the Iowa Fertilizer and Chemical Association followed Du Pont's lead with its own container recycling campaign later that year. DowElanco sponsored a 1990 television special aired on 118 stations that was intended to highlight for urbanites "how farmers, the agricultural chemical industry, university researchers, and government regulators are working together to eliminate potential water problems from developing." DowElanco spokespersons suggested that "you see a lot about environmental problems on the television news, but much less about what's being done to prevent potential problems from developing." The chemical industry also funded the creation of Foodwatch in 1990, a nonprofit organization dedicated to "safe, abundant food for all." The Chemical Manufacturer's Association also sponsored a booklet for Earth Day 1990, entitled "Earth Day Idea Bank," and other "informational" materials suggesting how the chemical industry supported agricultural sustainabilty and environmental responsibility.[39]

Agribusiness co-option of sustainable agriculture reached an art form in the print, radio, and television advertisements for agricultural chemicals in the first half of the 1990s. One advertisement appearing in *Wallaces' Farmer* in 1991 pictures a grizzled farmer whose finger is being grasped by an infant's hand. The accompanying passage reads, "From one generation to the next farmers have taken care of the land to preserve their unique way of life. And for more than 30 years, CIBA GEIGY has been there with them providing products that farmers need to produce the best crops possible."[40] Anyone who watches television in a farm state or has perused agricultural journals in recent years has noticed the deluge of images such as farmers holding children while viewing the "bounty of the land," wildlife bounding through farm fields, or farm youth splashing through clear streams as chemical firms tried to tell Americans that their industry was at the vanguard of agricultural environmentalism. Biotechnology and seed firms, often owned by the chemical giants, also ensured the public that they were developing herbicide-resistant crops, "which will be a lot safer for both the person applying the herbicide and for the environment." The engineering of less toxic chemicals also fit into the chemical industry's vision of sustainable agriculture, such as herbicides that quickly degrade or that bond to the soil to prevent leaching into groundwater supplies. The distinction between genuine improvements and an image designed for public consumption is, of course, arguable.[41]

By the mid-1990s, agribusiness's self-portrayal as environmentally benign wore thin with some farmers. Various farm commodity groups in Iowa and elsewhere complained in 1994 of the excessive environmental messages in the onslaught of chemical company advertising. The Iowa Corn Growers and other farm groups thought the ads depicted farmers as ruthless users of chemicals, thus defeating the intended purpose of defending farming practices. At the same time, the campaign inflated advertising budgets, which translated into higher costs for farmers. Farmers' fears seemed confirmed when, late in the summer of 1994, several fields that had received an application of DowElanco's Broadstrike, one of the new environmentally "friendly" chemicals, produced only

one-fifth as many plants per acre as is standard for an Iowa corn "jun- *was it*
gle."[42] A majority of farmers felt a keen sense of dependence on the effec- *on purpose*
tiveness of modern chemical fertilizers, pesticides, and herbicides.

THE INFLUENCE OF SUSTAINABLE AGRICULTURE

Ecological ideas from the permanent and sustainable agriculture movements have influenced American agriculture in at least five ways. First, ①
while we have argued that corporations and the academy co-opted the
language of sustainable agriculture, that process of rhetorical capture can
also be interpreted as a measure of the importance and influence of the
movement. Second, the sustainable agriculture movement prompted the ②
land-grant institutions to engage in new areas of agricultural research and
contributed to the introduction of coursework in agroecology. Third, the ③
movement increased the effectiveness of the federal conservation agencies and altered the conduct and focus of governmental agricultural policy. Fourth, the movement contributed to a general climate of information ④
that encouraged American farmers to experiment with new methods.
Fifth, the success of the movement in changing public perceptions of agri- ⑤
culture can be measured by a burgeoning market for organic produce.
Ultimately, the connection between ecology and agriculture has helped
fuel the development of an environmental ethic in the United States.

Co-option was a mixed bag, involving sincere individual and institutional change, as well as sleight of hand. While many supporters of the
original holistic, reformist conception of sustainable ecological agriculture often expressed chagrin at the dilution of the original imperatives
and models of the new farming, many professional people who believed
in sustainable agriculture perceived chinks in the armor of established
institutions, seeing an opportunity to influence the course of events. For
them, the adoption of ideas looked more like a successful transference
than co-option. Furthermore, the transformation of agency cultures and
behaviors and the sincere desire of many people in science and industry
to improve agriculture must be acknowledged. Farmers, scientists, and
agribusiness representatives, though not eager environmentalists, sometimes adopted lessons derived from ecology, as long as these insights
supported their own sense of stewardship and experience in the world of
production agriculture. Furthermore, lessons from ecology left some
room for interpretation. As Donald Worster commented, "Knowledge
offered by ecologists is deceptive in one vital respect: It does not afford a
general or comprehensive measure of what it means to be successful or
unsuccessful in agriculture." For Worster, a historian and a staunch advocate of sustainable agriculture, the American farmer was often "trapped

by his own past," and the field of ecology remained difficult to apply in practical ways. Worster enjoined "both science and agriculture" to look beyond narrow definitions and quick judgments, and to seek answers "from ethics and philosophy, from politics and social discourse, from the community at large trying to discover a new relationship to nature."[43]

For many years, farmers interested in organic and other alternative farming techniques carried out their own research. Robert Rodale started test plots to demonstrate the efficacy of his methods. For several reasons, the land-grant institutions simply did not address the topics that organic farmers needed information about. First, the structure of research funding created a situation where researchers asked questions created by the needs of industrialized agriculture. More specifically, over the past fifty years, major research universities have put more burdens on professors and researchers to bring in outside money to fund their own research. Utah State University, for example, tells new professors that if they are to qualify for tenure, by their third year their research needs to bring in a quarter of a million dollars in outside funding. Quite naturally, major corporations and agribusiness concerns not only have questions that need answers but also possess the money to fund research, and thus the research programs of land-grant colleges have been oriented toward answering the "how-to" questions of an agriculture that employs the philosophy of high technical inputs and mass-production techniques. There is no money to be made from reducing purchased chemical inputs or preserving heirloom varieties of squash; hence, many sustainable techniques will never attract corporate research funds. Researchers interested in sustainable agriculture have to compete for National Institutes of Health or USDA funding with high-technology projects in microbiology that carry considerable scientific cachet. In contrast to the growth of outside funding sources, the "formula funds" from the federal and state governments that land-grant colleges use to assist rural people have remained steady. Second, when farmers after World War II followed the advice of the university "experts" to increase the size of their operations and still went out of business en masse, the credibility of these experts dropped, but farmers' reliance on industrial techniques remained. Finally, a long-standing cultural rift between those behind the plow and those behind a desk made farmers skeptical of theoretical advice.[44]

As a result, many organic farmers thought experience provided a better teacher than theory from the colleges of agriculture. These farmers shared their knowledge in informal ways and through organized networks. While all farmers traditionally have watched others and learned from observation, those interested in sustainable agriculture found knowledge-sharing networks of vital importance. Examples of alternative farming information and support networks include the Ocooch

Grazers Network, the Wisconsin Women's Sustainable Farming Network, and the Practical Farmers of Iowa. Author Neva Hassanein suggests that the Western Wisconsin Sustainable Farming Network directly challenged the authority of agricultural science, labeling its workshops "winter institutes," a reminder of similar farmer-organized events during the early days of the land-grant colleges. Partly as a result of farmer dissatisfaction with the direction of land-grant research, and partly from internal reformation, the colleges began to respond to the needs of alternative farmers.[45]

Between the land-grant university's legitimized scientific expertise and the farmer's world of dirt, manure, and tractor hydraulics lies a sector of on-farm research trials that holds considerable promise and the confidence of those involved in alternative agriculture. The Practical Farmers of Iowa has actively promoted on-farm research by farmers since its inception in 1985. Establishing partnerships with other institutions, the PFI has shared in more than $2 million of projects and research funding. Significantly, the PFI frequently collaborates with Iowa State University faculty members, who help with research design. The PFI actually secures the funding for a cooperative extension position in sustainable agriculture.

Although the agricultural research establishment co-opted many of the ideals of sustainable ecological agriculture, portions of that same research establishment also changed its collective vision of agriculture in what could be described as an "ecological reappraisal" of its central beliefs and values. Distinguished political scientist Don Hadwiger addressed changes in the agricultural research establishment in 1982, noting that the establishment was once "privileged to determine U.S. agricultural policy in all its aspects . . . envied for its size, its aggressive leadership, its effective use of 'down home' imagery, and its successes both in economic productivity and political influence." Hadwiger noted that in an increasingly urban society, farm policy was going to be shaped, in part, by consumer interests and a tightening of federal subsidies for agriculture, as well as environmental interests. Establishment researchers, many of whom were naturally idealistic, responded to the ecological and cultural critique of their role in postwar agriculture. As Hadwiger noted, the establishment was not a faceless entity but was staffed with intelligent persons who could not help but recognize "out in the country enormous farm implements parked alongside decaying barns" and empty storefronts across rural America, the products of labor-saving technology and big-business farming.[46]

Questioning such traditional agricultural tenets as "the possibility of scientific mastery" and abandoning the monocultural "commodity form," a new breed of researchers emerged throughout the agricultural establishment devoted to "acknowledging the authority of other voices" and to working for a smaller-scale, decentralized, ecologically diverse, and economically sustainable agriculture. These researchers are dedicated to constructing a system of family and small-group-oriented farms "closely linked with nearby rural communities, supporting the economic, educational, and cultural vitality within those communities." In this view, food distribution networks and food-processing industries "would be closely connected to nearby food production so that consumers in local communities would benefit from the freshest, locally produced foods in season" and from "food-producing resources—land, water, technologies, marketing, processing, and distribution networks—much more democratically controlled and equitably distributed among many individuals." Gradually, researchers scattered through the traditional agricultural establishment have started to investigate the agronomic aspects of the new farming and the sustainable ideal.[47]

The experience of the Council for Agricultural Science and Technology represents institutional change and growing mainstream support for sustainable agriculture. The council's first director, Charles Black, had little regard for the environmental movement, feeling, like many others, that Rachel Carson had spawned an overreaction to the risks presented by agricultural pesticides. CAST's board of directors (all members were academics) included scientists who realized that the organization was engaged in extrascientific pursuits. While the organization was fulfilling its mission of interpreting scientific information for legislators, regulators, and the public, those interpretations were laden with Black's personal mission to respond to the environmentalists. The board brought in Bill Marian as director in 1985, going so far as to change the locks on the doors during this shift of personnel; it later hired Stan Olsen away from the Audubon Society. The organization fundamentally changed from fulfilling a prosecutorial role toward supplying unbiased scientific information on environmental and agricultural issues. CAST serves as the organizer of research, with well-qualified individuals at various institutions acting as part of a task force or research team. Examples of its work include a $750,000 grant from the EPA to study the impact of global climate change on American agriculture (1992) and reports on water quality and agriculture (1992), wetland policy issues (1994), public lands grazing (1996), diversifying crop production in the United States (1996), recommendations on proposed EPA pesticide rules (1998), and the benefits of biodiversity in agricultural systems (1999). Compared with the early days of the organization, the tone of these reports is scholarly, making substantial contributions to information regarding difficult problems for agriculture rather than adopting an obviously "green" or an "industrial" approach.

Academics who work on sustainable agriculture today are scattered throughout the disciplinary landscape in departments of agronomy, agricultural engineering, horticulture, forestry, and others. Most researchers are identified with a home department, but many find funding for particular projects through institutes that focus on sustainability, such as the Leopold Center for Sustainable Agriculture at Iowa State University or the Center for Sustainable Agricultural Systems at the University of Nebraska. Other educational organizations such as the Henry A. Wallace Institute for Alternative Agriculture also sponsor some research. Since the Iowa legislature established the Leopold Center when it passed the Iowa Groundwater Protection Act of 1987, the organization has funded over two hundred grants amounting to more than $9 million. In 1999, the center awarded grants to nineteen new and twenty-nine existing projects, ranging from about $3,000 to over $30,000. Projects included marketing studies, research investigating the use of manipulating predatory insects for better biological pest control, and a study of nitrogen conservation in swine manure compost.[48]

Critics would argue that while their hearts may be in the right place, some of the studies (such as examining better methods of swine carcass composting) are nothing but "business as usual" or one not oriented toward the central imperatives of a truly ecological agriculture. Is the institution making positive strides in the right direction, or is it hopelessly stuck in traditional ways of doing things, unable or unwilling to question the fundamental structures of industrial agriculture? Again, the struggle to define sustainable agriculture reveals fundamental differences in people's worldview. This issue also involves the nature of institutional change. The Iowa legislature gave the Leopold Center a limited mandate to "identify impacts of agricultural practices, contribute to the development of profitable farming systems that conserve natural resources, and cooperate with Iowa State University Extension to inform the public of new findings." This mandate falls far short of directing the center to revolutionize agriculture, to eliminate the use of chemical pesticides and herbicides, or to establish social justice for farmers. While the land-grant institutions have aided the progress of agriculture, the permanent and sustainable agriculture movements essentially questioned the trends of technological development and economic centralization that "progress" brought along with it. As in other instances of institutional change, the impetus and vision for change often come from outside the institution.

One measure of the influence of sustainable ideas in the world of land-grant research might be the relative proportion of funding devoted to "traditional" areas of research versus the share devoted to "sustainable" projects. While the Leopold Center expended $2.6 million during fiscal year 1998–99 (of which approximately $1.1 million went directly toward issues, research, and initiatives), Iowa State University directed almost $79 million through the College of Agriculture's experiment station. Depending on how it is calculated, the state's main funding source for research into sustainable agriculture spends only 1 to 3 percent of what the state's established agricultural research organization spends. Clearly, state-supported funding for research in alternative agricultural techniques remains a small piece of the institutional pie.[49]

Despite the limited extent of state support, university attention to alternative agriculture is growing. Yet, ultimately, the land-grant institutions will play the game both ways. As long as the money flows in, they will welcome any sort of "scientific" research program, despite the inevitable biases that creep in with industry-sponsored research. Already caught up in a pattern of corporate-funded research agendas, agriculture colleges have adopted sustainable projects to please an increasingly critical public.

FEDERAL POLICY

Sustainable ecological agriculture also has contributed to shifts in federal agricultural policy. Although an analysis of agriculture-related environmental regulations and laws could fill volumes, a few general trends and examples of legislation will illustrate how policy has shifted with the rise of sustainable agriculture. The federal farm apparatus grudgingly changed its response to environmental concerns and sustainable agriculture, eventually jumping on the sustainability bandwagon. Its first response came with the creation of the USDA's Science and Education Administration (SEA) in 1977. Although short-lived, the SEA did attempt to blend the concerns of environmentalists with those of the agricultural research establishment, in part by sponsoring research on integrated pest management. Also in 1977, former Wilderness Society lobbyist Rupert Cutler was appointed to the influential post of assistant secretary of agriculture for conservation, research and education at the USDA. Upon his appointment, Cutler confirmed that he shared Secretary of Agriculture Bob Bergland's determination to change the image of the USDA from that of the "servant of agribusiness to the servant of all the people, rural and urban, rich and poor, black and white. . . . we will show a sensitivity and concern for the quality of life, in terms of protecting environmental values."[50]

Impressed by some of the organic farm operations in Minnesota and a flurry of requests about organic farming, Bergland commissioned a USDA study on organic farming in 1979. The study's summary, "Report and Recommendations on Organic Farming" (1980), concluded that chemical-free organic farming was "being successfully practiced by a small minority of farmers across the nation and that these farmers are environmentally sound, energy conserving, productive, stable, and tended toward long-term sustainability." One result of the report was the appointment of one of its writers, Garth Youngberg, as organic farming coordinator at the USDA. The USDA report favoring a form of sustainable ecological agriculture received support a decade later in the findings of the National Research Council's favorable appraisal of alternative agriculture. In 1977, partially influenced by environmental concerns—erosion and the loss of prime farmland to nonfarm uses—the Carter administration also commissioned the National Agricultural Lands Study. During the late 1970s and early 1980s, states such as Maine and California recognized organic farming in various laws and statutes, and several environmental and activist groups, from the Izaak Walton League to Farm-Aid, also formed political support groups for sustainable agriculture.[51]

Around 1980, the political climate seemed to favor acceptance of sustainable agriculture within the agricultural policy establishment. But John Block (incoming secretary of agriculture under President Reagan in 1981), himself a heavy user of farm chemicals on his patch of Illinois earth, worked against USDA support for ecological agriculture, eventually demoting, then firing Garth Youngberg, while virtually ignoring legislation mandating research on organic farming. To the right of Block stood Interior Secretary James Watt, a notorious antienvironmentalist, who chafed at Block's support for increased soil conservation spending and would later become a vociferous opponent of sustainable agriculture.[52]

Yet the soil erosion panic of the late 1970s and early 1980s rescued federal support for sustainable agriculture in the 1980s. Despite the conservation programs of the 1930s, soil erosion problems had continued. While Congress created the Great Plains Conservation Program in 1956 (expanding it in 1969), by 1979 less than a third of its goal of turning 16 million acres of erodible cropland into grassland had been achieved. In fact, in response to prices buoyed by the opening of Russian and Chinese markets, farmers were plowing up grassland, converting back to cropping on the Great Plains. From 1973 to 1980, farmers in Weld County, Colorado, plowed up four thousand acres per year, with rates rising to fifteen thousand acres per year. By the time farmers expanded operations to take advantage of higher prices, prices had dropped, initiating what became known as the "farm crisis" of the 1980s. This soil erosion problem, together with public reaction to the Reagan administration's antienvironmentalism and the appeal of sustainable agriculture to an economically besieged farm population, led to a spate of agricultural-environmental legislation between 1985 and 1990.[53]

The monumental Food Security Act (FSA) of 1985 included a massive Conservation Reserve Program (CRP), a "sodbuster" provision halting the plow-up of erosion-prone land, and a "swampbuster" section designed to protect sensitive ecological areas from the plow. Significantly, "conservation compliance" provisions required farmers to put in place a conservation plan for highly erodible cropland or else lose their eligibility for federal price support programs. Conservation planner Frederick Steiner called this act the most important conservation legislation since the 1930s.[54]

The 1985 legislation also provided for USDA support for sustainable agriculture research and education, and the USDA even appointed an organic farming researcher to the Rodale Center, once the most vocal enemy of the agricultural establishment. In addition, the FSA funded and sponsored the Appropriate Technology Transfer for Rural Areas (ATTRA) project to spread sustainable ideas into the countryside and the Low-Input Sustainable Agriculture Program (LISA), beginning in 1987. LISA, later called the Sustainable Agriculture Research and Education Program (SARE), made *sustainable agriculture* a household word on the farm and funded numerous research, demonstration, and educational projects involved in sustainable agriculture.[55]

As a follow-up to the FSA, in 1990 Congress passed the Food, Agriculture, Conservation and Trade Act (FACTA), a piece of legislation that in many ways legitimizes over six decades of work for agricultural conservation and ecological agriculture while also pointing to the future of agricultural policy. FACTA offered incentives for farmers to adopt an "integrated farm management program" to promote three- to five-year small-grain and legume crop rotations; it also expanded the CRP (already designated to include 45 million acres of land) to include marginal pastureland, shelter belts, windbreaks, grass waterways, and contour strips in producing fields.

The legislation also included water quality incentives up of to $3,500 per year per farmer and a requirement for strict on-farm pesticides records; it also established tough standards for defining organic produce, while lessening cosmetic standards for fruits and vegetables as a concession to organic growers. Among its numerous provisions, FACTA attempted to increase SCS enforcement of conservation requirements by allowing SCS officials a more flexible response to noncompliant farmers, as opposed to former draconian penalties that officials were reluctant to enforce. FACTA also stipulated that $80 million be directed toward research and extension in sustainable agriculture and provided for the establishment of the Wetlands Reserve Program (WRP), designed to restore ecologically vital wetlands across rural America. Furthermore, FACTA provided for reforestation, conservation assistance for developing nations ("debt for nature" program), an integrated pest management program option to encourage the planting of legumes and grass crops on CRP acreage while allowing farmers to graze 50 percent of their set-aside acres, and income support to assist the transition to a new cropping system.

Although many farmers, researchers, and agribusiness representatives and policy makers resisted the environmental provisions of the 1990 farm bill, the FSA and FACTA nevertheless represented a continuing effort to reform American agriculture along environmental lines. While legislation is difficult to implement, and even harder to fund, advocates of sustainable, ecological agriculture could take heart in the realization that many of their long-cherished ideas had now gained formal recognition, albeit in altered form. Agricultural-environmental legislation since the 1930s has helped reduce soil erosion substantially, decreased water pollution, protected prime farmland and ecologically sensitive areas, provided necessary income to farmers, and helped legitimize sustainable agriculture as a "prime directive" in America's agricultural future.[56]

The "Freedom to Farm" bill of 1996 changed the outlook for conservation, as well as for the economics of contemporary farming. Steeped in free-market ideology, the legislation was intended to phase out most of the price supports for commodity production and ended the production controls put in place during the Great Depression. Without government meddling, the theory went, farmers could more effectively sell their products to markets uncorrupted by cumbersome bureaucracy. Ironically, farmers want it both ways—they welcome price supports while deploring the intrusions of government. Many farmers and the conservative farm groups like the Farm Bureau supported the 1996 legislation. The law effectively gutted some of the linkages between soil conservation and subsidy payments to farmers, removing the teeth from the 1985 FSA's conservation measures. By the late 1990s, however, farmers once again faced economic disaster as commodity prices dipped. In 1998, Congress passed a $5.9 billion emergency program for distressed farmers, a record sum. In 1999, Congress approved the largest farm bailout in history, allotting $8.7 billion, much of it going to supplement harvest income for grain, cotton, and soybean producers.[57]

PRACTICE

Sustainable, ecological agriculture also prompted a slowly growing proportion of American farmers to change their agricultural practices in recent years. Farmers seemed to rise above academic and industry debates over the meaning of sustainable agriculture, agreeing that it implied "a system that can function perpetually." As sustainable, ecological agriculture rose from its fledgling status, farmers across the land adopted various measures and methods designed to help them remain economically viable for the long term. At the same time, farmers could cite their attempts to preserve, as best as possible, what they and their society viewed as the environmental health of the land, water, air, and, to an extent, the rural community. Thus, while the world was not full of Dick Thompsons, Wes Jacksons, and New Alchemists, environmentalists and production agriculturists could agree that, by the mid-1990s, farming changes resulting from the quest for a sustainable and ecological agriculture had worked toward the betterment of the soil resource and the future of society.[58]

Many farmers have become better environmental stewards thanks in part to economic and political incentives, new technical information, a growing sense of environmental responsibility, and a devotion to redeveloping rural life and culture via rural economic diversification and thinking "beyond the bottom line." One Iowa farmer in his midforties illustrated the frustrations of mainstream agriculture during the 1990s when he complained: "I listened to Earl Butz, who said we should grow more food so that we could feed the world and we would never have to worry about prices again. It seems like that's all I've worried about since I got into farming." Another farmer of roughly the same age, who had embraced sustainable agriculture, was more upbeat, saying, "We're not out here chewing granola bars or anything, but it's amazing what happens when you let nature do what she wants."[59]

Within the last fifteen years, prodded by environmental and economic concerns, thousands of American farmers have practiced some of the methods first enunciated by the adherents of sustainable, ecological agriculture. It is hard to obtain reliable information on the number of farmers practicing alternative or organic agriculture, partly because of problems in definition. By 1994, farmers reported 1.5 million acres in organic production, but that figure underestimates actual acreage because not all land in organic production has been officially certified. In 1995, the USDA reported that more than five thousand U.S. farmers were using organic methods, mostly in vegetable and fruit production.[60] While relatively few farmers practice anything near the holistic, organic-type farming as originally conceived by its founders, the model is increasingly studied, and greater numbers of mainstream farmers have borrowed ideas from ecological agriculture, expanding their conception of stewardship beyond building terraces. More and more farmers are attempting to use fewer chemicals, employ more biological pest and disease controls, use more crop rotations and more cover and alternative crops, and reduce their tillage. In fact, one of the original tenets of ecological agriculture, the abandonment of the moldboard plow, had nearly been accomplished by the mid-1990s. By that time, many farmers were warming to the idea of making America "a green and permanent land."[61]

A measure of consumer interest in obtaining foods that are healthy or grown in an ecologically informed way can be found in a burgeoning market in organic foods. By 1995, 42 percent of mainstream stores carried some organic produce. By 1998, organic food sales topped $4.5 billion. In the late 1990s, natural foods were the fastest-growing retail market sector. In 1998, sales growth of organic food products exceeded 20 percent for the ninth consecutive year.[62] The net result is that farmers, even if not convinced of some particular merit of organic farming, will respond to market demands created by consumers who are concerned about the methods employed to grow their food.

ENVIRONMENTAL ETHICS

The sustainable agriculture movement has contributed to a larger trend in American environmental ethics. Lauren Soth, writing in 1989 in the nation's leading farm-state newspaper, the *Des Moines Register*, told his readers, "The current evolution towards something called sustainable agriculture [is] a reversal of exploitative practices. In America, this movement began outside the governmental apparatus of farm science and education. Farmers themselves and public crusaders for environmental protection are the movement's leaders." Orville Bidwell, another longtime agricultural observer and soil scientist, presaged Soth with a proclamation of a "New Age" of sustainable agriculture in 1986, which he thought "involves farming in the image of Nature and [is] predicated on the spiritual and practical notions and ethical dimensions of responsible stewardship and sustainable production of wholesome food." Ralph Grossi, of American Farmland Trust, echoed these sentiments in 1993; he wrote of the "Green Evolution" in agriculture, which he described as a gradual shift "toward principles of resource stewardship and marketplace economics, which we must recognize are not mutually exclusive goals!"[63]

Emerging from its roots in agriculture, the generalized concept of "sustainability" eventually earned a connotation equivalent to apple pie, and the cause of ecological farming and societal sustainability came to enjoy international support by the early 1990s. Nathaniel Adams, editor of the *Smithsonian* magazine, described the vigor of the sustainable ideal in 1993, noting, "The term 'sustainability,' which once meant little more than an ill-defined index of generalized worry about increasing environmental strains, has now begun to take on more concrete meaning. As a vital first step, a wide gamut of studies is under way on how to expand traditional national-income accounting in order to include measures of non-renewable resource consumption and other forms of adverse environmental impact." Interior Secretary Bruce Babbit also demonstrated the influence of sustainable ecological values in his pursuit of funding for the National Biological Survey and his promise to practice "ecosystem management" on federal land.[64]

IMPEDIMENTS TO SUSTAINABLE AGRICULTURE

Ecologically inspired agriculture has a long way to travel before it replaces industrialized agriculture, and many barriers still block the path toward a truly "permanent" agriculture. As our collective memory of the crisis of the 1970s and early 1980s faded, the sense of urgency that originally aided introduction of the new farming also weakened, only to return in the late 1990s. Many farmers still resist the ideas of ecological agriculture and continue to farm poorly, in the ecological sense, while others encountered technical and financial problems when they attempted to adopt an organic regime. Lingering pollution problems still plague agriculture, prime farmland continues to be devoured by "sluburban" sprawl, and soil erosion is still above acceptable rates on some of the nation's best land.[65]

Some problems are created by technological advance, and present considerable conundrums for science. Recent developments in biotechnology are a good example of how hope and suspicions come bundled together. Since scientific plant breeding got its start in Mendel's garden of peas, people have been "improving" crops by selecting the seeds of crops that possess desirable characteristics and crossing different varieties of a plant species to secure desired qualities such as larger ears of corn. Plant breeders have raised yields significantly during the twentieth century. Animal breeders, of course, used the same principles in developing cows that produce good milk or pigs that gain weight faster. What is different about plant breeding today is that scientists have reached directly into the chromosomes to separate a very specific trait from one species, then paste it onto the genetic makeup of an unrelated species. This is the "unnatural" part of the transaction that disturbs critics of the technology.[66]

Genetically altered commodity crops offered farmers several advantages and promised a technical solution to some environmental problems. Seed companies recently have introduced genetically altered varieties of corn and soybeans. One variety of soybean came to the seed drill "Roundup ready"—in other words, able to withstand a late application of the brand-name herbicide after the crop had attained considerable size. This enabled farmers to use herbicide for weed control several weeks later in the growth cycle. Weed control measures occur several times on a field during the growing season, and timing is critical, whether the farmer uses an herbicide or a mechanical cultivator. Genetically altered crops also promised to reduce the use of pesticides. If the genetic trait for resistance to a plant disease or a pest could be melded into a crop's genetic makeup, then later applications of pesticides would become unnecessary. The seed industry successfully developed such varieties, and by 1998, 22 out of 75 million acres planted to corn in the Midwest, or fully 29 percent of the corn crop, were genetically modified. Of all corn, soybeans, and cotton planted in the United States, by 1999 proportions of transgenic seed accounted for 20 to 45 percent. In 1966, 13 percent of Iowa farmers planting Bt corn decreased insecticide applications, and by 1998, 26 percent planting the new seeds used less insecticide.[67]

While biotechnology holds out the hope of reducing chemical inputs by creating disease- or insect-resistant crop varieties, it has also created unforeseen environmental problems. People who work in genetics have a high degree of confidence in the products of their labs. Yet this confidence is perhaps overstated when it comes to knowing what will happen when genetically modified organisms are placed in the great outdoors. In the case of Bt corn, scientists working for the seed company confidently predicted its deadly effects would be limited to a few species closely related to the target species, a moth with a voracious appetite for corn. Yet entomologist John Losey at Cornell University discovered that 50 percent of monarch caterpillars exposed to Bt corn pollen on milkweed leaves dropped dead within four days. Genetics firms hastened to reassure the public, suggesting that these results were observed only in a lab; in the field, pollen would travel only a limited distance, and thus it would not affect nontarget species of wildlife. Some farmers were left wondering how milkweed got into the middle of their fields, if plant pollen traveled only three feet, as the firms claimed. The other problem with Bt corn is that as the crop is used over the years, those pests that possess a resistance to Bt's poisonous effects will reproduce rapidly, eventually in such numbers that the plant breeders will need to go back to the drawing board to design a new variety of corn that would be poisonous to the new pest variety. It is important to realize that this game of cat and mouse between plant disease and plant breeders goes on constantly. The cycle of introducing a new plant variety resistant to a malady, through the disease organism's mutation and resurgence, leading to the need for a new variety, can be as short as three to five years. The same process goes on with the development of a pesticide—in a relatively short span of time, pests mutate and reproduce, requiring a new strain of pesticide. Organic growers are particularly concerned about Bt corn because the Bt organism is widely used in organic agriculture to control pests and has been referred to as their last line of defense.[68]

Farmers and researchers also face many political, social, and economic obstacles on the path to sustainability. The contentious and oft-shifting winds of agricultural policy keep farmers guessing on many issues, such as what they will do when CRP contracts on erosion-susceptible land end after the ten-year program expires, and what federal help they will receive with an uncertain role ahead for the USDA and agricultural subsidies in the age of diminished budgets and of conservative economic policies advanced by the Republican Party. Farmers and environmentalists scoff at the lack of compliance and enforcement of rules related to FSA and FACTA and at the loopholes created by farmers and corporations to skirt environmental provisions, such as those specified in the "swampbuster" directive.[69]

Furthermore, America apparently will lose hundreds of thousands of more small to midsize "family" farms in the very near future. The continued decline of family farms is a cultural and technical loss compounded by the fact that the average American farmer is over age sixty. The decline of people pursuing agriculture as a profession and lifestyle illustrates the concern expressed by many environmentalists and farm activists that agriculture and food production are increasingly controlled by corporate farms and contract farming. With the loss of independence and with reduced options for farm and rural people, a further loss occurs in the form of declining attention to the details of land stewardship that might be possible with a landowner who lives on-site and has the long-term health of the land in mind. Let us note that the ideal of small landholders using low-level technologies, and therefore having low impact on the land, is partly a mythical image. Amish agricultural practices in some places, for example, contribute to higher rates of erosion than the practices of neighboring farmers who use "modern" methods. While small landholders do not always use the best practices, it is hard to imagine a large corporation caring about the land in the way that small and independent farmers do. Especially in the alternative agriculture movement, farmers stress the idea of intergenerational responsibility and the farm as a family business enterprise.[70]

Author Marty Strange discusses two mythical conceptions of modern American farms. The first set of expectations depicts the family farm as a place that is owner operated, entrepreneurial, dispersed, diversified, at equal advantage in open markets, family centered, technologically progressive, and resource conserving and the family farmer as someone who strives for processes that are in harmony with nature and sees farming as a way of life. The second set of images conceives of farms that practice industrial agribusiness as industrially organized, financed for growth, large and concentrated, specialized, management centered, capital-intensive, at an advantage in controlled markets, standardized in the production processes, resource consumptive, and farmed as a business rather than as a family-centered enterprise. These two conceptions are mythical in that neither system exists in a pure form—very few farms actually fulfill all the conditions of the prototypes. Most farms today fall somewhere on a continuum between these two polar images. Indeed, part of the difficulty in analyzing a particular farm's economic problems lies in the fact that most farms utilize elements of both ideal systems. Strange notes that "the weight of community sanction is with the family farms that most emulate the industrial agribusiness model." This is the model of progressive farming in a society that embraces modernity. Yet all too often the progressive farmers end up filing for bankruptcy.[71]

THE MEANING OF SUSTAINABLE AGRICULTURE

The success of America's production-oriented and monoculture-dominated agricultural system depends very much on how one defines progress. For consumers, modern agriculture has brought a cornucopia of inexpensive, high-quality food. While the world's agricultural bounty is still not reliably or equitably distributed to all people, overall the green revolution did contribute to feeding a burgeoning world population. For large-scale farmers, corporate farms, and seed and chemical companies, industrialized agriculture is a rational system within which they have done quite well economically. Yet, as the critics of modern agriculture have pointed out, its focus is short-term and it places the functioning ecosystem rather far down on its list of objectives. There are legitimate concerns that industrialized agriculture may not be sustainable in the long run. That threat should be disconcerting.

To university researchers, progress means gaining a better understanding of nature in order to "improve" agriculture. Improvements in chemical fertilizers or corn genetics or machine technology often mean greater yields, but achieving those higher yields often requires more capital infusions to acquire the necessary technology. Unfortunately for the small farmer, improved yields mean lower commodity prices at delivery time, and hence improvements in agricultural method have not translated into financial well-being for American farmers. The search for "more," a dominant driver in American culture, has not brought prosperity.

The movements for permanent and sustainable agriculture always incorporated a social agenda as well as an ecological directive. Despite a booming economy in the 1990s that is bolstering a very wide and comfortable middle class, American society has nevertheless become increasingly divided economically as the bottom fifth of income sustained a growing number of people and the top fifth of income became ever more concentrated among a few. In the words of Secretary of Labor Robert Reich, "A society divided between haves and have-nots, . . . between the well-educated and the poorly educated," makes infertile ground for the growth of a "prosperous or stable society." Farmers were not immune to larger economic trends. From 1940 through the 1980s, the number of American farms dropped from over 6 million to approximately 2 million. As long as these inequities persist, and as long as farm labor (including migrant workers) does not share the prosperity of America, the social vision of the new agriculture still has a long way to go.[72]

For many farmers, the last eighty years have brought a fundamental and systemic financial insecurity, a poor reward for their risks and labors. Modern industrial agriculture has provided the conditions that have concentrated land, money, and control over technology and markets in fewer and fewer hands. Many farmers, like the Populists of 1890, argue that modern corporations have too much power and too much influence over public policy. Farm groups from the relatively liberal Iowa Farmers Union to the conservative Farm Bureau Federation share concerns over the concentration of agricultural industries. In 1999, the nation's largest pork processor, Smithfield Foods, attempted to take over the number two competitor, Murphy Family Farms. Farm leaders protested the consolidation, arguing that the processing market would no longer have any meaningful competition. The Iowa legislature enacted livestock price reporting laws, requiring processors to reveal the price they paid various suppliers for livestock, theoretically leveling the information playing field for smaller independent producers. Throughout the 1980s and 1990s, newspapers in North Carolina, Nebraska, Iowa, and other states were filled with information about concentration in the pork industry, as corporations built large hog confinement facilities with sewage lagoons. As critics had feared, these lagoons leaked or overflowed and burst, causing massive fish kills in rivers. Groundwater pollution from these industrialized barnyards has become a major worry for the Department of Natural Resources in several states.[73]

Biotechnology is contentious partly because it is seen as an instrument of concentration and industrialization. A flurry of lawsuits has been exchanged recently over seeds. Traditionally, farmers saved the best part of their crop as seed for the following year's planting. Seed companies have begun producing seed with a "terminator" gene, intended to be used only once. In 1998, Monsanto sued several farmers it claimed had violated the terms of their contract specifying that a crop's product not be used as a seed source. In 1999, several farmers and organizations teamed up to sue Monsanto in a class action lawsuit, charging that the corporation not only had rushed bioengineered seeds to market without sufficient safety measures but also had attempted to gain monopolistic control over world markets in corn and soybean seeds. As the advocates of sustainable agriculture point out, the issues of technology, economic equity for farmers, corporate control, and environmental health are closely linked.[74]

Ecological agriculture holds promise, even if farmers adopt it for purely economic reasons. If our measure for the success of ecological agriculture is land health, the motives involved matter less than the results of technique. The Practical Farmers of Iowa embody a very pragmatic approach to farming problems, concentrating on reducing costly inputs as a method of staying profitable. These farmers adopt techniques that make sense from an agronomic perspective, without necessarily subscribing to holistic notions or suspicions regarding chemicals that might motivate others who adopt the same techniques. Organic agriculture demonstrates one of the areas where ecologically inspired agriculture is making significant inroads into industrial agriculture's commanding presence. In this case, consumer preferences are forcing farmers to adopt methods that promise an improved degree of environmental friendliness. American consumers are becoming more like their counterparts in Europe, who are very particular not only about the purity of their food but also about taste. The market for organic produce has boomed in the United States over the past twenty years, and some growers are using organic methods not because they are convinced environmentalists but because the market niche promises increased profitability.[75]

While the issues surrounding modern agriculture are complex, and the problems difficult to solve given the current cultural atmosphere that resists regional planning and true cultural change, in its "permanent" and "sustainable" forms ecologically inspired agriculture has provided a beacon for individuals concerned about creating a future based on a true prosperity that is not solely economic in nature. Ecological agriculture sought to create a future society concerned with the long-term ecological health of both ecosystems and humans. For six decades the permanent and sustainable agriculture movements imparted ecological values, a sense of intergenerational responsibility, and an agenda of social equity. This movement still provides the vision and inspiration for modern agriculture to transcend its limitations and to link human artifice with nature's processes, creating a green and permanent land.

Notes

INTRODUCTION

1. Joseph Kahn and David E. Sanger, "Seattle Talks on Trade End with Stinging Blow to U.S.," *New York Times*, 5 December 1999, 1, 14; Marianne Means, "Biotech Scare Is More Politics Than Science," *Daily Tribune* (Ames, Iowa), 4 December 1999, A6; Tony Snow, "Infantile WTO Protest by Goof-Offs," *Des Moines Register*, 5 December 1999, 3AA; Barnaby J. Feder, "Public Fears Slow Biotechnology," *Daily Tribune* (Ames, Iowa), 20 December 1999, 1A, 8A.

2. NAS study cited in G. Tyler Miller Jr., *Sustaining the Earth*, 3d ed. (Belmont, Calif.: Wadsworth, 1998), 210, 220; see also Richard Heinberg, *Cloning the Buddha: The Moral Impact of Biotechnology* (Wheaton, Ill.: Quest Books, 1999).

3. Marty Strange, *Family Farming: A New Economic Vision* (Lincoln: University of Nebraska Press, 1988), 68–77.

4. David Barboza, "Hard Times Set In for Farmers," *Daily Tribune* (Ames, Iowa), 29 November, 1999, A1, A8.

5. Rick Welsh, "The Industrial Reorganization of U.S. Agriculture: An Overview and Background Report," Policy Studies Report No. 6 (Greenbelt, Md.: Henry A. Wallace Institute for Alternative Agriculture, April 1996); Strange, *Family Farming*, 77.

6. Heinberg, *Cloning the Buddha*, 19–20.

7. R. Douglas Hurt, *American Agriculture: A Brief History* (Ames: Iowa State University Press, 1994), 195–202; R. Douglas Hurt, *Agricultural Technology in the Twentieth Century* (Manhattan, Kans.: Sunflower University Press, 1991), 10; John L. Shover, *First Majority–Last Minority: The Transforming of Rural Life in America* (1976; De Kalb: Northern Illinois University Press, 1986), 143–70.

8. Thompson On-Farm Research, "Alternatives in Agriculture," 1999 Report, Boone, Iowa.

9. Osha Gray Davidson, *Broken Heartland: The Rise of America's Rural Ghetto* (Iowa City: University of Iowa Press, 1996), 35.

CHAPTER 1. SOIL AND THE CRISIS OF AMERICAN CIVILIZATION

1. L. H. Bailey, *The State and the Farmer* (New York: Macmillan, 1908), 59.

2. Page Smith, *Dissenting Opinions* (San Francisco: North Point Press, 1984), 3–13; Margaret Mead, *Keep Your Powder Dry* (New York: William Morrow, 1942), 193–94. On the American sense of crisis, see Sacvan Bercovitch, *The American Jeremiad* (Madison: University of Wisconsin Press, 1978).

3. Alan I. Marcus and Howard P. Segal, *Technology in America: A Brief History* (San Diego: Harcourt Brace Jovanovich, 1989), 255–314; Walter C. Lowdermilk, "The Eleventh Commandment," reprint from *American Forests* (January 1940),

box 141, "Friends of the Land," Morris L. Cooke Papers, Franklin D. Roosevelt Presidential Library, hereafter cited as Cooke Papers).

4. R. Douglas Hurt, *American Agriculture: A Brief History* (Ames: Iowa State University Press, 1994), 203–12, 221–22.

5. Ibid., 260–65.

6. Richard S. Kirkendall, *Social Scientists and Farm Politics in the Age of Roosevelt* (Columbia: University of Missouri Press, 1966); Arthur Schlesinger, *The Age of Roosevelt* (Boston: Houghton Mifflin, 1957); Rexford G. Tugwell, *Roosevelt's Revolution: The First Year, a Personal Perspective* (New York: Macmillan, 1977); Theodore Saloutos, *The American Farmer in the New Deal* (Ames: Iowa State University Press, 1982).

7. Cooke Papers, box 141, "Friends of the Land"; see Alan I. Marcus, *Agricultural Science and the Quest for Legitimacy* (Ames: Iowa State University Press, 1985); David Danbom, *The Resisted Revolution: The Country Life Movement in America* (Ames: Iowa State University Press, 1979); see also Liberty Hyde Bailey, *The Country Life Movement in the United States* (New York: Macmillan, 1913). On agricultural problems in the 1920s, see Wheeler McMillen, *Too Many Farmers* (New York: William Morrow, 1926); and David Hamilton, *From New Day to New Deal* (Chapel Hill: University of North Carolina Press, 1991); last quotation from Rexford G. Tugwell, "The Reason for Resettlement" (speech broadcast on the National Broadcasting Network, 2 December 1935), box 169, Rexford G. Tugwell Papers, Franklin D. Roosevelt Presidential Library (hereafter cited as Tugwell Papers).

8. Rexford G. Tugwell, "Down to Earth." *Current History* 44 (July 1936); 32–38; Henry A. Wallace, *New Frontiers* (New York: Reynal and Hitchcock, 1934), 242; Morris L. Cooke, "Is America Doomed Agriculturally?" In the *Philadelphia Evening Ledger,* August 1936, found in Cooke Papers, box 327; Paul B. Sears, "Death from the Soil." *American Mercury* 42 (December 1937); 441; Hugh H. Bennett quoted in *Soil Conservation* 5 (May 1940); 277; Charles D. Jarrett, "Erosion Control Drama," *The Land Today and Tomorrow* (c. 1935).

9. Edward Faulkner, *Uneasy Money* (Norman: University of Oklahoma Press, 1945), 35; Hugh H. Bennett, "Program of the Soil Conservation Service" (paper presented to the Eighth Southwestern Soil and Water Conservation Conference, Tyler, Texas, 8–9 July 1936), file 8, box 10, Hugh H. Bennett Papers, Archives of American Agriculture, Special Collections, Parks Memorial Library, Iowa State University (hereafter cited as Bennett Papers); script of *The Land* quoted from Russell Lord and Kate Lord, *Forever the Land* (New York: Harper & Brothers, 1951), 30.

10. Walter C. Lowdermilk, *Conquest of the Land Through Seven Thousand Years* (Washington, D.C.: USDA, 1948), 2–5; Stuart Chase, *Rich Land, Poor Land* (New York: McGraw-Hill, 1936), 342–46; P. H. Walser, "Erosion Finished the Mayans," *The Land Today and Tomorrow* 2 (January 1935): 7.

11. Walter C. Lowdermilk, "Other Lands: Dispatches from Japan," *The Land* 11 (summer 1951); 209–11; Pearl S. Buck, "The Land and People of China," *China and America: A Chronicle of Cultural Relations* 1 (October 1948): 3; Paul B. Sears, *Deserts on the March* (Norman: University of Oklahoma Press, 1935), 11–12; Paul Sears, "Human Ecology," *The Land* 10 (spring 1951): 24.

12. Louis Bromfield, *A Few Brass Tacks* (New York: Harper & Brothers, 1948), 102; Neil M. Clark, "Peasant Sage," in Lord and Lord, *Forever the Land*, 289; J. I. Rodale, *The Organic Front* (Emmaus, Pa.: Rodale Press, 1948), 11–12; Sears, *Deserts on the March*, 169; G. V. Jacks and R. O. Whyte, *The Rape of the Earth: A World Survey of Soil Erosion* (London: Faber and Faber, 1939), 18.

13. Sears, *Deserts on the March*, 120; Hugh H. Bennett, Address to the Sixth

Southwest Soil and Water Conservation Conference (8–9 July 1935), Bennett Papers, box 10, file 8.

14. Hugh H. Bennett, "Soil Conservation" (address before the Forty-first Annual Session, Illinois Farmers Institute, Belleville, Illinois, 20 February 1936, Bennett Papers, box 10, file 12.

15. Louis Bromfield, *Pleasant Valley* (New York: Harper & Brothers, 1945), 103; Hugh H. Bennett, "Unmaking a Continent" (address before the Brooklyn Institute of Arts and Sciences, Brooklyn Academy of Music, 22 April 1937, Bennett Papers, box 1, file 15; Faulkner, *Uneasy Money,* 53.

16. *The Plow That Broke the Plains* (Washington, D.C.: USDA, 1937); *The River* (Washington, D.C.: Farm Security Administration, 1937); Lord and Lord, *Forever the Land,* 31.

17. Faulkner, *Uneasy Money,* 18–19; Edward Faulkner, *Plowman's Folly* (Norman: University of Oklahoma Press, 1943), 19; Bromfield, *A Few Brass Tacks,* 116–17; see also Randal Beeman, "Louis Bromfield Versus the 'Age of Irritation,'" *Environmental History Review* 17 (spring 1992): 77–92; and Randal Beeman, "The Trash Farmer: Edward Faulkner and the Origins of Sustainable Agriculture, 1943–1953," *Journal of Sustainable Agriculture* 4 (winter 1993): 91–102.

18. Louis Bromfield, *Out of the Earth* (New York: Harper & Brothers, 1950), xii–xiii, 5–6; Bromfield, *A Few Brass Tacks,* 11; Faulkner, *Plowman's Folly,* 3–7, 22–23, 52–53; Faulkner, *Uneasy Money,* 102–7; Edward Faulkner, *A Second Look* (Norman: University of Oklahoma Press, 1947), 26–27; Edward Faulkner, *Soil Restoration* (London: Michael Joseph, 1953), 110–23.

19. Bromfield, *A Few Brass Tacks,* 11, 90–95; Ralph Borsodi, "The Case Against Farming as a Big Business," *The Land* 5 (winter 1945–46): 25–28; Louis Bromfield, "The High Cost of Poor Farming," *The Land* 5 (winter 1945–46): 446–49; Charles E. Kellogg, "A Challenge to America's Soil Scientists," *Proceedings of the Soil Science Society of America* 25 (November–December 1961): 419–23.

20. Many criticisms of past mistreatment of soil resources were echoed in the Great Plains Committee, *The Future of the Great Plains* (Washington, D.C.: GPO, 1936); Ellen Bromfield-Geld, *The Heritage: A Daughter's Memories of Louis Bromfield* (New York: Harper & Brothers, 1962), 83–84; Bromfield, *Out of the Earth,* 14–15; "Deplores Farming Evils," *Science News Letter,* 3 July 1943, 43; Hugh H. Bennett quoted in *Town Meeting: Bulletin of America's Town Meeting of the Air* 5 (11 March 1940); 19–20; Wallace, *New Frontiers,* 239.

21. Morris L. Cooke, quoted in "Clippings," Cooke Papers, box 327.

22. Marcus and Segal, *Technology in America,* 114–15, 204–5, quote on 207.

23. William S. Graebner, *The Age of Doubt: American Thought and Culture in the 1940s* (Boston: Twayne, 1991), 69–100; Bailey, *Country Life Movement in the United States,* 14–15, 49; see also Herbert M. Hamlin, ed., *Readings Related to the Objectives for Agriculture* (Ames, Iowa: Collegiate Press, 1934), 137–62.

24. Hugh H. Bennett, "Soil Conservation," Bennett Papers, box 10, file 12; Hugh Bennett, "Soil Conservation: Our Common Concern" (speech to Farm and Home Week, East Lansing, Michigan, 28 January 1948), Bennett Papers, box 11, file 36; Paul B. Sears quoted in Lord and Lord, *Forever the Land,* 271; see also Gove Hambridge, "Soils and Men: A Summary," in *Soils and Men: Yearbook of Agriculture 1938* (Washington, D.C.: GPO, 1938), 3.

25. Hugh H. Bennett, "Program of the Soil Conservation Service," Bennett Papers, box 10, file 8; Cooke Papers, "Friends of the Land," box 141.

26. Stuart Chase quoted in Lord and Lord, *Forever the Land,* 64; Fairfield Osborn quoted in Henry F. Pringle, "A Prodigal Agriculture Can't Feed the

World," *Saturday Evening Post,* 11 September 1948; for more on this ethical "shift," see Samuel P. Hays, *Beauty, Health and Permanence: Environmental Politics in the United States, 1955–1985* (Cambridge: Cambridge University Press, 1987), 13–35; and Aldo Leopold, *A Sand County Almanac* (1953; reprint, New York: Oxford University Press, 1966), 217–41.

27. J. E. Noll cited in Lord and Lord, *Forever the Land,* 59; Chester C. Davis cited on page 190.

28. Lewis Mumford, "Power and Culture" (speech delivered to a special session of the Third World Power Conference, 11 September 1936), Cooke Papers, box 280, "3rd World Power Conference"; Marcus and Segal, *Technology in America,* 270–76; see also Randal Beeman, "'Chemivisions': The Forgotten Promises of the Chemurgy Movement," *Agricultural History* 68 (winter 1994): 23–45.

29. Rexford G. Tugwell, "The Outlines of a Permanent Agriculture" (c. 1935), Tugwell Papers, box 69; E. G. Cheney and T. Schantz-Hantzen, *This Is Our Land* (St. Paul, Minn.: Webb, 1940), 48–49.

30. Lowdermilk, *Conquest of the Land,* 33.

31. Hugh H. Bennett, "Soil Conservation," National Archives, Great Plains Region, Kansas City, Missouri, Records Group 114, box 97, "Hugh H. Bennett."

32. Rexford G. Tugwell, *The Diary of Rexford G. Tugwell: The New Deal, 1932–35* (New York: Greenwood Press, 1962); Rexford G. Tugwell, *The Battle for Democracy* (New York: Columbia University Press, 1935); Rexford G. Tugwell, *The Brains Trust* (New York: Viking, 1968); Tugwell, *Roosevelt's Revolution.*

33. Rexford G. Tugwell, "Conservation Redefined," Tugwell Papers, box 69.

34. On contemporary planning, see Oswin W. Willcox, *Reshaping Agriculture* (New York: Norton, 1934); Morris L. Cooke, *Our Cities Awake* (New York: Doubleday, 1918); Jean Christie, "New Deal Resources Planning: The Proposals of Morris L. Cooke," *Agricultural History* 53 (July 1979): 507–606; Bushrod W. Allin, "Historical Background of the United States Department of Agriculture" (lecture delivered to the Agricultural Workers of the United States Department of Agriculture and the North Carolina State College for Agriculture and Engineering, Raleigh, North Carolina, 4 October 1940), Bushrod W. Allin Papers, Archives of American Agriculture, Special Collections, Parks Memorial Library, Iowa State University (hereafter cited as Allin Papers), box 1, file 8; Harry J. Carman and Rexford G. Tugwell, "The Significance of American Agricultural History," *Agricultural History* 12 (April 1938): 100–103.

35. Rexford G. Tugwell, "Earthbound: The Problem of Planning and Survival," *Antioch Review,* winter 1949–50, Tugwell Papers, Speech and Writings File, box 69; Tugwell quoted in *Washington Star,* 29 June 1941, Tugwell Papers, Press Clippings, box 27, file 1; Rexford G. Tugwell, "Your Future and Your Nation" (commencement address, University of New Mexico, 10 June 1935), Speech and Writings File, 1935–37, box 57.

36. Rexford G. Tugwell, "Resettlement Administration" (speech given at Olympic Auditorium, Los Angeles, 28 October 1935), Tugwell Papers, Speech and Writings File, 1935–37, box 57; Sherman E. Johnson, "Definitions of Efficient Farming," *Land Policy Review* 2 (September–October 1939): 22–23.

37. Bushrod W. Allin, "Is Planning Compatible with Democracy?" (speech given to the Society for Social Research, University of Chicago, 22 August 1936), Allin Papers, box 1, file 1.

38. Henry A. Wallace memo to Hugh H. Bennett, 6 June 1935, Henry A. Wallace Papers, University of Iowa Library, Microfilm IA 20–845 (hereafter cited as Wallace Papers).

39. Franklin D. Roosevelt quoted in Edgar B. Nixon, ed., *Franklin D. Roosevelt*

and Conservation, vol. 2 (Hyde Park, N.Y.: National Archives, 1957), 68–69; Morris L. Cooke, "Is the United States a Permanent Country?" *Forum and Century* 49 (January–June 1938): 236–40; Bushrod Allin and Ellery A. Foster, "The Challenge of Conservation," and Hugh H. Bennett, "Our Soil Can Be Saved," both in *Yearbook of Agriculture 1940* (Washington, D.C.: USDA, 1940), 416–37.

40. Cyril G. Hopkins, *Soil Fertility and Permanent Agriculture* (Boston: Ginn, 1910).

41. Ralph Borsodi, *Flight from the City: The Story of the New Way to Family Security* (New York: Harper & Brothers, 1933); quotes from Frank Owsley, "The Pillars of Americanism" (1935), reprinted in Robert M. Crunden, ed., *The Superfluous Men: Conservative Critics of American Culture, 1900–1945* (Austin: University of Texas Press, 1977), 164–207; on Henry Ford's Village Industry concept, see Marcus and Segal, *Technology in America,* 270–72; and Reynold Wik, "Henry Ford's Science and Technology for Rural America," *Technology and Culture* 3 (summer 1962): 247–58.

42. Rexford G. Tugwell, "The Place of Government in a National Land Program" (address to joint meeting of the American Economists Association, the American Statisticians Association, and the Farm Economic Association, Philadelphia, 29 January 1933), Tugwell Papers, Speech and Writings File, 1932–33, box 55.

43. Rexford G. Tugwell, "Farm Relief and a Permanent Agriculture," *Annals of the American Academy of Political and Social Science,* March 1929, Tugwell Papers, box 55; Rexford G. Tugwell, "An Outline of a Permanent Agriculture" (n.d.), Tugwell Papers, box 69.

44. Tolley and Wilson quoted from anthology in the Cooke Papers, box 141; Wallace, *New Frontiers,* 248; Wallace quoted in Nixon, *Franklin D. Roosevelt and Conservation,* 144–45; see also Morris L. Cooke, "An Engineer Blueprints a New America," *New York Times Magazine,* 15 November 1936, 4–5, 19; and Charles E. Kellogg, *The Soils That Support Us* (New York: Macmillan, 1941), 273–91.

45. Hugh H. Bennett, "A Major Effort at Erosion Control," *The Land Today and Tomorrow* 1 (October 1934): 1–5; Hugh H. Bennett, "Emergency and Permanent Control of Wind Erosion on the Great Plains," *Scientific Monthly,* November 1938, 381–99; Hugh H. Bennett, "A New Farm Movement Takes Rapid Root," *Soil Conservation* 6 (February–March 1941): 1; T. B. Chambers, "Field Operations of the SCS" (radio broadcast on NBC network, 7 August 1936), National Archives, Great Plains Region, Kansas City, Missouri, CPR7-NA-KC, RG 114, box 1; Bushrod W. Allin, "The County Planning Project: A Cooperative Approach to Agricultural Planning" (address to the American Farm Economists Association, Philadelphia, 28 December 1939), Allin Papers, box 4.

46. Rexford G. Tugwell, "The Resettlement Idea," *Agricultural History* 33 (October 1959): 159–63; see also Russell Lord and Paul Johnstone, *A Place on Earth: A Critical Appraisal of Subsistence Homesteads* (Washington, D.C.: USDA, 1942); Raymond P. Duncan, *A Federal Resettlement Project: Granger Homesteads* (Washington, D.C.: Catholic University of America, 1937), 6–22, 164–73.

47. Morris L. Cooke to Franklin D. Roosevelt, 31 January 1937, FDR Library, FDR OF-728-736, box 1; Ward Shepard, *Food or Famine: The Challenge of Erosion* (New York: Macmillan, 1945), 206; Lord and Lord, *Forever the Land,* 52–54.

CHAPTER 2. AN ECOLOGICAL BASIS FOR CULTURE AND AGRICULTURE

1. Hugh H. Bennett, "Permanent Systems of Farming," Bennett Papers, box 10, file 35.

2. Keith R. Benson, "From Museum Research to Laboratory Research: The

Transformation of Natural History into Academic Biology," in *The American Development of Biology,* ed. Ronald Rainger, Keith R. Benson, and Jane Maienschein (Philadelphia: University of Pennsylvania Press, 1988), 49–86.

3. Roderick Nash, *The Rights of Nature: A History of Environmental Ethics* (Madison: University of Wisconsin Press, 1989), 55–67; Orlando Park, "Observations Concerning the Future of Ecology," *Ecology* 26 (January 1945): 1–9; Frank Egerton, ed., *History of American Ecology* (New York: Arno Press, 1977); Leslie A. Reals and James H. Brown, eds., *Foundations of Ecology: Classic Papers with Commentaries* (Chicago: University of Chicago Press, 1984); Richard Overfield, "Charles E. Bessey: The Impact of the 'New' Botany on American Agriculture, 1880–1910," *Technology and Culture* 16 (April 1975): 162–81.

4. "Comments," *Ecology* 19 (1938): 164–66; Barrington Moore, "The Scope of Ecology," *Ecology* 1 (1920): 1–13; Richard Brewer, "A Brief History of Ecology," *Papers of the C. C. Adams Center for Ecological Studies* 1 (1960): 1–13.

5. Ronald C. Tobey, *Saving the Prairie: The Life Cycle of the Founding School of American Plant Ecology, 1895–1955* (Berkeley: University of California Press, 1981); Donald Worster, *Nature's Economy: A History of Ecological Ideas,* 2d ed. (Cambridge: Cambridge University Press, 1994), 205–20; Nash, *Rights of Nature,* 56–57.

6. Worster, *Nature's Economy,* 238–40; Frank B. Golley, *A History of the Ecosystem Concept in Ecology: More Than the Sum of the Parts* (New Haven, Conn.: Yale University Press, 1993), 22–24.

7. Golley, *History of the Ecosystem Concept,* 22–34; Worster, *Nature's Economy,* 18, 21–22, 209–12; Nash, *Rights of Nature,* 57–60.

8. Frederic E. Clements and Victor E. Shelford, *Bio-ecology* (New York: Wiley, 1939); Nash, *Rights of Nature,* 57.

9. See also Eugene Cittadino, "The Failed Promise of Human Ecology," in *Science and Nature: Essays in the History of the Environmental Sciences,* ed. Michael Shortland (Oxford: British Society for the History of Science, 1993), 251–84; Juan Ilerbaig, "Allied Sciences and Fundamental Problems: C. C. Adams and the Search for Method in Early American Ecology" (paper presented at the History of Science Society, Kansas City, October 1998).

10. Clements and Shelford, *Bio-ecology,* 1–9.

11. Worster, *Nature's Economy,* 232; Paul Sears, "Science and the Living Landscape," *Harper's,* July 1939, 213; Paul B. Sears, *Life and Environment: The Interrelations of Living Things* (New York: Columbia University Press, 1939), cover insert.

12. Louise E. Howard, *The Earth's Green Carpet* (Emmaus, Pa.: Rodale Press, 1947), 15–24; see also Thomas F. Gieryn, *Cultural Boundaries of Science: Credibility on the Line* (Chicago: University of Chicago Press, 1999), 233–35, esp. 234–35.

13. Edward H. Graham, *Natural Principles of Land Use* (London: Oxford University Press, 1944), 230–31; Russell Lord and Kate Lord, *Forever the Land* (New York: Harper & Brothers, 1951), 192; Jonathan Forman and Ollie Fink, *Water and Man: A Study in Ecology* (Columbus, Ohio: Friends of the Land, 1950), xv.

14. Walter P. Taylor, "What Is Ecology and What Good Is It?" *Ecology* 17 (July 1936): 345; see also Thomas Dunlap, *Saving American Wildlife* (Princeton, N.J.: Princeton University Press, 1988), 76–77; Nash, *Rights of Nature,* 55–86.

15. Worster, *Nature's Economy,* 173–74, 212–13; Nash, *Rights of Nature,* 43; Anna Bramwell, *Ecology in the Twentieth Century: A History* (New Haven, Conn.: Yale University Press, 1989).

16. Sears, *Life and Environment, The Interrelations of Living Things,* 129–32; Paul Sears, "Darwin and the Living Landscape," in *From the Land,* ed. Nancy Pittman (New York: Island Press, 1990), 406–7; Paul Sears, "Science and the Living Land-

scape," *Harper's*, July 1939, 207. See also Douglas R. Weiner, *Models of Nature: Ecology, Conservation, and Cultural Revolution in Russia* (Bloomington: Indiana University Press, 1988).

17. Sears, *Life and Environment*, 11, 62–66, 129–35; Sears, "Human Ecology," *Land* 10 (spring 1951): 23–26, esp. 24.

18. Sears, *Life and Environment*, 11–135; Paul Sears, "The Importance of Ecology in the Training of Engineers," *Science*, 4 July 1947.

19. Paul B. Sears, "The Conditions of Life," *The Land* 5 (summer 1946): 239–44; see also Paul B. Sears, *This Is Our World* (Norman: University of Oklahoma Press, 1937), 280; and Curt Meine, "The Farmer as Conservationist: Leopold on Agriculture," in *Aldo Leopold: The Man and His Legacy*, ed. Thomas Tanner (Ankeny, Iowa: Soil Conservation Society of America, 1987), 39–52.

20. Charles E. Little, ed., *Louis Bromfield at Malabar: Writings on Farming and Country Life* (Baltimore: Johns Hopkins University Press, 1988), 154–55; Louis Bromfield, *Out of the Earth* (New York: Harper & Brothers, 1950), 8.

21. Sears, "Conditions of Life," 244. See Liberty Hyde Bailey, *The Outlook to Nature* (New York: Macmillan, 1911), 1–11; Charles E. Kellogg, "A Challenge to American Soil Scientists: On the Occasion of the 25th Anniversary of the Soil Science Society of America," *Proceedings of the Soil Science Society of America* 25 (November–December 1961): 419–21.

22. Sir Albert Howard, *The Soil and Health: A Study of Organic Agriculture* (New York: Devin-Adair, 1947), 30–31, 257–60; Sir Albert Howard, *An Agricultural Testament* (London: Oxford University Press, 1940), ix–223; see also Philip Conford, ed., *The Organic Tradition: An Anthology of Writings on Organic Farming, 1900–1950* (London: Green Books, 1988).

23. Hugh H. Bennett, "Adjustment of Agriculture to Its Environment" (address to the Fortieth Annual Meeting of the Association of American Geographers, 18 September 1943), Bennett Papers, box 10, file 50.

24. See also F. C. Bishop, "Entomology in Relation to Conservation," *Journal of Economic Entomology* 31 (February 1938): 1–10.

25. Herbert C. Hanson, "Ecology in Agriculture," *Ecology* 20 (April 1939): 111–17.

26. Ibid.

27. Edward H. Graham, "Ecology and Land Use," *Soil Conservation* 6 (November 1940): 123–26; Edward H. Graham, "Soil Erosion as an Ecological Process," *Scientific Monthly* 55 (July 1942): 2.

28. Edward Ackerman, "The Geographic Meaning of Land Use," and Edward H. Graham, "The Biologist's Viewpoint," both in the special "Symposium —the Ecological Approach to Land Use" in the *Journal of Soil and Water Conservation* 1 (October 1946): 55–70, esp. 64; Edward H. Graham, *Natural Principles of Land Use* (London: Oxford University Press, 1944), 226.

29. J. P. J. Van Vuren, *Soil Fertility and Sewage* (New York: Dover, 1948), 21–37, esp. 29; Thomas J. Barrett, *Harnessing the Earthworm* (Boston: Bruce Humphries, 1947), 9–75; J. I. Rodale, *The Organic Front* (Emmaus, Pa.: Rodale Press, 1948), 15.

30. See Leonard Wickenden, *Make Friends with Your Land* (New York: Devin-Adair, 1949), 1–130; Ehrenfield Pfeiffer, *Soil Fertility, Renewal and Preservation: Biodynamic Farming and Gardening* (London: Faber and Faber, 1947), 15–186; R. P. Faulkner, *Garden Manures and Fertilisers: Embodying Special Recommendations for Fruit, Vegetables and Flowers* (London: Collingridge, 1949), 24–30; Charles E. Kellogg, *The Soils That Support Us* (New York: Macmillan, 1941), 14–66.

31. Louis Bromfield, "Trash Farming at Malabar," *The Land* 4 (summer 1945):

322; portions of this section originally appeared in Randal Beeman, "Louis Brom-field Versus the 'Age of Irritation,'" *Environmental History Review* 17 (spring 1993): 77–92.

32. Bromfield, *Out of the Earth*, 297; Louis Bromfield, *A Few Brass Tacks* (New York: Harper & Brothers, 1948), 2–7.

33. *Louis Bromfield's Malabar Farm*, brochure from Malabar Farm State Park, Richland County, Ohio (Columbus: State of Ohio, n.d.); David Anderson, *Louis Bromfield* (New York: Twayne, 1964); Little, *Louis Bromfield at Malabar*, 1–15. Spe-cial thanks to Andrew Ware and Clive Edwards of Ohio State University for addi-tional biographical information.

34. Louis Bromfield, "Pleasant Valley," *Farm Quarterly* 1 (Autumn 1946): 33–36.

35. Ellen Bromfield Geld, *The Heritage: A Daughter's Memories of Louis Brom-field* (New York: Harper & Brothers, 1962), 68–75, esp. 69.

36. Louis Bromfield, "Ecology at Malabar," *The Land* 7 (winter 1949): 515.

37. Bromfield, *Out of the Earth*, 42; Little, *Louis Bromfield at Malabar*, 30, 90–102, 132.

38. Bromfield, "Ecology at Malabar," 515–17; Louis Bromfield, "Spring," *Farm Quarterly* 8 (spring 1952): 68–70; Bromfield, *Out of the Earth*, 35–36; Little, *Louis Bromfield at Malabar*, 26, 40–41, 90–102.

39. Some of this material on Edward Faulkner appeared in Randal Beeman, "The Trash Farmer: Edward Faulkner and the Origins of Sustainable Agricul-ture, 1943–1953," *Journal of Sustainable Agriculture* 4 (winter 1993): 91–102; Edward Faulkner, *Plowman's Folly* (Norman: University of Oklahoma Press, 1943); Edward Faulkner, *Uneasy Money* (Norman: University of Oklahoma Press, 1945); Edward Faulkner, *A Second Look* (Norman: University of Okla-homa Press, 1947); Edward Faulkner, *Soil Restoration* (London: Michael Joseph, 1953).

40. Faulkner, *Soil Restoration*, 42–43, 66, 104–9; Faulkner, *A Second Look*, 26, 182; Faulkner, *Plowman's Folly*, 43; Faulkner, *Uneasy Money*, 28–36.

41. Faulkner, *Plowman's Folly*, 3–9, 46–53, 104–9; Faulkner, *Soil Restoration*, 13, 20–122; Faulkner, *A Second Look*, 61, 81, 92, 126; Faulkner, *Uneasy Money*, 28–36, 53, 100–105. See also Edward Faulkner, "Do We Need More Tile? A Critical Note on Artificial Drainage," *The Land* 2 (winter 1941–42): 29–34.

42. Faulkner, *Plowman's Folly*, 12–13, 104–5; Faulkner's idealistic view of Asian peasant agriculture was informed by F. H. King's *Farmers of Forty Centuries, or Permanent Agriculture in China, Korea and Japan* (Emmaus, Pa.: Rodale Press, 1947).

43. Faulkner, *Plowman's Folly*, 26–107; Faulkner, *A Second Look*, 18–41, 110–35; Faulkner, *Soil Restoration*, 32–33, 206–7; see John F. Hensler, "My Faulknerizer," *The Land* 4 (winter 1945): 83–84. Faulkner later admitted he briefly used some manufactured fertilizer in the 1930s; see Hugh H. Bennett, "The Abolition of the Plow," *New Republic*, 10 October 1943, 83, 453–54; see also Bromfield, "Trash Farming at Malabar," 321–25.

44. See "Design for Plenty," in *Food at the Grass Roots: The Nation's Stake in Soil Minerals* (Knoxville: Tennessee Valley Authority, 1947), 5–15; William Vogt, "The Survival of Man," *Conservation in the Americas* 5 (October 1947): 1–8.

45. David Danbom, "Romantic Agrarianism in Twentieth-Century America," *Agricultural History* 65 (fall 1991): 1–12.

46. Bromfield, *A Few Brass Tacks*, 2–9; Bromfield, *Out of the Earth*, 297–98; see also Winfield Scott and Joseph B. Paul, *Permanent Agriculture: A Textbook of Gen-*

eral Agriculture (New York: Wiley, 1941); A. Whitney Griswold, *Farming and Democracy* (New Haven, Conn.: Yale University Press, 1952), 14–15; Louis Bromfield, "Foreword," in P. Alston Waring and Walter Magnes Teller, *Roots in the Earth: The Small Farmer Looks Ahead* (New York: Harpers, 1943), vii.

47. Bromfield quoted in Little, *Louis Bromfield at Malabar,* 46–48, 75.

48. E. B. White, "Malabar Farm," *New Yorker,* 8 May 1944, 104; Rexford G. Tugwell, "This Ugly Civilization" (book review), Tugwell Papers, box 69.

49. Bromfield, *A Few Brass Tacks,* 112, 199.

50. Faulkner, *Uneasy Money,* 38–97; Faulkner, *Soil Restoration,* 125, 203; Faulkner, *Plowman's Folly,* 159.

51. Hugh H. Bennett, "Businessmen and Soil Conservation," Bennett Papers, box 13, file 27; Hugh H. Bennett, "Permanent Systems of Farming," Bennett Papers, box 10, file 30; John Bird, "Jobs for Half a Million," *Saturday Evening Post,* 27 November 1943, 20–21; Hugh H. Bennett, "The Economy and Soil Conservation" (speech to Banker-Farmer Meeting, Pulaski Virginia, 25 March 1949), Bennett Papers, box 13, file 26; Hugh H. Bennett, "The Utilities' Stake in Soil Conservation" (speech to Annual Meeting of the Edison Electrical Institute, Atlantic City, New Jersey, 3 June 1948), Bennett Papers, box 12, file 1; Hugh H. Bennett, *Elements of Soil Conservation* (New York: McGraw-Hill, 1947), 1–9.

52. Louis Bromfield quoted in Wellington Brink, *Big Hugh: The Father of Soil Conservation* (New York: Macmillan, 1951), ix; Hugh H. Bennett to Conservation Workshop for Teachers, Murray, Ky., 1949, Bennett Papers, box 12, file 37; Faulkner, *Soil Restoration,* 206–7; see also Louis Bromfield, *Reader's Digest,* August 1943, 111–18.

53. Faulkner, *Plowman's Folly,* 160–61; Faulkner also quoted from "proceedings," *The Land* 4 (winter 1945): 4; Louis Bromfield, "Foundation for Life" (review of Sir Albert Howard's *The Soil and Health*), in *The Land* 6 (spring 1947): 69; Jonathan Forman and Ollie Fink, eds., *Soil, Food and Health: "You Are What You Eat"* (Columbus, Ohio: Friends of the Land, 1948), 11–35; see also "The Farmer's Stake in Diet and Jobs," *Country Gentleman,* April 1946, 30–31; J. I. Rodale, *The Organic Front* (Emmaus, Pa.: Rodale Press, 1948), 9–14; Evelyn B. Balfour, *The Living Soil and the Haughley Experiment* (New York: Universe, 1976), 12–32.

54. Walter C. Lowdermilk, *Palestine: Land of Promise* (New York: Harper & Brothers, 1945), 15, 19–20; on world government, see William S. Graebner, *The Age of Doubt: American Thought and Culture in the 1940s* (Boston: Twayne, 1991), 71–74; see also Paul Boyer, *By the Bomb's Early Light: American Thought and Culture at the Dawn of the Atomic Age* (New York: Pantheon, 1985), 29–170; on Tugwell and the world government movement, see "Reflections on Our Preliminary Discussion of Planning and Cautions for the Future," Tugwell Papers, "World Constitution" box 50; see also "The Policy of the United World Federalists" and other materials in Kenneth A. Carlander Papers, University Archives, Parks Memorial Library, Iowa State University, boxes 1–4.

55. Faulkner, *Soil Restoration,* 33; Shepard, *Food or Famine: The Challenge of Erosion* (New York: Macmillan, 1945), 36–55.

56. Hugh H. Bennett, "Permanent Peace—A World's Soil Problem" (address to the Seventh Annual Meeting of Friends of the Land, Houston, 7 November 1947), Bennett Papers, box 11, file 32; "Good soil is the hub" quote taken from pamphlet prepared by the Fifth Annual Texoma Soil Clinic, Madill, Okla., 11 June 1948, located in Bennett Papers, "Correspondence File," box 1; Walter C. Lowdermilk, "The Flag Is on the Plow," speech located in Henry A. Wallace Vice-Presidential Papers, FDR Library, box 45, "Lob-Lou."

57. On international aspects of permanent agriculture, see Faulkner, *A Second Look*, 176–77; see also "Wallace Encourages International Cooperation," *Courier-Journal* (Louisville), October 1942, located in Tugwell Papers, box 14, file 4; see also Bert D. Robinson, "'The Shape of a Better World' Seen in Land Meeting in Louisville and Memphis," *Soil Conservation* 8 (December 1942): 127–31; Hugh H. Bennett, "Permanent Peace: A World's Soil Problem," Bennett Papers, box 14, file 4; see also Hugh H. Bennett, "Soil Conservation and National Security" (speech at Staunton, Va., 3 August 1950), Bennett Papers, box 13, file 26; and Hugh H. Bennett, "Conservation Against the Background of War" (speech presented ca. October 1941), Bennett Papers, box 10, file 35.

CHAPTER 3. THE PUBLIC LIFE OF PERMANENT AGRICULTURE

1. Russell Lord to Morris L. Cooke, 14 November 1939, Cooke Papers, box 144, "Russell Lord."
2. See Richard Griffin, *The World of Robert Flaherty* (New York: Capo Press, 1972), 139–47; Richard Barsam, *The Vision of Robert Flaherty: The Artist as Myth and Filmmaker* (Bloomington: Indiana University Press, 1986), 72–84; William T. Murphy, *Robert Flaherty: A Guide to Reference and Research* (Boston: G. K. Hall, 1978), 31–37; Paul Rotha, *Robert Flaherty: A Biography* (Philadelphia: University of Pennsylvania Press, 1983); "Beauty, Danger and Terror," *The Land* 1 (autumn 1941): ii–iv; the script of *The Land* is reprinted in Russell Lord and Kate Lord, *Forever the Land* (New York: Harper & Brothers, 1951), 21–35.
3. Aldo Leopold, *A Sand County Almanac* (1953; reprint, New York: Oxford University Press, 1966), 225; Hugh H. Bennett, "Effective Soil Conservation Demands Level Thinking" (speech to Seventh Annual Meeting of Friends of the Land, Milwaukee, 20 September 1947), Bennett Papers, box 11, file 20; Aldo Leopold, "Land Use and Democracy," *Audubon* 44 (September 1947): 359–65; Hugh H. Bennett, "The Coming Technological Revolution on the Land" (speech presented at Princeton University, 2 October 1946), box 12, file 37, Bennett Papers, Archives of American Agriculture, Parks Memorial Library, Iowa State University.
4. National Commission on Conservation Education, *Report of the National Commission on Policies in Conservation Education* 1 (February 1948): 1–5; George E. Barnes, "Conservation in the Classroom," *Soil Conservation* 6 (October 1940): 87–89; Hugh H. Bennett, "Education for Soil Conservation," *National Education Association Journal* 30 (January 1941): 8–11.
5. Louis Bromfield, *Pleasant Valley* (New York: Harper & Brothers, 1945), 260–62; Russell Lord, "If My Land Cry," *The Land* 3 (summer 1943): 70.
6. Hugh H. Bennett to Morris L. Cooke, 13 July 1938, Cooke Papers, box 140; on Friends of the Land, see Cooke Papers, boxes 140–44; see also Lord and Lord, *Forever the Land*, 46–195; and Bromfield, *Pleasant Valley*, 260–65.
7. The founding manifesto is located in Cooke Papers, boxes 140–41; see also Lord and Lord, *Forever the Land*, 1–10; final quote from Rexford Tugwell, "Proceedings," *The Land* 4 (winter 1945).
8. Correspondence between Russell Lord and Rexford Tugwell, Tugwell Papers, box 14, "Russell Lord."
9. "Personal Mention," *The Land* 5 (summer 1946): 139; Lord and Lord, *Forever the Land*, 114, 196; on financial affairs, see Cooke Papers, box 141, files 1 and 2, "Friends of the Land."
10. Lord and Lord, *Forever the Land*, 74–109, 179–80, 340–41.

11. Randal Beeman interview with Professor David E. Wright (Department of History of Science, Michigan State University) in Little Rock, Arkansas, June 1994; Bromfield quoted in "Review," *Farm Journal* 5 (summer 1950): 266–67.

12. See "Proceedings," *The Land* 2 (July 1942): 81–136; "Proceedings," *The Land* 6 (Summer 1947): 134–36; Lord, *Forever the Land,* 178, 334–45; Charles Little, ed., *Louis Bromfield at Malabar: Writings on Farming and Country Life* (Baltimore: Johns Hopkins University Press, 1988), xviii; see also file "Friends of the Land," PA box 25–562, box 14–279, Ohio State Historical Society, Columbus, Ohio.

13. Hugh H. Bennett, "Education for Soil Conservation," *National Education Association Journal* 30 (January 1941).

14. "Land Week," *The Land* 10 (winter 1950–51): 586–87; see also Lord and Lord, *Forever the Land,* 40–41, 194–213, 256–59; "Proceedings," *The Land* 5 (autumn 1946): 193.

15. Evidence of the credence given to Bromfield, Bennett, and Cooke is suggested in correspondence with Vice President Henry A. Wallace in the Microfilm Papers of Henry A. Wallace, University of Iowa Library.

16. Hugh H. Bennett, "Conservation Farming is High Production Farming" (speech presented in Athens, Ga., 1 March 1943), Bennett Papers, box 10, file 47; Vernon G. Carter, "Education, Resources and This War," *National Education Association Journal* 32 (February 1943): 41–42; Otis W. Freeman, "Conservation as a Post-war Problem," *Education* 65 (January 1945): 316–22.

17. See Sir Albert Howard, "Mr. Faulkner Has a Touch of Genius," *The Land* 3 (1943–44): 155–61; see also entire issues of *The Land* 4 (summer 1943), and *The Land* 5 (autumn 1946); on attention to Faulkner, see H. A. Wallace to Russell Lord, 4 October 1943, Wallace Microfilm Papers, IA 25–290; Hugh H. Bennett, "The Abolition of the Plow," *New Republic* 4 (October 1943): 154–57; "Down with the Plow," *Time,* 26 July 1943, 44; on Faulkner's walk, see Edward Faulkner, *A Second Look* (Norman: University of Oklahoma Press, 1947), vii–10; on support from the permanent agriculture camp, see John F. Hensler, "My Faulknerizer," *The Land* 4 (winter 1945): 83–84; Lord and Lord, *Forever the Land,* 38; Louis Bromfield, "Trash Farming at Malabar," *The Land* 4 (winter 1945): 83–84; Edward Faulkner and Richard Bradfield, "To Plow or Not to Plow," *House and Garden,* March 1944, 100–101.

18. Lord and Lord, *Forever the Land,* 338–40; Chester C. Davis, "Unfinished Business," *The Land* 5 (winter 1945–46): 101–3; Henry B. Miller to Harry S. Truman, 17 February 1951, Harry S. Truman Presidential Library, Independence, Missouri, Harry S. Truman White House Central Files (hereafter cited as Truman Papers), President's Personal File, OF 660, box 1555.

19. On criticisms of Faulkner, see William A. Albrect, "The Indictment Will Not Stand," H. E. Middleton, "In the Face of Known Facts," F. L. Duley, "No Contribution or Check . . . Too Many Assumptions," Firman Bear, "Faulkner's Folly," and Paul W. Chapman, "Shall We Change Symbols," all in *The Land* 3 (summer 1943): 71–79.

20. Emil Truog, "Plowman's Folly Refuted," *Harper's,* July 1944, 73–177; see also Emil Truog, "Organics Only?—Bunkum!" *The Land* 5 (autumn 1946): 315–23; Donald P. Hopkins, *Chemicals, Humus and the Soil* (London: Faber and Faber, 1945), 237–39.

21. Paul Appleby, "Appetite First," *Nation,* 25 September 1943, 348–51; for opposition to the "coercive" aspect of permanent agriculture, see Karl B. Mickey, *Man and the Soil* (Chicago: International Harvester, 1945), 96–97; Clarence Armstrong, "Ridiculous," *Nation,* 13 November 194, 567; see also "The Farmer and the

Plow," *Nation*, 12 June 1944, 714; and "Two Revolutions in Plowing," *Nation*, 9 October 1943, 412–13.

22. Russell Lord, "Shocking!" *Nation*, 13 November 1943, 567; Faulkner, *A Second Look*, 3–12, 81; Edward Faulkner, *Soil Restoration* (London: Michael Joseph, 1953), 20–29, 198.

23. See *The Land* (1950): 309, 311, and 350; see also L. G. Samsel, "Is Special Equipment Needed for Stubble Mulch Farming?" *Journal of Soil and Water Conservation* 1 (October 1946): 67–70.

24. Jonathan Forman, "Words, Words, Words," *The Land* 11 (summer 1952): 177.

25. P. V. Cardon, "Our Aim: An Introduction," in *Grass: The Yearbook of Agriculture, 1948*, ed. Alfred Stefferud (Washington, D.C.: USDA, 1948), 1.

26. Little, *Louis Bromfield at Malabar*, 221.

27. True D. Morse, "Watch Out Before You Buy That Farm," *Science Digest* 16 (December 1944): 64–66; "If GI Joe Goes Back to the Land," *Fortune*, September 1944, 166–68; "Poor Time to Start Farming," *Wallaces' Farmer*, 7 April 1945, 6; Harold Titus, "Please! No More Crackpot Land Schemes for Veterans," *Saturday Evening Post*, 18 November 1944, 24–25, 47–48; "Reconversion on the Farm," *Business Week*, 24 February 1945, 123; "To Hold Up Farm Incomes," *Wallaces' Farmer*, 6 October 1945, 1; see also National Association of State Universities and Land Grant Colleges, *Postwar Agricultural Policy* (National Association of State Universities and Land Grant Colleges, October 1944), 39–47.

28. Alan I. Marcus and Howard P. Segal, *Technology in America: A Brief History* (San Diego: Harcourt Brace Jovanovich, 1989), 280–83; see also Crop Engineering Research Branch, *List of Publications* (Beltsville, Md.: USDA, 1967).

29. USDA Report, "The Fertilizer Situation for 1947–48," Official Correspondence, box 7, "Fertilizer," Clinton P. Anderson Papers, Harry S. Truman Presidential Library, Independence, Missouri.

30. Arthur C. Bunce, "Using Our Soils for War Production," *Wartime Farm and Food Policy*, Pamphlet No. 7 (Ames: Iowa State College Press, 1943), 1–29; Claude R. Wickard, "Moving Forward Together" (speech presented to Kiwanis Club, Richmond, Ind., 9 May 1945), box 48, "Speeches January–June 1945," Claude R. Wickard Papers, Harry S. Truman Presidential Library, Independence, Missouri (hereafter cited as Wickard Papers); Faulkner, *Soil Restoration*, 107; Clarence J. McCormick, "Strengthening the Family Farm" (speech presented to Annual Meeting of the Production and Marketing Administration, Chicago, Ill., 12 December 1950), Official File 1 (1949) to 1 (January–March, 1951), Truman Papers, box 2, file 5.

31. Charles F. Brannan to Allan B. Kline, 15 September 1950, Official File 1 (1949) to 1 (January–March 1951), Truman Papers, box 2, file 4.

32. N. E. Dodd to Harry S. Truman, 23 July 1947, Official File 1, Truman Papers, box 1, file 3.

33. Harry S. Truman, "Prepared Statement," 13 June 1952, President's Personal File 6113, Truman Papers; on poor funding for agricultural conservation and interagency divisions, see Clarence J. McCormick, "Conservation Production" (speech presented to State Meeting of SCS District Conservationists, Columbus, Ohio, 17 February 1952), Official File 1 (February 1952), Truman Papers, box 3, file 5; Clarence J. McCormick, "Agriculture's Role in the Nation's Peace Program" (speech presented to Production Marketing Association County and Community Committeemen, Huron, S.D., 15 February 1952), Official File 1 (February 1952), Truman Papers, box 3, file 5; Milton Eisenhower, "Do We Get Our Money's Worth Out of Soil Conservation?" *Farm Journal*, March 1948; Charles F. Brannan

to State Agricultural Department Heads, 9 November 1951, Official File 1 (April–June 1951) to (March 1952), Truman Papers, box 3, file 4; Clarence J. McCormick to Democratic Banquet, Kansas City, Kans., 25 January 1952, Official File 1 (April–June 1951) to (March 1952), Truman Papers, box 3, file 5; on the push for a decentralized soil conservation, see "America's Crossroads," *American Soil Conservation District News* 2 (1 November 1951): 1.

34. See comments in *Nature* 37 (March 1944): 145; Alexander F. Skutch, "The Tangled Strands of Conservation," *Nature* 47 (May 1954): 258–60; Bernard Devoto, "Conservation: Down and On the Way Out," *Harper's*, August 1952, 66–74; on politics and conservation, see J. B. Oakes, "Conservation: The Party Platforms," *New York Times*, 3 August 1952; on Resources for the Future (RSFF) see Cooke Papers, box 157; on the decline of Friends of the Land, see material in Tugwell Papers, box 14, "Russell Lord," and in Cooke Papers, boxes 140–44; see also Jonathan Forman, "Growth and Change," *The Land* 11 (winter 1953): 351–52; and *The Land* 13 (spring 1954): 87–99.

35. Russell Lord, "The Whole Landscape: An Appraisal," *The Land* 11 (winter 1951): 413.

36. Paul B. Sears, *The Biology of the Living Landscape* (London: Allen Unwin, 1964); Paul Sears, "Ethics, Aesthetics and the Balance of Nature," in *Perspectives on Conservation*, ed. Henry Jarrett (Baltimore: Johns Hopkins University Press, 1958), 106–14; Vernon Gill Carter and Tom Dale, *Topsoil and Civilization* (Norman: University of Oklahoma Press, 1955), 257–75.

37. Robert M. Salter, "The Job Ahead" (speech to National Association of Soil Conservation Districts, Cleveland, Ohio, 28 February 1952), General Correspondence, Cooke Papers, box 157, "Robert M. Salter."

38. Charles R. Koch, "William Albrect Sums Up a Career in Soil Research," *Farm Quarterly* 15 (winter 1960); Charles Walters, ed., *The Albrect Papers*, vol. 2 (Kansas City: Acres USA, 1975), ix–182, esp. 112–16; Lewis Herber, *Our Synthetic Environment* (New York: Knopf, 1962), 1–239; Johnson D. Hill and Walter E. Stuermann, *Roots in the Soil: An Introduction to a Philosophy of Agriculture* (New York: Philosophical Library, 1964), 14–20; on traces of ecological agriculture in the land-grant colleges in the late 1950s, see George D. Scarseth, *Man and His Earth* (Ames: Iowa State University Press, 1962), 64–116, 181–99; and Firman E. Bear, *Earth: The Stuff of Life* (Norman: University of Oklahoma Press, 1962); Firman E. Bear, ed., *Soil Science: Food for America's Future* (New York: McGraw-Hill, 1960), 3–16.

39. Helen Nearing and Scott Nearing, *Living the Good Life: How to Live Safely and Sanely in a Troubled World* (1954; reprint, New York: Schocken Books, 1970), 3–177; Helen Nearing and Scott Nearing, *Continuing the Good Life: Half a Century of Homesteading* (New York: Schocken Books, 1979), 1–185; see also John A. Saltmarsh, *Scott Nearing: An Intellectual Biography* (Philadelphia: Temple University Press, 1991), 245–64.

CHAPTER 4. SOIL AND THE CRISIS OF HUMANITY

1. Samuel P. Hays, "From Conservation to Environment: Environmental Politics in the United States Since World War II," *Environmental Review* 6 (fall 1982): 14–41; Donald Fleming, "Roots of the New Conservation Movement," in *Perspectives in American History*, ed. Donald Fleming and Bernard Bailyn (New York: Macmillan, 1971), 7–63; and Kirkpatrick Sale, *The Green Revolution: The American Environmental Movement, 1962–1992* (New York: Hill and Wang, 1993).

2. Osha Gray Davidson, *Broken Heartland: The Rise of America's Rural Ghetto* (Iowa City: University of Iowa Press, 1996), 15–16; John L. Shover, *First Majority-Last Minority: The Transforming of Rural Life in America* (De Kalb: Northern Illinois University Press, 1986), 252.

3. Davidson, *Broken Heartland,* 28; Shover, *First Majority–Last Minority,* 252.

4. Davidson, *Broken Heartland,* 28; Shover, *First Majority–Last Minority,* 252; see also Orville L. Freeman, "Statement," in *Food and Agriculture: A Program for the 1960s* (Washington, D.C.: USDA, 1962), 1–5.

5. Lester R. Brown, *Foreign Agricultural Economic Report No. 11* (Washington, D.C.: USDA, 1963), 1–10; see also Lester R. Brown Oral History Interview Transcript, AC 74–185, Lyndon B. Johnson Presidential Library, University of Texas, Austin, Texas (hereafter cited as LBJ Library); Lily Kay, *The Molecular Vision: Caltech, the Rockefeller Foundation, and the Rise of the New Biology* (New York: Oxford University Press, 1993).

6. Fairfield Osborn, ed., *Our Crowded Planet: Essays on the Pressures of Population* (New York: Doubleday, 1962), 7–23; see also Fairfield Osborn, *The Limits of Earth* (Boston: Little, Brown, 1953), 3–5; Fairfield Osborn, *Our Plundered Planet* (Boston: Little, Brown, 1948), vii–201; Erik Eckholm, *Losing Ground: Environmental Stress and World Food Prospects* (New York: Norton, 1976), 1–23; Paul R. Ehrlich, *The Population Bomb* (New York: Ballentine Books, 1968); Garrett Hardin, "The Tragedy of the Commons," *Science,* 30 July 1968, 99; and Michael Hamilton, ed., *This Little Planet* (New York: Scribner, 1970).

7. William A. Albrect, "Wastebasket of the Earth," *Bulletin of Atomic Scientists* 17 (October 1961): 335–40.

8. James Whorton, *Before Silent Spring: Pesticides and Public Health in Pre-DDT America* (Princeton, N.J.: Princeton University Press, 1974); Pete Daniel, "A Rogue Bureaucracy: The USDA Fire Ant Campaign of the Late 1950s," *Agricultural History* 64 (spring 1990): 91–121; Stewart Udall, Oral History Interview, Tape 1 of 1, 16 December 1969, LBJ Library.

9. See Linda J. Lear, "Bombshell in Beltsville: The USDA and the Challenge of Silent Spring," *Agricultural History* 66 (spring 1992): 151–70; Linda J. Lear, *Rachel Carson: Witness for Nature* (New York: Henry Holt, 1997); Thomas R. Dunlap, *DDT: Scientists, Citizens, and Public Policy* (Princeton, N.J.: Princeton University Press, 1981); Frank M. Graham, *Since Silent Spring* (Boston: Houghton Mifflin, 1970); John H. Perkins, *Pesticides and Politics: Insects, Experts and the Insecticide Crisis* (New York: Plenum, 1982); Christopher J. Bosso, *Pesticides and Politics: The Life Cycle of a Public Issue* (Pittsburgh: University of Pittsburgh Press, 1987).

10. Barry Commoner, *Science and Survival* (New York: Viking, 1963), 10–22; Dorothy M. Slusser and Gerald H. Slusser, *Technology: The God That Failed* (Philadelphia: Westminster Press, 1971), 80–105.

11. Alan I. Marcus and Howard P. Segal, *Technology in America: A Brief History* (San Diego: Harcourt Brace Jovanovich, 1989), 315–64.

12. Barry Commoner, *The Closing Circle: Nature, Man and Technology* (New York: Knopf, 1971), 153–295.

13. See collections of the Green Center (New Alchemy Institute), Archives of American Agriculture, Special Collections, Parks Memorial Library, Iowa State University. John Todd, quote from *New Alchemy Institute Bulletin,* 2 November 1971, located in "The New Alchemy Institute: Search for an Alternative Agriculture," *Science,* 28 February 1975, 728.

14. John L. Hess and Karen Hess, "The Green Revolution," in *Political Ecology, ed.* Alexander Cockburn and James Ridgeway (New York: Times Books, 1979), 180–89.

15. Kai Curry-Lindhal, *Conservation for Survival: An Ecological Strategy* (New York: William Morrow, 1972), 305–7.

16. Barry Commoner, "Summary of the Conference: On the Meaning of Ecological Failures in International Development," in *The Careless Technology: Ecology and International Development*, ed. M. Taghi Farvar and John P. Milton (Garden City, N.Y.: Natural History Press, 1972), xxi–xxix; Susan DeMarco and Susan Sechler, *The Fields Have Turned Brown: Four Essays on World Hunger* (Washington, D.C.: Agribusiness Accountability Project, 1975), 63; Robert Steffen to MacDonald R. Mitchell, 18 April 1971, box 1, file 2, Archives of American Agriculture, Special Collections, Parks Memorial Library, Iowa State University, Ames, Iowa (hereafter cited as Steffen Papers).

17. Richard Merrill quoted in "New Alchemy Institute: Search for an Alternative Agriculture," *Science*, 28 February 1975, 727; Robert Steffen to Mrs. Richard Weirc, 27 June 1972, Steffen Papers, box 1, file 2.

18. Jim Hightower, *Hard Tomatoes, Hard Times: A Report of the Agribusiness Accountability Project on the Failure of America's Land Grant College Complex* (Cambridge, Mass.: Schenkman, 1973); for a more conspiratorial view, see Charles Walters, *Angry Testament* (Kansas City: Halcyon House, 1969); see also Robert Steffen, draft of article for *Organic Farming*, Steffen Papers, box 1, file 2; Jackson, *New Roots for American Agriculture* (San Francisco: Friends of the Earth, 1980), 38; Morton Rothstein, "The Big Farm: Abundance and Scale in American Agriculture," *Agricultural History* 49 (October 1975): 583–97; Wayne D. Rassmussen, "The Impact of Technological Change on American Agriculture, 1862–1962," *Journal of Economic History* 22 (December 1962); Wayne D. Rassmussen, "Advances in American Agriculture: The Mechanical Tomato Harvester as a Case Study," *Technology and Culture* 9 (October 1968): 531–43; Sam B. Hilliard, "The Dynamics of Power: Recent Trends in Mechanization on the Farm," *Technology and Culture* 13 (January 1972): 1–24.

19. Wendell Berry, *The Unsettling of America: Culture and Agriculture* (San Francisco: Sierra Club, 1977), 19.

20. Ibid., 143–69; see also Wendell Berry, *What Are People For?* (San Francisco: North Point Press, 1990), 123–25; Wendell Berry, *Home Economics* (San Francisco: North Point Press, 1987), 123–36.

21. Commoner, *Closing Circle*, 284.

CHAPTER 5. ECOLOGICAL INSPIRATION FOR AGRICULTURE

1. On the quasi-spiritual aspect of sustainable agriculture, see Mike Gangwer, "Sustainability and American Agriculture," *Pacific Northwest Sustainable Agriculture* 4 (December 1992): 7; see also Geoffrey R. Lilburne, "Theology and Land Use," *Vital Speeches* 53 (15 December 1986): 139–41; Jay P. Wagner, "Monks Making Changes on the Farm," *Des Moines Register*, 10 July 1994, 1J.

2. Frank N. Egerton, "Changing Concepts of the Balance of Nature," *Quarterly Review of Biology* 48 (1973): 322–50, esp. 324, 335, 341.

3. Donald Worster, *Nature's Economy: A History of Ecological Ideas*, 2d ed. (Cambridge: Cambridge University Press, 1994), 294–311; Frank B. Golley, *A History of the Ecosystem Concept in Ecology: More Than the Sum of the Parts* (New Haven, Conn.: Yale University Press, 1993), 109–40, esp. 135.

4. Worster, *Nature's Economy*, 306; Golley, *History of the Ecosystem Concept*, 95.

5. Stanley A. Cain, "Population Ecology" (speech presented to the American Assembly on the Population Dilemma, Alma, Mich., 9 April 1967), AC 69-12,

Stanley A. Cain Papers, LBJ Library (hereafter cited as Cain Papers); Stanley A. Cain, "The Importance of Ecology in Land Use Planning" (speech presented to Conferencio Latino Americana, 27 March 1968), AC 69-12, Cain Papers; Stanley A. Cain, "The Political Ecology of Conservation" (speech presented to Annual Convention of the Federation of Western Outdoor Clubs, 5 September 1965), AC 69-12, Cain Papers; on the limitations of analysis, see Stanley A. Cain, "Man and His Environment" (speech presented to International Horticultural Congress, College Park, Maryland, 19 August 1966), AC 69-12, Cain Papers.

6. Cain, "Man and His Environment."

7. Paul B. Sears, "Ecology: A Subversive Subject," Robert B. Platt and John N. Wolfe, "Introduction," W. Frank Blair, "The Case for Bio-ecology," and Eugene P. Odum, "The New Ecology," all in *Bioscience* 14 (July 1964): 9–43; see also Paul B. Sears, *Where There Is Life* (New York: Dell, 1962), 21–41, 176–87.

8. Paul Sears quoted in "The Environmental Revolution," a proposal for a National Education Network television series on the environment, ca. 1965, WHCF 648, box 19, 1–8, Richard Goodwin Papers, LBJ Library; Osborn Segerberg, *Where Have All the Flowers, Fishes, Birds, Trees, Water, and Air Gone?* (New York: Van Rees, 1971), 90–95; Charles A. Reich, *The Greening of America* (New York: Random House 1970, 1971), 382–83, 425.

9. An extreme vision of ecological holism is Clive Enthwhistle, "Holopolis: Herald of a Great Society," (2 July 1965), box 19 (648) Goodwin Papers; Reich, *Greening of America*, 1–17.

10. News accounts are located in boxes 1–11, file boxes 1 and 2, Scott and Helen Nearing Papers, Mugar Library, Special Collections, Boston University.

11. On Scott and Helen Nearing, see Roy Reed, "The Nearings: After 43 Years on the Land, They're Still 'Living the Good Life,'" *New York Times,* 7 May 1975; Peter Gelzing, "The Counter–Culture Pioneers," *Boston Herald,* 17 June 1979; "Scott Nearing: The Man and the Monument, 1883–1983," *New Socialist* 9 (spring 1983): 101–7.

12. On 1970s communalism, see Juliette de Bairacli Levy, *Nature's Children* (New York: Schenken, 1971); "Prophets of a Good Life," *Newsweek,* 14 September 1970, 102–3; John Thompson, "Getting Away from It All," *Harper's,* November 1970, 129–30; John N. Cook, "Scott Nearing's Ninety-three-Year Plan," *Horticulture* 55 (November 1976): 23–30; see also E. F. Schumacher, *Small Is Beautiful: Economics As If People Mattered* (London: Blond Briggs, 1973); Greg Watson, "Who Was Bucky Fuller, and Why Is the Geodesic Dome the Least of His Ideas?" *New Alchemy* 13 (fall 1983): 14; on the New Alchemy Institute, see Kate Eldred, "Promise Rediscovered: New Alchemy's First Twenty Years," *New Alchemy* 11 (fall 1981): 4–18.

13. Wade Green, "The New Alchemists," *New York Times Magazine,* 8 August 1976, 4, 13, 32, 42; Paul T. Libassi, "The Transmuted Farm," *The Sciences* 15 (August/ September 1975): 11–15.

14. See Robert Steffen papers at the Archives of American Agriculture, Special Collections, Parks Memorial Library, Iowa State University; see also Fred Thomas, "Boys Town Farm Boss 'Conservationist of the Year,'" *Omaha Sunday World-Herald,* ca. September 1975; Robert Steffen to Mr. Dave Garcia, Redding, Calif., ca. 1971, Steffen Papers, file 1, box 2; Robert Steffen, draft of article "Agriculture and Your Environment," October 1971, Steffen Papers; file 2, box 1; Dave Sink, "Boys Town Ends Organic Farming," *Omaha Sun,* 13 October 1977, 1.

15. Garth Youngberg, "The Alternative Agriculture Movement," *Policy Studies Journal* 6 (summer 1978): 524–30; on consumer demands, see Richard Merrill,

"Ecosystem Farming," in *Radical Ecology,* ed. Alexander Cockburn and James Ridgeway (New York: Times Books, 1979), 217–28.

16. On the persistence of holistic thought in the 1950s, see William A. Albrect, "Wastebasket of the Earth," *Bulletin of Atomic Scientists* 17 (October 1961): 335–40; George D. Scarseth, *Man and His Earth* (Ames: Iowa State University Press, 1962), 64–116; Firman E. Bear, *Earth: The Stuff of Life* (Norman: University of Oklahoma Press, 1962); Lewis Herber, *Our Synthetic Environment* (New York: Knopf, 1962), 1–239.

17. Orville L. Freeman, "Agriculture 2000: Resources" (speech presented to National Association of Soil and Water Conservation Districts, Cincinnati, Ohio, 6 February 1967), box 16, Daniel Pierson Papers, LBJ Library.

18. See Orville L. Freeman, "Statement," in *Food and Agriculture: A Program for the 1960s* (Washington, D.C.: USDA, 1962), iii–vii; Orville L. Freeman, "Rural Resources in the 1960s" (speech presented to the National Conference on Land and People, Washington, D.C., 15 January 1962), box 11, Orville L. Freeman Papers, John F. Kennedy Presidential Library, Boston, Massachusetts; Orville L. Freeman, "Conservation of Man's Total Environment" (speech presented at USDA, June 1967), box 25, Freeman Papers; Orville L. Freeman, "Remarks to International Shade Tree Conference," Philadelphia, Pennsylvania, 29 August 1967, box 25, Ceil Bellinger Office Files, LBJ Library.

19. Roger Mitchell, "Agronomy in a Global Age," in *Agronomy in Today's Society,* ed. J.W. Pendleton, American Society of Agronomy Special Publication No. 33 (Madison, Wisc.: American Society of Agronomy, 1978), 1–5.

20. Wesley F. Buchele, "Healing This Wounded Earth: An Agricultural Engineer's Proposal," *Webbs Ag World* 1 (December 1975): 1–5; see also Lloyd F. Seatz, ed., *Ecology and Agricultural Production* (Knoxville: University of Tennessee Press, 1973).

21. Charles V. Kidd, "The Evolution of Sustainability," *Journal of Agricultural and Environmental Ethics* 3 (1992): 2–23; see also Ernest Callenbach, *Ecotopia: The Notebook and Reports of William Weston* (New York: Bantam, 1975).

22. Lester R. Brown, *The Twenty-ninth Day: Accommodating Human Needs and Numbers to the Earth's Resources* (New York: Norton, 1978), 16–25.

23. Gerald O. Barney, *The Global 2000 Report to the President—Entering the 21st Century,* vol. 1 (New York: Pergamon, 1980), 3, 94–100; see also Jeremy Rifkin, *Entropy: Into the Greenhouse World* (New York: Viking, 1980), 52.

24. Lester Brown, *Building a Sustainable Society* (New York: Norton, 1981); Robert Theobald, ed., *Futures Conditional* (Indianapolis: Bobbs-Merrill, 1972); Pierre Eliot Trudeau, "Remarks on the Opening of the New Alchemists Ark, Spry Point, Prince Edward Island," ca. 1980, Papers of the New Alchemy Institute/Green Center, Archives of American Agriculture, file 8, box 1; Erik Eckholm, *Losing Ground: Environmental Stress and World Food Prospects* (New York: Norton, 1976); Richard A. Falk, *This Endangered Planet: Prospects and Proposals for Human Survival* (New York: Random House,1971), 260–63; James C. Coomer, "The Nature of the Quest for a Sustainable Society," Paul R. Ehrlich, "Diversity and the Stable State," Tom Stonier, "Science, Technology and Emerging Post-industrial Society," and Edward Clark and W. John Coletta, "Ecosystem Education: A Strategy for Social Change," all in *Quest for a Sustainable Society,* James C. Coomer, ed. (New York: Pergamon, 1979), 1–31, 70–88, 183–200.

25. Schumacher, *Small Is Beautiful,* 28–30; Bill Mollison, *Permaculture: A Designer's Manual* (Tyalgum, Australia: Tagari, 1988), 507–10; Wes Jackson, *New Roots for American Agriculture* (San Francisco: Friends of the Earth, 1980), 82–89;

on defining sustainability, see Gordon K. Douglass, "The Meanings of Agricultural Sustainability," in *Agricultural Sustainability in a Changing World Order.* ed. Gordon K. Douglass (Boulder, Colo.: Westview Press, 1984), 3–15; and Robert Rodale, "The Past and Future of Regenerative Agriculture," in *Sustainable Agriculture and Integrated Farming Systems,* ed. Thomas C. Edens, Cynthia Fridgen, and Susan L. Battenfield (East Lansing: Michigan State University Press, 1985), 312–17.

26. Wendell Berry, *What Are People For?* (San Francisco: North Point Press, 1990), 125; see also Wendell Berry, *A Continuous Harmony: Essays Cultural and Agricultural* (San Diego: Harcourt Brace Jovanovich, 1970), 86–168; Wendell Berry, *Standing by Words* (San Francisco: North Point Press, 1983), 64–79; Wendell Berry, *Home Economics* (San Francisco: North Point Press, 1990), 123–92.

27. Cornucopia Project, *Empty Breadbasket: The Coming Challenge to America's Food Supply and What We Can Do About It* (Emmaus, Pa.: Rodale Press, 1981), 111–77.

28. See Claude Aubert, "Conversion to Biological Agriculture," in *Basic Techniques in Ecological Farming,* ed. Stuart Hall (Boston: Bagel, 1978), 22–25.

29. J. Artie Browning, "Relevance of Knowledge About Natural Ecosystems to Develop Pest Management Programs for Agroecosystems," *Proceedings of the American Phytopathological Society* 1 (1974): 191–95.

30. V. G. Thomas and P. G. Kevan, "Basic Principles of Agroecology and Sustainable Agriculture," *Journal of Agricultural and Environmental Ethics* 3 (1993): 1–19.

31. Stephen D. Gliesman, "An Agroecological Approach to Sustainable Agriculture," in *Meeting the Expectations of the Land: Systems in Sustainable Agriculture and Stewardship,* ed. Wes Jackson, Wendell Berry, and Bruce Colman (San Francisco: North Point Press, 1984), 153–59.

32. Miguel Altieri, *Agroecology: The Scientific Basis of Alternative Agriculture* (Berkeley: Division of Biological Control, University of California, 1983), 129–31.

33. Miguel Altieri and Helen Vukasin, *Environmentally Sound Small-Scale Agricultural Projects: Guidelines for Planning* (Berkeley: Godel, 1988), 4–16.

34. Altieri, *Agroecology,* 30–31.; see also C. Ronald Carroll, John H. Vandermeer, and Peter Rosset, *Agroecology* (New York: McGraw-Hill, 1990).

35. Richard R. Harwood, *Organic Farming Research at the Rodale Center* (Emmaus, Pa.: Rodale Press, 1982), 3–4.

36. Ibid., 3–4; Borlie L. Schmidt, "Organics on the Farm and in the Garden," *Science, Food and Agriculture,* March 1984, 23–26.

37. Rodale, "Past and Future of Regenerative Agriculture, 312–17.

38. H. H. Koepf, *Biodynamic Agriculture: An Introduction* (Spring Valley, N.Y.: Anthroposophic Press, 1976), 1–15; see also H. H. Koepf, "Soil Management," Heinz Grotzke, "Thoughts on Biodynamics," and Anne E. Marshall, "A Goethian Approach to Agriculture," all in *Biodynamics* 133 (winter 1980): 1–65; on the history of biodynamic agriculture, see Fredrich Sattler and Eckard V. Westinghausen, *Biodynamic Farming Practice* (Cambridge: Cambridge University Press, 1992), 1–12.

39. Masanobu Fukuoka, *The One Straw Revolution: An Introduction to Natural Farming* (Emmaus, Pa.: Rodale Press, 1978); see also Emily M. Bernstein, "Chinese Use Old Ways to Advance," *Des Moines Register,* 15 August 1993.

40. James Risser, "A Revolution in the Making on Iowa, Nebraska Farms," *Des Moines Register,* 12 June 1989; Thompson On-Farm Research, 1999 Report "Alternatives in Agriculture," 1–1.

41. Anne Schauer, ed.. *The Thompson Farm On-Farm Research* (Emmaus, Pa.: Rodale Press, 1991), 14–15; see also the Regenerative Agriculture Association, *The Thompson Farm: Nature's Ag School* (Emmaus, Pa.: Rodale Press, 1985); Patrick Slattery, "Iowa State Discovers Nature's Ag School," reprint from *New Farm* (September–October 1982): 1–10.

42. Risser, "A Revolution in the Making on Iowa, Nebraska Farms."

43. "Intentional Communities: Some Inside Views," *Mother Earth News*, July–August 1984, 82–85; and Ernest Bauer, "Living the Good Life," *Mother Earth News Special*, spring 1989, 66–68; see also "Strip Intercropping Interest Grows," *Sustainable Farming News* 24 (December 1993): 1–2; Ecology Action, *Bountiful Gardens Catalog 1985* (Willits, Calif.: Ecology Action, 1985); Matthew Werners, "Earthworms: Renewers," *Sustainable Farming News* 3 (fall 1990): 1–2; *Missouri Farm* 7 (July–August 1990), entire issue; *BioOptions* 3 (fall 1983), esp. 1–6; Steve Van Gorder, "Alternative Aquaculture," *Alternative Aquaculture Network*, winter 1985, 1–2; "Seeds of Revolution: New, Low-Cost Crops Backed as an 'Alternative Agriculture' to Save U.S. Farmers," *Wall Street Journal*, 10 January 1986; Susan Kirr, "Ecologically Correct Clothes Made of Marijuana," *Des Moines Register*, 6 November 1994.

44. Keith Schneider et al., "The Regreening of America," *New Age Journal*, March 1986, 50–56, 85–88, 91, 93; Jane E. Brody, "Organic Farming Moves Toward Middle America," *New York Times Large Type Weekly*, 14 October 1985; Danita Allen, "Organic Farmers Sell 3$ Corn, 7$ Beans, 4.50$ Wheat," *Successful Farming* 84 (April 1986): 10-A; on infiltration into mainstream agriculture, see William Lockeretz and Sarah Wernck, "Commercial Organic Farming in the Corn Belt in Comparison to Conventional Practices," *Rural Sociology* 45 (winter 1980): 711.

45. Mollison, *Permaculture*, ix–12; on the intellectual atmosphere of permaculture, see J. E. Lovelock, *Gaia: A New Look at Life on Earth* (London: Oxford University Press, 1979).

46. Mollison, *Permaculture*, ix–4.

47. Paul T. Libassi, "A Transmuted Farm," *The Sciences* 15 (August/September 1975): 11–19; Nicholas Wade, "New Alchemy Institute: Search for an Alternative Agriculture," *Science* 187 (February 1975): 727–29; James K. Page Jr. and Wilson Clark, "The New Alchemy: How to Survive in Your Spare Time," *Smithsonian* 5 (February 1975): 82–89.

48. "Natural Farming," *New Alchemy Quarterly* 11 (spring 1983): 3–4; on the tools of permaculture, see *Whole Earth Epilog*, located in file 4, box 1, Green Center (New Alchemy Institute), Archives of American Agriculture, Parks Library; Walter Truett Anderson, "New Alchemy: Saving the World with Yankee Ingenuity?" *New Age Journal*, November 1984, 32–37; "Interview: John Todd," *Omni*, August 1984, 76–83.

49. Evan Eisenberg, "Back to Eden," *Atlantic Monthly*, November 1989, 57–74; Jackson, *New Roots for American Agriculture*; Wes Jackson and Marty Bender, "New Roots for American Agriculture," *Journal of Soil and Water Conservation* 36 (December 1981): 322–23; Wes Jackson, "Ecosystem Agriculture: The Marriage of Ecology and Agriculture," in *Global Perspectives on Agroecology and Sustainable Agriculture Systems*, vol. 1, ed. Patricia Allen and Debra Van Husen (Santa Cruz: University of California–Santa Cruz, 1989), 3–17; James Risser, "The Land Institute Forges the Future of Agriculture," *Des Moines Register*, 13 June 1984; Joan Morrison, "Land Institute's Perennial Grains Tempt Taste Buds," *Topeka Capitol-Journal*, 5 October 1992.

50. Wes Jackson and Marty Bender, "Horses or Horsepower," *Soft Energy Notes* 5 (July–August 1982): 70–73, 87; see also *Land Report* 4 (1987).

51. Wes Jackson, "On Becoming Native to This Place" (Twenty-eighth Paul Errington Memorial Lecture, Iowa State University, 24 March 1992); Wes Jackson, fund-raising letter on Matfield Green project, 1 April 1994; see also "Book Previews," *Land Report*, spring 1993, 25.

52. See C. Arden-Clarke, *The Environmental Effect of Conventional and Organic/Biological Farming Systems* (Oxford: Political Ecology Research Group, 1980), 64–66; Jennifer Curtis, with Lawrie Mott and Tom Kuhnle, *Harvest of Hope: The Potential for Alternative Agriculture to Reduce Pesticide Use;* "Farming, Wildlife Can Co-exist," *Wallaces' Farmer,* 12 March 1991, 68–69; C. Dean Freudenberger, *Global Dust Bowl* (Minneapolis, Minn.: Augsburg Fortress, 1990).

53. Robert C. Oelhaf, *Organic Agriculture : Economic and Ecological Comparisons with Conventional Methods* (New York: Wiley, 1978), 228; Charles C. Geisler, J. Tadlock Cowan, Michael R. Hattery, and Harvey M. Jacobs, "Sustained Land Productivity: Equity Consequences of Alternative Agricultural Technologies," in *The Social Consequences and Challenges of New Agricultural Technologies,* ed. Gigi M. Berardi and Charles C. Geisler (Boulder, Colo.: Westview, 1984), 213–36; Rod Swoboda, "Pegging the Costs of Low-Input Farming," *Wallaces' Farmer,* 13 February 1990, 12–13; James Risser, "Study Cites 'Exciting Implications' of Organic Farming," *Des Moines Register,* 11 November 1983; on the societal benefits of sustainable ecological agriculture, see Wanda Schmidt, "Cultivation of Mind and Soil," *Ecology and Farming* 2 (1991): 1; Thomas L. Dobbs and John D. Cole, "Potential Effects on Rural Economies of Conversion to Sustainable Farming Systems," *American Journal of Alternative Agriculture* 7 (1992): 70–75; Paul Lasley, Eric Hoiberg, and Gordon Bultena, "Is Sustainable Agriculture an Elixir for Rural Communities?" *American Journal of Alternative Agriculture* 8 (1993): 133–42; Jerry Aaker, *Livestock for a Small Planet: The Role of Animals in a Just and Sustainable World* (Washington, D.C.: Heifer Project International, 1994), 87–92.

CHAPTER 6. THE PUBLIC LIFE OF SUSTAINABLE AGRICULTURE

1. Randal Beeman, personal observation.

2. "Big Promoter Is Farm Boss at Boy's Town," *Omaha World-Herald,* 12 November 1971, 13.

3. Wendell Berry, *The Unsettling of America: Culture and Agriculture* (San Francisco: Sierra Club, 1977).

4. Evan Eisenberg, "Back to Eden," *Atlantic Monthly,* November 1989, 57–74.

5. Ibid., 65; on Wes Jackson as a communicator, see Brian Button, "Speaker: Follow Nature's Example," *Iowa State University Daily,* 26 March 1992, 1, 3; Karen Uhlenruth, "Roots of a Revolution," *Kansas City Star,* 27 June 1992, E1, E6–E7; Douglas Hand, "Breadbasket Ecology," *American Health* 8 (September 1989): 66–68; Barbara Joseph, "Ceremony Marks Plowing of Prairie," *Topeka Capital Journal,* 22 November 1992, 1H.

6. R. Neil Sampson, *Farmland or Wasteland: A Time to Choose* (Emmaus, Pa.: Rodale Press, 1981), 5–10; see also Frederick R. Steiner, *Soil Conservation in the United States: Policy and Planning* (Baltimore: Johns Hopkins University Press, 1990), 184–85.

7. Sampson, *Farmland or Wasteland,* 12–13; Lauren Soth, *The Farm Policy Game Play by Play* (Ames: Iowa State University Press, 1989); see also Don Muhm, "In Celebration of Soil Conservation," *Des Moines Register,* 20 September 1984, 1T.

8. Lauren Soth, "For Energy, Topsoil Crises, Rotation May Be the Answer,"

Des Moines Register, 3 April 1979; Robert Steffen, Statement to Secretary of Agriculture Bob Bergland, 4 December 1979, Steffen Papers, box 1, file 4; Jim Head, "Futuristic Farm Looks at Tomorrow's Farming," *Wallaces' Farmer,* 6 June 1979, 10.

9. Osha Gray Davidson, *Broken Heartland: The Rise of America's Rural Ghetto* (Iowa City: University of Iowa Press, 1996), 17, 35.

10. Mike Williams, "Back to Basics: Sustainable Agriculture Both Praised and Questioned," *Iowa Farmer Today,* 12 August 1988, 14A; Lauren Soth, "Just How Bad Is It on the Farm?" *Des Moines Register,* 3 February 1986; "Soil Erosion and the Iowa Soil 2000 Program" (Ames: ISU Cooperative Extension Service, PM-1056, July 1982), 1–8; Marty Strange, *Family Farming: A New Economic Vision* (Lincoln: University of Nebraska Press, 1986), 13–30.

11. Thompson On-Farm Research, 1999 Report "Alternatives in Agriculture," Boone, Iowa, 1-1–1-19; Jerry Perkins, "Practical Farmers Looking for Ways to Grow," *Des Moines Register,* 8 February 1987, 1A, 2F; Practical Farmers of Iowa, *Newsletter,* spring 1989, 1–6; Mike Williams, "Innovation: Keeps Farm in Spotlight" and "Sustainable Agriculture Attracts International Attention," *Iowa Farmer Today,* 13 August 1988, 1A; 15A; "PFI Farm Tours," *Des Moines Register,* 7 August 1994, 3G; Nancy Kimball, "Personal Goals Steer Farmers' Sustainable Efforts," *Iowa Farmer Today,* 13 August 1988, 14A; Finn Bullers, "The New Farm: Manure, Common Sense," *Ames Daily Tribune,* 4 April 1987, A1, A7; Jerry Perkins, "Activism Takes Iowa Woman to Top of Farm Group," *Des Moines Register,* 6 March 1994, 1J.

12. Ron Rosmann, personal communication, 2 January 2000; Practical Farmers of Iowa, "What is P.F.I.?" flyer, n.d. [c. 1986].

13. See also brochure *Prairie Festival 1994: The Pattern Which Connects* (Salina, Kans.: Land Institute, 1994); see also entire issue of *The Land Report,* no. 46 (Spring 1993).

14. On the New Alchemy Institute's role, see box 1, files 2–12, Green Center/ New Alchemy Instititute Papers, Archives of American Agriculture, Special Collections, Parks Memorial Library, Iowa State University.

15. "Interest in Sustainable Ag Rising as Requests for Technical Information Balloon," *ATTRA News,* May 1991, 2; Kerr Center for Sustainable Agriculture, "Newsletter," May/June 1993, 1–8; Andrew Ware, "Louis Bromfield Sustainable Ag Library Launched," *Sustainable Agriculture News,* spring 1992, 1; "Leopold Center Educational Programs," New Release (September 1992); Raymond P. Poincelot, "From the Editor," *Journal of Sustainable Agriculture* 1 (1990): 1–3; Iowa Division–United Nations Association, *Beyond Rio: Earth Charter Iowa* (Iowa City: Iowa Division-United Nations Association, 1993), 1–12; Lynn Betts, "Better Land, Better Water," *Wallaces' Farmer,* 26 February 1991, 6, 8; "Lines on the Land," *Wallaces' Farmer,* October 1991, 35.

16. Wheeler McMillen, *Bugs or People?* (New York: Appleton-Century, 1965), 1, 10, 22, 28.

17. Jamie L. Whitten, *That We May Live* (Princeton, N.J.; D. Van Nostrand, 1966), 208–16.

18. Donald Hornig to Joseph Califano, Memo, 28 February 1968, White House Central Files SP2-3/1968/NR, box 129, LBJ Library.

19. Diedre Cox, "Borlaug: Rights Must Take Back Seat to Needs," *Iowa State University Daily,* 10 February 1978, 1, 9; William Inman, "Nobel Winner Raps Antipesticide Movement," *Ames Daily Tribune,* 29 June 1985, C7; Norman Borlaug, "The Green Revolution: Can We Make It Meet Expectations?" *Proceedings of the American Phytopathological Society: Symposium on World Food* 1 (1977): 6–8.

20. Lauren Soth, "Soil Erosion: Getting Better or Worse?" *Des Moines Register,* 26 September 1983; Lauren Soth, "Hiding Soil Losses Under Increased Productivity," *Des Moines Register,* 10 January 1983, 1J.

21. Paul E. Waggoner, "How Much Land Can Ten Billion People Spare for Nature?" Council for Agricultural Science and Technology, Task Force Report No. 121 (Ames, Iowa: February 1994).

22. Soth, "Hiding Soil Losses Under Increased Productivity," 1J; Theodore W. Schultz, "A Dissenting Opinion on Soil Erosion," *Des Moines Register,* 20 June 1982, 1C; "Economist Says Erosion Fears Exaggerated," *Des Moines Register,* 18 March 1982, 5B; Julian Simon and Herman Kahn, *The Resourceful Earth: A Response to Global 2000* (New York: Basil Blackwell, 1984), 1–27, 39–45, 200–219.

23. James Risser, "As Costs Soar, More Farmers Going 'Organic,'" *Des Moines Register,* 10 June 1984, 1A, 9A.

24. Council for Agricultural Science and Technology, *Alternative Agriculture Scientists' Review,* CAST Special Publication No. 16 (Ames, Iowa: CAST, 1990), vii–3, 84–85.

25. Lauren Soth, "Case for Sustainable Agriculture," *Des Moines Register,* 5 May 1989, 10A; Council for Agricultural Science and Technology, *Long-Term Viability of U.S. Agriculture,* CAST Report No. 114 (Ames, Iowa: CAST, 1988), 1–7.

26. CAST, *Alternative Agriculture Scientists' Review,* 131–37; on recent antagonism between sustainable agriculture and the establishment view see Leonard Gianessi, "The Quixotic Quest for Chemical-Free Farming," *Issues in Science and Technology* 10 (fall 1993): 29–36; see also Council for Agricultural Science and Technology, *How Much Land Can Ten Billion People Spare For Nature?* CAST Task Force Report No. 121 (Ames, Iowa: CAST, 1994); Gene Logsdon, "Death of a Sacred Cow," *Ohio Magazine,* May 1992, 30–49, 56–59; Bob Holmes, "Can Sustainable Agriculture Win the Battle of the Bottom Line?" *Science,* 25 June 1993, 1893–95.

27. Jack Early, speech presented to the American Society of Agricultural Consultants, McClean, Virginia, 1980, in *Opportunities in Times of Crisis: Proceedings of the Annual Meeting of the American Society of Agricultural Consultants* 1 (1980): 117–20; see also Jim Ruen, "Agricultural Research and Food Safety: A 130–Year Success Story," *Across the Table* (1992): 12–14; Richard J. Mahoney, *A Commitment to Greatness* (St. Louis, Mo.: Monsanto, 1988); Gordon Berg, "We Are Winning the Ag Pollution Battle," *Farm Chemicals* 145 (October 1982): 98; Lisa Heacox, "Ground Water Contamination Not Widespread," *Farm Chemicals* 154 (March 1991): 68; Dixie Lee Ray, "Let Consumers Know the Facts," *Farm Chemicals* 155 (January 1992): 25; Dorothy Schumck, "CDPA Braces for the 1990s," *Farm Chemicals* 154 (March 1991): 68; Dale Darling, "Other Comments," *Journal of Soil and Water Conservation* 48 (July–August 1993): 3–5; Lindsay Brown, "Sustainable Agriculture: What Is It?" *Across the Table* (1991): 1–2; Francois Lepine, "Shut Down Leopold," *Iowa State University Daily,* 26 February 1993, 4.

28. Terry Gips, "Sustainable Agriculture Defined," *New Alchemy Quarterly,* no. 38 (winter 1989–90): 4; Dana Jackson, "The Relationship Between Organic and Sustainable Agriculture," *Land Report,* no. 45 (November 1992): 14, 15.

29. Michael R. Dicks, "What Will Be Required to Guarantee Sustainability of U.S. Agriculture in the 21st Century?" *Journal of Alternative Agriculture* 7 (1992): 190–95.

30. Dennis R. Keeney, "Toward a Sustainable Agriculture: Need for Clarification of Concepts and Terminology," *American Journal of Alternative Agriculture* 4 (1989): 101–5; Dennis R. Keeney, "The Future of Leopold Center," in *Farming Systems for Iowa: Seeking Alternatives* (Ames, Iowa: Leopold Center for Sustainable

Agriculture, 1990), 19–20; J. Patrick Madden, "What Is Alternative Agriculture?" *American Journal of Alternative Agriculture* 4 (1989): 32–34; Harold F. Breimeyer, "Defining Sustainable Agriculture," *Missouri Farm*, July–August 1990, 14.

31. William Lockeretz, "Commentary: Open Questions in Sustainable Agriculture," *American Journal of Alternative Agriculture* 3 (fall 1988): 174–81.

32. Ibid., 178–79; Tim T. Phipps, Pierre Crosson, and Kent A. Price, eds., *Agriculture and the Environment: Report of the National Center for Food and Agricultural Policy* (Washington, D.C.: Resources for the Future, 1986), 3–28; Pierre Crosson, "What Is Alternative Agriculture?" *American Journal of Alternative Agriculture* 4 (1989): 28–31; Sandra S. Batie and Daniel B. Taylor, "Assessing the Character of Agricultural Production Systems: Issues and Implications," *American Journal of Alternative Agriculture* 6 (1991): 184–87; Hugh Lehman, E. Anne Clark, and Stephen F. Weise, "Clarifying the Definition of *Sustainable Agriculture*," *Journal of Agricultural and Environmental Ethics* 6 (1993): 127–43; Riley E. Dunlap, Curtis E. Beus, Robert E. Howell, and Jack Wand, "What Is Sustainable Agriculture? An Empirical Examination of Faculty and Farmer Definitions," *Journal of Sustainable Agriculture* 3 (1992): 5–40; "Get Acquainted with LISA," *Pacific Northwest Sustainable Agriculture* 3 (June 1991): 7.

33. Cheryl Long, "Certified Organic: A Guarantee of Pure, Wholesome Food," *Organic Gardening*, November/December 1999, 44–45.

34. On the no-till revolution, see J. C. Siemens and W. R. Oschwald, *Corn-Soybean Tillage Systems: Erosion Control, Effects on Crop Production, Costs* (St. Joseph, Mich.: American Society of Agricultural Engineers, 1976), 1–18; Office of Planning and Evaluation, *Minimum Tillage: A Preliminary Technology Assessment* (Washington, D.C.: USDA, 1975); "There's a Revolution Going On in Those Fields," *Worthington (Minn.) Globe*, 22 December 1978, 17; Don Muhm, "ISU Study Says Terracing May Not Pay," *Des Moines Register*, 24 February 1984, 5S, 8S; Larry Reichenbeg, "Here's What Successful No-Till Planters Must Do Right," *Successful Farming*, May 1980, 24–25; Charles E. Sommers, "Control Vegetation for Successful No-Till Corn," *Successful Farming*, April 1980, 34–35; "Tillage: Latest Research Will Be Our Own," *Successful Farming*, March 1978, 23–24; "Cut Costs, Tillage, But Not Yields," *Farm Journal*, December 1981, 19; "Farm Journal's Machinery Update," *Farm Journal*, Mid-January 1982, 20; Darrell Smith, "Corn-Barley-Soybean Strips Slow Hillside Erosion," Lynn Betts, "Switch Entirely to No-Till in One Season," *Wallaces' Farmer*, 13 February 1983, 118–19: Rod Swoboda, "Blowing Beans into the Ground," *Wallaces' Farmer*, May 1994, 6–8; on conservation tillage, see also box 5, file 27, David Staniforth Papers, University Archives, Parks Memorial Library, Iowa State University.

35. "A Giant Step or a Springtime Skip?" *Newsweek*, 4 May 1970, 26–28; on corporate co-option of the environmental movement, see Carl Deal, *The Greenpeace Guide to Anti-environmental Organizations* (Berkeley, Calif.: Odonian Press, 1993); Steve Kufrin, "Reduced Tillage Saves Soil, Labor and Fuel for Farmers," reprint from *Swift County (Minn.) Monitor-News*, October 1980, 1–2; Don Muhm, "No-Tillage Innovators in Iowa Save Both Fuel and Soil," *Des Moines Register*, 5 September 5, 1982, 2F; James Risser, "Reduced Tillage Adding to State Water Pollution," *Des Moines Register*, 22 January 1984, 1A, 8A; Terry Cacek, "Organic Farming: The Other Conservation Farming System," *Journal of Soil and Water Conservation* 39 (November–December 1984): 65–68.

36. Rollie Henkes, "The Mainstreaming of Alternative Agriculture," *Furrow*, September–October 1985, 10–15; "DMI Yield-Till Gets More Grain from Your Fields!" *Wallaces' Farmer*, August 1991, 19; "Stop Pollution! Knife into the Seed

Zone," *Wallaces' Farmer,* February 1990; "This Spring Launch Your Conservation Campaign with a Little Green Paint," *Wallaces' Farmer,* 9 January 1990, advertising insertion between pages 42 and 43.

37. "Sustainable Agriculture: Perspectives from Industry," *Journal of Soil and Water Conservation* 48 (January–February 1990): 31–33.

38. "Big Changes Ahead in How You Control Weeds," *Wallaces' Farmer,* 8 January 1991, 38; "What's on His Mind?" *Wallaces' Farmer,* August 1991, 31.

39. "We're All Getting Together" (Des Moines: Iowa Fertilizer and Chemical Association, 1992); Rod Swoboda, "Recycling Chemical Jugs . . . the Right Thing to Do," *Wallaces' Farmer,* July 1991, 24–25; Monte Sesker, "Recycling Herbicide Containers Begins," *Wallaces' Farmer,* 12 March 1991, 62; "National Agriculture Week TV Program Examines Water Quality Issues," *Wallaces' Farmer,* 13 March 1990, 16–17; Charlotte Sine, "FoodWatch Needs You!" *Farm Chemicals* 153 (March 1990): 28; Robyn A. Dill, "Food Safety Meeting Grabs Attention," *Farm Chemicals* 153 (March 1990): 30–31; "Earth Day 1990 Needs Your Attention," *Farm Chemicals* 153 (March 1990): 13; ML Communications, ed., "Atrazine and 'Modern' Corn Production," *Wallaces' Farmer,* January 8, 1991, CG1–CG11.

40. CIBA GEIGY advertisement in *Wallaces' Farmer,* 8 June 1991, CG12.

41. "Big Changes Ahead in How You Control Your Weeds," 38; "Weed Scientist Redirects Herbicide Research Program," *Ag Bioethics Forum* 4 (December 1992): 1, 5; "Biotechnology and Sustainable Agriculture," *Ag Bioethics Forum* 2 (January 1990): 1–3, 8; see also Preston Smith, "Jim Mosely: The Real Ag Voice at EPA," *Farm Chemicals,* January 1990, 28–29; Dennis R. Keeney, "The Role of Input Dealers in Sustainable Agriculture," *Leopold Letter* (fall 1991): 3.

42. Dirck Steimel, "Farmers Worry About the Image of Ag Chemical Ads," *Des Moines Register,* 6 February 1994, 1J; "Broadstrike Struck Corn, Farmers Say," *Des Moines Register,* 11 September 1994, 5B.

43. Donald Worster, "Some Cautionary Thoughts on a Marriage Proposal," *Land Report,* no. 36 (fall 1989): 12–13.

44. Neva Hassanein, *Changing the Way America Farms: Knowledge and Community in the Sustainable Agriculture Movement* (Lincoln: University of Nebraska Press, 1999), 14–22; Lisa Jones, "Searching for Pasture," *High Country News* 31 January 2000, 1, 13–15; Louis Jacobson, "Fleeced," *Lingua Franca,* September 1998, 9–10.

45. Hassanein, *Changing the Way America Farms,* 46.

46. Don Hadwiger, *The Politics of Agricultural Research* (Lincoln: University of Nebraska Press, 1982), 1–10, 198–202; "Farm Chemicals," *Wallaces' Farmer,* 8 October 1990, WF1.

47. Paul B. Thompson and Bill A. Stout, "Beyond the Large Farm," in *Beyond the Large Farm: Ethics and Research Goals for Agriculture,* ed. Paul B. Thompson and Bill A. Stout (Boulder, Colo.: Westview Press, 1991), 270–74; Gail Feenstra, "Should the Food System Be Decentralized?" *Sustainable Agriculture News* 4 (summer 1992): 6–7; see also Terry L. Cacek, "Biological Farming and Wildlife Conservation," in *Proceedings of the Management Alternatives for Biological Farming Workshop II,* ed. Robert Dahlgren (Ames: Iowa State University Cooperative Wildlife Research Unit, 1985), 2–4; W. Arden Sheets, "Can It Be Done?" *Pacific Northwest Sustainable Agriculture News* 3 (June 1991): 7; Board of Agriculture–National Research Council, *Sustainable Agriculture: Research and Education in the Field* (Washington, D.C.: National Academy Press, 1991), 1–108, 387–92; Gene Meyer, "Research Shifts to Small Farms: Scientists Looking at Less Costs, More Natural Innovations," *Kansas City Times,* 21 February 1981, D1, D26; Galen Bridge,

"Is Whole-Farm Conservation Planning the Answer?" *Journal of Soil and Water Conservation* 48 (July–August 1993): 296–98; Richard Nagleby and David L. Schertz, "Conservation Tillage: A Hot, New Idea from the Distant Past," and Kenneth A. Cook, "Alternative Agriculture," both in *Our American Land: 1987 Yearbook of Agriculture*, ed. William Whyte (Washington, D.C.: USDA, 1987), 165–67, 244–46; "Managing Your Crop to Protect Your Environment," *Wallaces' Farmer*, 10 April 1990, 56–57; William B. Lacy, "Can Agricultural Colleges Meet the Needs of Sustainable Agriculture?" *American Journal of Alternative Agriculture* 8 (1993): 40–43.

48. Jeri Neal, "Leopold Center Awards $404,000 to New Projects, Renews 29 Others," *Leopold Letter* 11, no. 2 (summer 1999): 1–8.

49. 1998 Annual Report, College of Agriculture, Iowa State University, Ames, Iowa; 1998–99 Annual Report, Leopold Center for Sustainable Agriculture, Iowa State University, Ames, Iowa, 9.

50. Hadwiger, *Politics of Agricultural Research*, 198–202; "Rupert Cutler: The Environmentalist in the Farmer's Backyard," *Science*, April 1977, 505–7; John P. Reganold, Robert I. Papendick, and James F. Parr, "Sustainable Agriculture in the United States: An Overview," *Proceedings of the First International Symposium in Natural Resource Management for a Sustainable Agriculture*, 1 (1990): 447–48.

51. Garth Youngberg and Frederick H. Buttel, "Public Policy and Socio-Political Factors Affecting the Future of Sustainable Farming Systems," in *Organic Farming: Current Technology and Its Role in Sustainable Agriculture*, ed. D. F. Bezdicek, American Society for Agronomy Special Publication No. 46 (Madison, Wis.: ASA, 1984), 167–86; Tim Lehman, "Failed Land Reform: The Politics of the 1981 National Agricultural Lands Study," *Environmental History Review* 14 (spring/summer 1990): 129–49; Guy Gugliotta, "13 Years Later, Farm Policy Sees Light," *Des Moines Register*, 10 July 1994, 1J; James Risser, "Bill to Study Organic Farmers Presented," *Des Moines Register*, 22 April 1983, 1F.

52. Lauren Soth, "Next Step in Soil Saving: Mild Regulation of Farms," *Des Moines Register*, 17 January 1983, 10A; Lauren Soth, "Cutting Erosion with Carrot, Stick," *Des Moines Register*, 27 June 1982; Darwin C. Hall, Brian P. Baker, Jacques Franco, and Desmond A. Jolly, "Organic Food and Sustainable Agriculture," *Contemporary Policy Issues* 7 (October 1989): 47–73; James Risser, "USDA, Chemical Firms Move to Trip Organics Bill," *Des Moines Register*, 14 June 1984, 1A, 10A.

53. Steiner, *Soil Conservation in the United States*, xii, 104.

54. Ibid., xiii, 175.

55. George Turman, "The National Center for Appropriate Technology," *ATTRAnews*, September 1990, 1; Elizabeth Henderson, "NOFA Gets LISA Grant," *Natural Farmer*, spring 1989, 1; "USDA Funds Sustainable Agriculture Network," *Sustainable Agriculture News*, fall 1991, 1–2; Neill Schaller, "Background and Status of the Low-Input Sustainable Agriculture Program," in Board of Agriculture-National Research Council, *Sustainable Agriculture: Research and Education in the Field* (Washington, D.C.: National Academy Press, 1991), 22–31; Council for Agricultural Science and Technology, *Ecological Impacts of Federal Conservation and Cropland Reduction Programs*, CAST Task Force Report No. 117 (Ames, Iowa: CAST, 1990), 1–23; William K. Reilly, "Agriculture and the Environment," *Vital Speeches* 53 (December 15, 1986): 136–39; see also Ted Napier, ed., *Implementing the Conservation Title of the Food Security Act of 1985* (Ankeny, Iowa: Soil and Water Conservation Society of America, 1990); federal legislation often accompanied or was followed by state legislation supporting sustainable agriculture; see John Pesek, "The History of the Leopold Center," in *Farming Systems for Iowa: Seeking*

Alternatives (Ames, Iowa: Leopold Center for Sustainable Agriculture, 1990), 33–37.

56. Jennifer Dorsch and John Walter, "Green and Global," *Successful Farming,* December 1990, 15–17; Dave Chaney and Dave Campbell, "1990 Farm Bill: Implications for California," *Sustainable Agriculture News,* spring 1991, 14–15; "Can You Use Sustainable Options of New Farm Bill?" *Wallaces' Farmer,* March 1991, 54; Rod Swoboda, "Pesticide Records," *Wallaces' Farmer,* December 1991, 11; "New Water Quality Project Expands Big Spring Effort," *Wallaces' Farmer,* November 1991, 30; Sara Wyant, "Fielding a New Farm Bill," *Soybean Digest,* April 1990, 54–56; Sara Handrick, "Back to Nature: New Program Takes Wetlands Out of Production— For Good," *Iowa Agriculturist* (spring 1994), 16–17; George Anthan, "Sizing Up CRP's Balance Sheet," *Des Moines Register,* 6 March 1994, 1J; Dirck Steimel, "Wetlands Reserve Program Proves Hit in Iowa," *Des Moines Register,* 31 July 1994, 1J; Council for Agricultural Science and Technology, *Water Quality: Agriculture's Role,* CAST Task Force Report No. 120 (Ames, Iowa: CAST, 1992), 1–16; "Organic Foods Act," *Farm Chemicals* 153 (March 1990): 27; Toyna Haigh, "The Challenge of National Organic Standards," *Land Report,* no. 45 (fall 1992): 16–17.

57. "Clinton Signs $8.7 Billion Package to Help Farmers," *Tribune* (Ames, Iowa), 23 October, 1999, A1, A4.

58. "What Is Sustainable Agriculture?" *Wallaces' Farmer,* September 1991, 70; "Would Sustainable Ag Help or Hurt Your Profitability?" *Wallaces' Farmer,* 12 March 1991, 47.

59. "Profile," *Des Moines Register,* 26 June 1994, 3J; "Profile," *Des Moines Register,* 15 August 1993, 3J.

60. Organic Trade Association, Web site at www.ota.com, and the Organic Farming Research Foundation, www.ofrf.com.

61. David Ehrenfeld, "Beyond the Farming Crisis," *Technology Review* 90 (July 1987): 47–56; John Walter, "Environment," *Successful Farming,* January 1992, 63; John Walter, "Farmers Decide What's Sustainable," *Successful Farming,* December 1992, 24–25; "Farm Progress Show," *Wallaces' Farmer,* September 1993, 37; Larry Stone, "Fire Dies Out as Best Way to Manage Prairies," *Des Moines Register,* 20 March 1994, 12D; Tom J. Bechman, "A Tale of Two Weed Control Strategies for the 1990s," *Wallaces' Farmer,* December 1991, 12–13; James Risser, "As Costs Soars, More Farmers Going Organic," *Des Moines Register,* 10 June 1984, 1A, 9A; Jay P. Wagner, "Sold on Mixed Vegetables," *Des Moines Register,* 26 June 1994, 1J; "More Alternative Crops," *Wallaces' Farmer,* August 1991, 19; on alternative crops see the entire issue of *Missouri Farm,* November–December 1990; Kent Parker, "No-Till Farming: Evolution, Not Revolution," *Des Moines Register,* 6 December 1981, F1–F2; "Profile," *Des Moines Register,* 12 September 1993, 3J; John M. Cross, "Decade of Ecofallow is all the Proof He Needs," reprint from *Nebraska Farmer,* 4 July 1981; Hugh Sidey, "A 'Cultural Revolution,'" *Des Moines Register,* 5 July 1992, F1–F2.

62. Organic Trade Association, Web site at www.ota.com.

63. Lauren Soth, "Case for Sustainable Agriculture," *Des Moines Register,* 5 May 1989, 10A; Orville Bidwell, "Where Do We Stand on Sustainable Agriculture?" *Journal of Soil and Water Conservation* 41 (September–October 1986): 317–20; Ralph Grossi, "A Green Evolution: Retooling Agricultural Policy for Greater Sustainability," *Journal of Soil and Water Conservation* 48 (July–August 1993): 285–88; Mike Krapfl, "Butterfly Blues," *Tribune* (Ames, Iowa), 5 June 1999, A1, A4.

64. Nathaniel Adams, "Smithsonian Horizons," *Smithsonian* 24 (September 1993): 10; Lester R. Brown, "Sustaining World Agriculture," and Edward C. Wolf,

"Raising Agricultural Productivity," both in *State of the World 1987: A Worldwatch Report on Progress Towards a Sustainable Society*, ed. Linda Starke (New York: Norton, 1987): 122–56; Paul Lewis, "Environmental Aid for Poor Nations Agreed at UN," *New York Times*, 5 April 1992, 1; Technical Advisory Committee to the Consultative Group of International Agricultural Research, *Sustainable Agriculture Production: Implications for International Research* (Rome: UN-FAO, 1989), 1–71; Shareen Hertel, *The World Economy in Transition: Prospects for Sustainability, Equity and Prosperity* (New York: UN-USA, 1993), 1–20; Micah Morrison, "Babbit's Gambit: Interior Designs," *Insight*, 9 August 1993, 6–13.

65. Jeffery Sinn, "How Are Soil Erosion Control Programs Working?" *Journal of Soil and Water Conservation* 48 (July–August 1993): 254–59; Kenneth Pins and George Anthan, "Ag Groups Take Aim at the Green Giants," *Des Moines Register*, 22 February 1994, 5A; Jerry Perkins, "Iowans Ready for Wetlands Battle," *Des Moines Register*, 25 December 1994, 1J; Rob Swoboda, "Farmers Don't Realize Full Benefits of IPM," *Wallaces' Farmer*, 14 August 1990, 54; Larry Stone, "Iowans Speak Out on Stream Rules," *Des Moines Register*, 12 September 1993, 2J; Dirck Steimel, "Farmers Fear Missouri Plan," *Des Moines Register*, 13 November 1994, 1J; "Non-Chemical Farms Lag in Profitability," *Wallaces' Farmer*, 14 August 1990, 54; John Bongaarts, "Can the Growing Human Population Feed Itself?" *Scientific American*, March 1994, 36–41; Linda Kanamine, "Proposal Promises More 'Protection' in Pesticide Laws," *USA Today*, September 22, 1993, 4A; Michael Arnst, "Herbicides Imperil Water in Midwest," *Chicago Tribune*, October 19, 1994, 1, 4, 8; Dirck Steimel, "Big Hog Farms Spark Debate," *Des Moines Register*, 27 February 1994, 1J; George Anthan, "Urban Sprawl Ruins Best Land," *Des Moines Register*, 19 September 1993, 1J; George Anthan, "Experts See Precious Soil at Risk," *Des Moines Register*, 18 November 1993, 1A; Dirck Steimel, "Weeds Resist Herbicide Punch," *Des Moines Register*, 7 August 1994, 1J; Suzanne Possehl, "Its Budget Slashed, Russian Seed Bank Fights for Life," *New York Times*, 23 March 1993, B7.

66. Richard Heinberg, *Cloning the Buddha: The Moral Impact of Biotechnology* (Wheaton, Ill.: Quest Books, 1999).

67. Diane Heldt, "ISU Study: Farmers Reduce Insecticide Use with Bt Corn," *Tribune* (Ames, Iowa), 20 November 1999, B1, B3.

68. John E. Losey, Linda S. Rayor, and Maureen E. Carter, "Transgenic Pollen Harms Monarch Larvae," *Nature* 399, no. 6733 (1999): 214; Yvonne Baskin, "Into the Wild," *Natural History*, October 1999, 34–37; Gary Paul Nabhan, "The Killing Fields: Monarchs and Transgenic Corn," *Wild Earth* 9 (winter 1999/2000): 49–52; Carol Kaesuk Yoon, "Reassessing Ecological Risks Of Genetically Altered Crops," *New York Times*, 3 November 1999, A1, A22; Walter Truett Anderson, "Food Without Farmers: The Biotech Revolution in Agriculture," *The Futurist* 24 (January–February 1990): 16–21; Jack R. Kloppenburg Jr., *First the Seed: The Political Economy of Plant Biotechnology, 1492–2000* (Cambridge: Cambridge University Press, 1988), 277; Cary Fowler and Pat Mooney, *Shattering: Food, Politics and the Loss of Genetic Diversity* (Tucson: University of Arizona Press, 1990): 1–101; "Workshop on Herbicide Tolerant Crops," *Ag Bioethics Forum* 3 (August 1991): 2; Donald Worster, *The Wealth of Nature* (New York: Oxford University Press, 1993), 142–55.

69. Kenneth A. Cook, *So Long CRP!* (Washington, D.C.: Environmental Working Group, 1994), 1–39; Center for Resource Economics, *Farm Bill 1990 Revisited: Agenda for the Environment and Consumers* (Washington, D.C.: CRE, 1992), 2–34; *White Paper: The Next Generation of U.S. Agricultural Conservation Policy* (Ankeny, Iowa: Soil and Water Conservation Society of America, 1993), 1–40.

70. Marty Strange, "Control Corporate Farming," *Des Moines Register*, 8 March 1994, 1C; Jerry Perkins, "Farm Forum Coming," *Des Moines Register*, 20 February 1994, 1J; George Anthan, "Land Ownership Increasingly Concentrated," *Des Moines Register*, 9 August 1992, 3A; Craig Canine, "A Farewell to Farms," *Harrowsmith Country Life* 33 (June 1991): 30–29; Dirck Steimel, "Number of Farms Keeps Slipping," *Des Moines Register*, 19 November 1993, 1A; Michael A. Lev, "Finding New Blood for Farms," *Des Moines Register*, 19 February 1995, 1J; Kenneth Pins, "Agriculture Weighs Costs of Progress," *Des Moines Register*, 20 March 1994, 1J; K. V. Johnson, "Family Farms Rapidly Slipping into History," *USA Today*, 7 February 1995, 7A; Lynne Heasley, "Uncertain Boundaries: Mixing Science and History, Property and Nature in the Kickapoo Valley, Wisconsin" (paper presented at American Society for Environmental History, Tucson, Arizona, 14–18 April, 1999).

71. Strange, *Family Farming*, 39.

72. Robert Reich quoted in Catherine S. Manegold, "Department: Work a Polarized Place," *Kansas City Star*, 24 November 1994, C1; Strange, *Family Farming*, 176.

73. Mike Glover, "Farm Leaders Worried About Concentration," *Tribune* (Ames, Iowa), 23 October 1999, A1.

74. David Barboza, "Monsanto Sued over Use of Biotechnology in Developing Seeds," *New York Times*, 15 December, 1999, C1, C10.

75. Rick Weiss, "A Crop of Questions: Gene-Altered Foods May Offer Benefits, but How Safe Are They?" *Washington Post National Weekly Edition*, 23 August 1999, 6–7.

Selected Bibliography

ARCHIVAL SOURCES

Iowa State University, Ames, Iowa
Archives of American Agriculture, Special Collections, Parks Memorial Library
   Bushrod W. Allin Papers
   Hugh H. Bennett Papers
   Green Center/New Alchemy Institute Papers
   Robert Steffen Papers
University Archives
   Kenneth A. Carlander Papers
   William Murray Papers
   David Staniforth Papers

Harry S. Truman Presidential Library, Independence, Missouri

   Clinton P. Anderson Papers
   Daniel L. Goldy Papers
   Clarence J. McCormick Papers
   Wesley McCune Papers
   Harry S. Truman, White House Central Files
   Claude G. Wickard Papers

Lyndon B. Johnson Presidential Library, University of Texas, Austin, Texas

   David Angelvine Papers
   John A. Baker Papers
   Ceil Bellinger Office Files
   Lester R. Brown Oral History Interview Transcripts
   Stanley A. Cain Papers
   Environmental Services Administration, Records of
   Orville L. Freeman Papers
   James Gaither Papers
   Richard Goodwin Papers
   Robert Hardesty Papers
   Lyndon B. Johnson Presidential Papers, White House Central Files
   Office of Science and Technology, Records of
   Daniel Pierson Papers
   Stewart Udall Oral History Interview Transcripts
   United States Department of Agriculture, Records of

John F. Kennedy Presidential Library, Boston, Massachusetts

   Orville L. Freeman Papers

Mugar Library, Special Collections, Boston University

  Scott and Helen Nearing Papers

National Archives, Great Plains Region, Kansas City, Missouri

  Soil Conservation Service, Records of (Record Group 114)

Franklin D. Roosevelt Presidential Library, Hyde Park, New York

  Morris L. Cooke Papers
  Franklin D. Roosevelt Office Files
  Rexford G. Tugwell Papers
  Henry A. Wallace Vice-Presidential Papers
  Claude G. Wickard Papers

University of Iowa Library, Iowa City, Iowa

  Henry A. Wallace (Microfilm) Papers

BOOKS AND BOOK CHAPTERS

Aaker, Jerry. *Livestock for a Small Planet: The Role of Animals in a Just and Sustainable World*. Washington, D.C.: Heifer Project International, 1994.
Albrect, William A. *Good Horses Require Good Soils*. Chicago: Horse and Mule Association of America, 1948.
Alihan, Milla Aissa. *Social Ecology: A Critical Analysis*. New York: Columbia University Press, 1938.
Allin, Bushrod W., and Ellery A. Foster. "The Challenge of Conservation." *Yearbook of Agriculture 1940*. Washington D.C.: USDA, 1940.
Altieri, Miguel. *Agroecology: The Scientific Basis of Alternative Agriculture*. Berkeley: Division of Biological Control, University of California, 1983.
Altieri, Miguel, and Helen Vukasin. *Environmentally Sound Small-Scale Agricultural Projects: Guidelines for Planning*. Berkeley: Godel, 1988.
Anderson, David. *Louis Bromfield*. New York: Twayne, 1964.
Andrews, E. Benjamin. *The Call of the Land*. New York: Orange Judd, 1913.
Bailey, Liberty Hyde. *The State and the Farmer*. New York: Macmillan, 1908.
——. *The Country Life Movement in the United States*. New York: Macmillan, 1913.
Balfour, Evelyn B. *The Living Soil and the Haughley Experiment*. New York: Universe, 1976.
Barney, Gerald O., ed. *The Global 2000 Report to the President—Entering the 21st Century*. Vol. 1. New York: Pergamon, 1980.
Barrett, Thomas J. *Harnessing the Earthworm*. Boston: Bruce Humphries, 1947.
Barsam, Richard. *The Vision of Robert Flaherty: The Artist as Myth and Filmmaker*. Bloomington: Indiana University Press, 1986.
Bathurst, Effie G. *Large Was Our Bounty: Natural Resources and the Schools*. Washington, D.C.: National Education Association, 1948.
Bear, Firman E. *Soil Science: Food for America's Future*. New York: McGraw-Hill, 1960.

――――. *Earth: The Stuff of Life*. Norman: University of Oklahoma Press, 1962.

Belasco, Warren J. *Appetite for Change: How the Counterculture Took on the Food Industry, 1966–1988*. New York: Pantheon, 1989.

Bender, Jim. *Future Harvest: Pesticide-Free Farming*. Lincoln: University of Nebraska Press, 1994.

Bennett, Hugh H. *Elements of Soil Conservation*. New York: McGraw-Hill, 1947.

Berry, Wendell. *A Continuous Harmony: Essays Cultural and Agricultural*. San Diego: Harcourt Brace Jovanovich, 1970.

――――. *The Unsettling of America: Culture and Agriculture*. San Francisco: Sierra Club, 1977.

――――. *Standing by Words*. San Francisco: North Point Press, 1983.

――――. *Home Economics*. San Francisco: North Point Press, 1987.

――――. *What Are People For?* San Francisco: North Point Press, 1990.

Black, John Donald, and Maxine Enlow Keifer. *Future Food and Agriculture Policy: A Program for the Next Ten Years*. New York: McGraw Hill, 1948.

Bonnifield, Paul. *The Dust Bowl*. Albuquerque: University of New Mexico Press, 1979.

Borsodi, Ralph. *Flight from the City: The Story of the New Way to Family Security*. New York: Harper and Brothers, 1933.

Borsodi, Ralph, O. E. Baker, and M. L. Wilson. *Agriculture in Modern Life*. New York: Harper & Brothers, 1939.

Bosso, Christopher J. *Pesticides and Politics: The Life Cycle of a Public Issue*. Pittsburgh: University of Pittsburgh Press, 1991.

Boyer, Paul. *By the Bomb's Early Light: American Thought and Culture at the Dawn of the Atomic Age*. New York: Pantheon, 1985.

Bramwell, Anna. *Ecology in the Twentieth Century: A History*. New Haven, Conn.: Yale University Press, 1989.

Brink, Wellington. *Big Hugh: The Father of Soil Conservation*. New York: Macmillan, 1951.

Brinser, Ayers, and Ward Shepard. *Our Use of the Land*. New York: Harper & Brothers, 1939.

Bromfield, Louis. *Pleasant Valley*. New York: Harper & Brothers, 1945.

――――. *A Few Brass Tacks*. New York: Harper & Brothers, 1948.

――――. *Out of the Earth*. New York: Harper & Brothers, 1950.

Bromfield-Geld, Ellen. *The Heritage: A Daughter's Memories of Louis Bromfield*. New York: Harper & Brothers, 1962.

Bronfenbrenner, Martin. *Academic Encounter: The American University in Japan and Korea*. New York: Crowell-Collier, 1962.

Brown, Lester. R. *The Twenty-ninth Day: Accommodating Human Needs and Numbers to the Earth's Resources*. New York: Norton, 1978.

――――. *Building a Sustainable Society*. New York: Norton, 1981.

――――. "Sustaining World Agriculture." In *Vital Signs 1992: Trends That Shape Our World*, edited by Linda Starke, 96–99. New York: Norton, 1992.

Buck, John Lossing. *Chinese Farm Economy: A Study of 2866 Farms in Seventeen Localities and Seven Provinces in China*. Chicago: University of Chicago Press, 1930.

Bunce, Arthur C. *The Economics of Soil Conservation*. Ames: Iowa State University Press, 1942.

Callenbach, Ernest. *Ecotopia: The Notebook and Reports of William Weston*. New York: Bantam, 1975.

Cardon, P. V. "Our Aim: An Introduction." In *Grass: The Yearbook of Agriculture, 1948*, edited by Alfred Stefferud. Washington, D.C.: USDA, 1948.

Carroll, C. Ronald; John H. Vandermeer, and Peter Rosset, eds. *Agroecology*. New York: McGraw-Hill, 1990.

Carter, Vernon Gill, and Tom Dale. *Topsoil and Civilization*. Norman: University of Oklahoma Press, 1955.

Chapman, Paul W., Frank W. Fitch Jr., and Curry L. Veatch. *Conserving Soil Resources: A Guide to Better Living*. Atlanta: Turner E. Smith, 1950.

Chase, Stuart. *Rich Land, Poor Land*. New York: McGraw-Hill, 1936.

Cheney, E. G. and T. Schantz-Hantzen. *This is Our Land*. St. Paul, Minn.: Webb, 1940.

Cittadino, Eugene. "The Failed Promise of Human Ecology." In *Science and Nature: Essays in the History of the Environmental Sciences*, edited by Michael Shortland, 251–84. Oxford: British Society for the History of Science, 1993.

Clements, Frederick E., and Victor E. Shelford. *Bio-ecology*. New York: Wiley, 1939.

Commoner, Barry. *Science and Survival*. New York: Viking, 1963.

———. *The Closing Circle: Nature, Man and Technology*. New York: Knopf, 1971.

Conford, Phillip, ed. *The Organic Tradition: An Anthology of Writings on Organic Farming, 1900–1950*. London: Green Books, 1988.

Cook, Kenneth A. *So Long CRP!* Washington, D.C.: Environmental Working Group, 1994.

Cooke, Morris L. *Our Cities Awake*. New York: Doubleday, 1918.

Coomer, James C., ed. *Quest for a Sustainable Society*. New York: Pergamon, 1979.

Cornucopia Project. *Empty Breadbasket: The Coming Challenge to America's Food Supply and What We Can Do About It*. Emmaus, Pa.: Rodale Press, 1981.

Crunden, Robert M., ed. *The Superfluous Men: Conservative Critics of American Culture, 1900–1945*. Austin: University of Texas Press, 1977.

Curry-Lindhal, Kai. *Conservation for Survival: An Ecological Strategy*. New York: William Morrow, 1972.

Danbom, David B. *The Resisted Revolution: Urban America and the Industrialization of Agriculture, 1900–1930*. Ames: Iowa State University Press, 1979.

Daryee, William B. *A Living from the Land*. New York: McGraw-Hill, 1934.

Davidson, Donald. *I'll Take My Stand*. New York: Harper & Brothers, 1930.

Davidson, Osha Gray. *Broken Heartland: The Rise of America's Rural Ghetto*. Iowa City: University of Iowa Press, 1996.

Deal, Carl. *The Greenpeace Guide to Anti-environmental Organizations*. Berkeley: Odonian Press, 1993.

DeMarco, Susan, and Susan Sechler. *The Fields Have Turned Brown: Four Essays on World Hunger*. Washington, D.C.: Agribusiness Accountability Project, 1975.

Duggan, Raymond R. *A Federal Resettlement Project: Granger Homesteads*. Washington, D.C.: Catholic University of America, 1937.

Dunlap, Thomas R. *DDT: Scientists, Citizens, and Public Policy*. Princeton, N.J.: Princeton University Press, 1981.

———. *Saving American Wildlife*. Princeton, N.J.: Princeton University Press, 1988.

Eckholm, Erik. *Losing Ground: Environmental Stress and World Food Prospects*. New York: Norton, 1976.

Egerton, Frank N. "The History and Present Entanglements of Some General Ecological Perspectives." In *Humans as Components of Ecosystems*, edited by Mark J. McDonnell and Steward T. A. Pickett, 9–23. New York: Springer-Verlag, 1993.

Falk, Richard A. *This Endangered Planet: Prospects and Proposals for Human Survival*. New York: Random House, 1971.

Faulkner, Edward. *Plowman's Folly*. Norman: University of Oklahoma Press, 1943.

------. *Uneasy Money.* Norman: University of Oklahoma Press, 1945.

------. *A Second Look.* Norman: University of Oklahoma Press, 1947.

------. *Soil Restoration.* London: Michael Joseph, 1953.

Faulkner, R. P. *Garden Manures and Fertilisers: Embodying Special Recommendations for Fruit, Vegetables and Flowers.* London: Collingridge, 1949.

Fleming, Donald. "Roots of the New Conservation Movement." In *Perspectives in American History,* edited by Donald Fleming and Bernard Bailyn, 7–63. New York: Macmillan, 1971.

Forman, Jonathan, and Ollie Fink, eds. *Soil, Food and Health: "You Are What You Eat."* Columbus, Ohio: Friends of the Land, 1948.

------. *Water and Man: A Study in Ecology.* Columbus, Ohio: Friends of the Land, 1950.

Fowler, Cary, and Pat Mooney. *Shattering: Food, Politics and the Loss of Genetic Diversity.* Tucson: University of Arizona Press, 1990.

Freeman, Orville L. "Statement." In *Food and Agriculture: A Program for the 1960s.* Washington, D.C.: USDA, 1962.

Freudenberger, C. Dean. *Global Dust Bowl.* Minneapolis, Minn.: Augsburg Fortress, 1990.

Geisler, Charles C., J. Tadlock Cowan, Michael R. Hattery, and Harvey M. Jacobs. "Sustained Land Productivity: Equity Consequences of Alternative Agricultural Technologies." In *The Social Consequences and Challenges of New Agricultural Technologies,* edited by Gigi M. Berardi and Charles C. Geisler, 213-36. Boulder: Westview, 1984.

Gliesman, Stephen D. "An Agroecological Approach to Sustainable Agriculture." In *Meeting the Expectations of the Land: Systems in Sustainable Agriculture and Stewardship,* edited by Wes Jackson, Wendell Berry, and Bruce Colman, 153-59. San Francisco: North Point Press, 1984.

Golley, Frank B. *A History of the Ecosystem Concept in Ecology: More Than the Sum of the Parts.* New Haven, Conn.: Yale University Press, 1993.

Goodman, Gordon T., R. W. Edwards, and J. M. Lambert. *Ecology and the Industrial Society.* New York: Wiley, 1964.

Graebner, William S. *The Age of Doubt: American Thought and Culture in the 1940s.* Boston: Twayne, 1991.

Graham, Edward H. *Natural Principles of Land Use.* London: Oxford University Press, 1944. Reprint 1969, Greenwood Press.

Graham, Frank M. *Since Silent Spring.* Boston: Houghton Mifflin, 1970.

Great Plains Committee. *The Future of the Great Plains.* Washington, D.C.: GPO, 1936.

Griffin, Richard. *The World of Robert Flaherty.* New York: Capo Press, 1972.

Griswold, A. Whitney. *Farming and Democracy.* New Haven, Conn.: Yale University Press, 1952.

Hadwiger, Don. *The Politics of Agricultural Research.* Lincoln: University of Nebraska Press, 1982.

Hall, Bolton. *Three Acres and Liberty.* New York: Macmillan, 1910.

Hall, Stuart, and Pierre Ott, eds. *Basic Techniques in Ecological Farming.* Basel, Switzerland: Birkhäuser Verlag, 1982.

Hambridge, Gove. "Soils and Men: A Summary." In *Soils and Men: Yearbook of Agriculture 1938.* Washington, D.C..: GPO, 1938.

Hamilton, David. *From New Day to New Deal.* Chapel Hill: University of North Carolina Press, 1991.

Hamilton, Michael, ed. *This Little Planet.* New York: Scribner, 1970.

Hamlin, Herbert M., ed. *Readings Related to the Objectives for Agriculture.* Ames, Iowa: Collegiate Press, 1934.

Hardin, Charles M. *The Politics of Agriculture: Soil Conservation and the Struggle for Power in Rural America.* Glencoe, Ill.: Free Press, 1952.

Harwood, Richard R. *Organic Farming Research at the Rodale Center.* Emmaus, Pa.: Rodale Press, 1982.

————. "A History of Sustainable Agriculture." In *Sustainable Agriculture Systems,* edited by Clive Edwards, 3–19. Ankeny, Iowa: Soil and Water Conservation Society, 1990.

Hassanein, Neva. *Changing the Way America Farms: Knowledge and Community in the Sustainable Agriculture Movement.* Lincoln: University of Nebraska Press, 1999.

Hays, Samuel P. *Beauty, Health and Permanence: Environmental Politics in the United States, 1955–1985.* Cambridge: Cambridge University Press, 1987.

Heasley, Lynne, and Raymond Guries. "Forest Tenure and Cultural Landscapes: Environmental Histories in the Kickapoo Valley." In *Who Owns America? Social Conflict over Property Rights,* edited by Harvey Jacobs, 182–207. Madison: University of Wisconsin Press, 1998.

Heinberg, Richard. *Cloning the Buddha: The Moral Impact of Biotechnology.* Wheaton, Ill.: Quest Books, 1999.

Held, R. Burnell, and Marion Clawson. *Soil Conservation in Perspective.* Baltimore: Johns Hopkins University Press, 1965.

Henderson, Lawrence J. *The Fitness of the Environment: An Inquiry into the Biological Significance of the Properties of Matter.* New York: Macmillan, 1913.

Herber, Lewis. *Our Synthetic Environment.* New York: Knopf, 1962.

Hertel, Shareen. *The World Economy in Transition: Prospects for Sustainability, Equity and Prosperity.* New York: UN-USA, 1993.

Hess, John L., and Karen Hess. "The Green Revolution." In *Political Ecology,* edited by Alexander Cockburn and James Ridgeway, 180–89. New York: Times Books, 1979.

Hightower, Jim. *Hard Tomatoes, Hard Times: A Report of the Agribusiness Accountability Project on the Failure of America's Land Grant College Complex.* Cambridge, Mass.: Schenkman, 1973.

Hill, Johnson D., and Walter E. Stuermann. *Roots in the Soil: An Introduction to a Philosophy of Agriculture.* New York: Philosophical Library, 1964.

Hopkins, Cyril G. *Soil Fertility and Permanent Agriculture.* Boston: Ginn, 1910.

Hopkins, Donald P. *Chemicals, Humus and the Soil.* London: Faber and Faber, 1945.

Howard, Sir Albert. *An Agricultural Testament.* London: Oxford University Press, 1940.

————. *The Soil and Health: A Study of Organic Agriculture,* New York: Devin-Adair, 1947.

Howard, Louise E. *The Earth's Green Carpet.* Emmaus, Pa.: Rodale Press, 1947.

Hurt, R. Douglas. *The Dust Bowl: An Agricultural and Social History.* Chicago: Nelson Hall, 1981.

————. *American Agriculture: A Brief History.* Ames: Iowa State University Press, 1994.

Inge, M. Thomas, ed. *Agrarianism in American Literature.* New York: Odyssey Press, 1969.

Jacks, G. V., and R. O. Whyte. *The Rape of the Earth: A World Survey of Soil Erosion.* London: Faber and Faber, 1939.

Jackson, Wes. *New Roots for American Agriculture.* San Francisco: Friends of the Earth, 1980.

————. "Ecosystem Agriculture: The Marriage of Ecology and Agriculture." In *Global Perspectives on Agroecology and Sustainable Agriculture Systems*, Vol. 1, edited by Patricia Allen and Debra Van Husen, 3–17. Santa Cruz: University of California–Santa Cruz, 1989.

Kains, M. G. *Five Acres and Independence.* New York: Greenburg, 1935.

Katz, Robert. *A Giant in the Earth.* New York: Stein and Day, 1973.

Kay, Lily. *The Molecular Vision: Caltech, the Rockefeller Foundation, and the Rise of the New Biology.* New York: Oxford University Press, 1993.

Kellogg, Charles E. *The Soils That Support Us.* New York: Macmillan, 1941.

King, F. H. *Farmers of Forty Centuries, or Permanent Agriculture in China, Korea and Japan.* Emmaus, Pa.: Rodale Press, 1947.

Kingsland, Sharon. *Modeling Nature: Episodes in the History of Population Ecology.* Chicago: University of Chicago Press, 1985.

Kirkendall, Richard S. *Social Scientists and Farm Politics in the Age of Roosevelt.* Columbia: University of Missouri Press, 1966.

Kloppenburg, Jack. *First the Seed: The Political Economy of Plant Biotechnology, 1492–2000.* Cambridge: Cambridge University Press, 1988.

Koepf, H. H. *Biodynamic Agriculture: An Introduction.* Spring Valley, N.Y.: Anthroposophic Press, 1976.

Lappé, Francis Moore, and Joseph Collins. *Food First: The Myth of Scarcity.* Boston: Houghton Mifflin, 1977.

Lear, Linda J. *Rachel Carson: Witness for Nature.* New York: Henry Holt, 1997.

Leopold, Aldo. *A Sand County Almanac.* 1953. Reprint, New York: Oxford University Press, 1966.

Levy, Juliette de Bairacli. *Nature's Children.* New York: Schenken, 1971.

Little, Charles E. *Green Fields Forever: The Conservation Tillage Revolution in America.* Washington, D.C.: Island Press, 1986.

————, ed. *Louis Bromfield at Malabar: Writings on Farming and Country Life.* Baltimore: Johns Hopkins University Press, 1988.

Lord, Russell. *The Care of the Earth: A History of Husbandry.* New York: Mentor, 1962.

Lord, Russell, and Kate Lord. *Forever the Land.* New York: Harper & Brothers, 1951.

Lord, Russell, and Paul Johnstone. *A Place on Earth: A Critical Appraisal of Subsistence Homesteads.* Washington, D.C.: USDA, 1942.

Lovelock, J. E. *Gaia: A New Look at Life on Earth.* London: Oxford University Press, 1979.

Lowdermilk, Walter C. *Palestine: Land of Promise.* New York: Harper & Brothers, 1945.

————. *Conquest of the Land Through Seven Thousand Years.* Washington, D.C.: USDA, 1948.

Mahoney, Richard J. *A Commitment to Greatness.* St. Louis, Mo.: Monsanto, 1988.

Marcus, Alan I. "Back to the Present: Historians' Treatment of the City as a Social System During the Reign of the Idea of Community." In *American Urbanism,* edited by Zane Miller, 7–10. Westport, Conn.: Greenwood Press, 1987.

————. *Agricultural Science and the Quest for Legitimacy.* Ames: Iowa State University Press, 1985.

Marcus, Alan I., and Howard P. Segal. *Technology in America: A Brief History.* San Diego: Harcourt Brace Jovanovich, 1989.

Marsh, George Perkins. *Man and Nature: or Physical Geography as Modified by Human Nature.* 1864. Reprint. Cambridge, Mass.: Harvard University Press, 1967.

Matusow, Allan J. *Farm Policies and Politics in the Truman Years*. Cambridge, Mass.: Harvard University Press, 1967.

McCoy, Donald R. *The Presidency of Harry S. Truman*. Lawrence: University Press of Kansas, 1984.

McIntosh, Robert P. "The Background and Some Current Problems of Theoretical Ecology." In *Conceptual Issues in Ecology*, edited by Esa Saarinen, 1–61. Dordrecht: D. Reidel, 1982.

McMillen, Wheeler. *Too Many Farmers*. New York: William Morrow, 1926.

———. *Bugs or People?* New York: Appleton-Century, 1965.

Mead, Margaret. *Keep Your Powder Dry*. New York: William Morrow, 1942.

Meine, Curt. "The Farmer as Conservationist: Leopold on Agriculture." In *Aldo Leopold: The Man and His Legacy*, edited by Thomas Tanner. Ankeny, Iowa: Soil Conservation Society of America, 1987.

Merrill, Richard. "Ecosystem Farming." In *Radical Ecology*, edited by Alexander Cockburn and James Ridgeway, 217–28. New York: Times Books, 1979.

Mickey, Karl B. *Man and the Soil*. Chicago: International Harvester, 1945.

Mollison, Bill. *Permaculture: A Designer's Manual*. Tyalgum, Australia: Tagari, 1988.

Murphy, William T. *Robert Flaherty: A Guide to Reference and Research*. Boston: G. K. Hall, 1978.

Myrick, Susan. *Our Daily Bread*. Danville, Ill.: Interstate Publishers, 1950.

Napier, Ted, ed. *Implementing the Conservation Title of the Food Security Act of 1985*. Ankeny, Iowa: Soil and Water Conservation Society of America, 1990.

National Research Council (Board of Agriculture). *Sustainable Agriculture: Research and Education in the Field*. Washington, D.C.: National Academy Press, 1991.

Nash, Roderick. *The Rights of Nature: A History of Environmental Ethics*. Madison: University of Wisconsin Press, 1989.

Nearing, Scott, and Helen Nearing. *Living the Good Life: How to Live Safely and Sanely in a Troubled World*. New York: Schocken Books, 1970.

———. *Continuing the Good Life: Half A Century of Homesteading*. New York: Schocken books, 1979.

Nixon, Edgar B., ed. *Franklin D. Roosevelt and Conservation*. Vol 2. Hyde Park, N.Y.: National Archives, 1957.

Oelhaf, Robert C. *Organic Agriculture: Economic and Ecological Comparisons with Conventional Methods*. New York: Wiley, 1978.

Osborn, Fairfield. *Our Plundered Planet*. Boston: Little, Brown, 1948.

———. *The Limits of Earth*. Boston: Little, Brown, 1953.

———, ed. *Our Crowded Planet: Essays on the Pressures of Population*. New York: Doubleday, 1962.

Pesek, John. "The History of the Leopold Center." In *Farming Systems for Iowa: Seeking Alternatives*, 33–37. Ames, Iowa: Leopold Center for Sustainable Agriculture, 1990.

Peterson, Merril D. *The Jefferson Image in the American Mind*. New York: Oxford University Press, 1960.

Pfeiffer, Ehrenfield. *Soil Fertility, Renewal and Preservation: Biodynamic Farming and Gardening*. London: Faber and Faber, 1947.

Phipps, Tim T., Pierre R. Crosson, and Kent A. Price. *Agriculture and the Environment*. Washington, D.C.: Resources for the Future, 1986.

Quick, Herbert. *On Board the Good Ship Earth: A Survey of World Problems*. Indianapolis: Bobbs-Merrill, 1913.

Raeburn, Paul. *The Last Harvest: The Genetic Gamble That Threatens to Destroy American Agriculture*. Lincoln: University of Nebraska Press, 1995.

Regenerative Agriculture Association. *The Thompson Farm: Nature's Ag School.* Emmaus, Pa.: Rodale Press, 1985.

Reich, Charles A. *The Greening of America.* New York: Random House, 1970.

Riesch, A. L. *Conservation Under FDR.* New York: Praeger, 1983.

Robbins, Roy M. *Our Landed Heritage: The Public Domain, 1776–1970.* 2d ed. Lincoln: University of Nebraska Press, 1976.

Roberts, Isaac Phillips. *Ten Acres Enough.* New York: Orange Judd, 1918.

Rodale, J. I. *The Organic Front.* Emmaus, Pa.: Rodale Press, 1948.

Rodale, Robert. "The Past and Future of Regenerative Agriculture." In *Sustainable Agriculture and Integrated Farming Systems,* edited by Thomas C. Edens, Cynthia Fridgen, and Susan L. Battenfield, 312–17. East Lansing: Michigan State University Press, 1985.

Ross, Edward Alsworth. *The Changing Chinese: The Conflict of Oriental and Western Culture in China.* New York: Century, 1912.

Rotha, Paul. *Robert Flaherty: A Biography.* Philadelphia: University of Pennsylvania Press, 1983.

Rubenstein, Richard. *The Cunning of History: The Holocaust and the American Future.* New York: Harper and Row, 1978.

Sale, Kirkpatrick. *The Green Revolution: The American Environmental Movement, 1962–1992.* New York: Hill and Wang, 1993.

Saloutos, Theodore. *The American Farmer in the New Deal.* Ames: Iowa State University Press, 1982.

Saltmarsh, John A. *Scott Nearing: An Intellectual Biography.* Philadelphia: Temple University Press, 1991.

Sampson, R. Neil. *For the Love of the Land: A History of the National Association of Soil Conservation Districts.* Leagues City, Tex.: National Association of Soil Conservation Districts, 1985.

Scarseth, George D. *Man and His Earth.* Ames: Iowa State University Press, 1962.

Schauer, Anne, ed. *The Thompson Farm On-Farm Research.* Emmaus, Pa.: Rodale Press, 1991.

Schlesinger, Arthur. *The Age of Roosevelt.* Boston: Houghton Mifflin, 1957.

Schumacher, E. F. *Small Is Beautiful: Economics As If People Mattered.* London: Blond Briggs, 1973.

Scott, James Cameron. *Health and Agriculture in China.* London: Faber and Faber, 1949.

Scott, Winfield, and Joseph B. Paul. *Permanent Agriculture: A Textbook of General Agriculture.* New York: Wiley, 1941.

Sears, Paul B. *Deserts on the March.* Norman: University of Oklahoma Press, 1935.

———. *This Is Our World.* Norman: University of Oklahoma Press, 1937.

———. *Life and Environment: The Interrelations of Living Things.* New York: Columbia University Press, 1939.

———. "Ethics, Aesthetics and the Balance of Nature." In *Perspectives on Conservation,* edited by Henry Jarrett, 106–14. Baltimore: Johns Hopkins University Press, 1958.

———. *Where There Is Life.* New York: Dell, 1962.

———. *The Biology of the Living Landscape.* London: Allen Unwin, 1964.

Seatz, Lloyd F., ed. *Ecology and Agricultural Production.* Knoxville: University of Tennessee Press, 1973.

Segerberg, Osborn. *Where Have All the Flowers, Fishes, Birds, Trees, Water, and Air Gone?* New York: Van Rees, 1971.

Shepard, Ward. *Food or Famine: The Challenge of Erosion.* New York: Macmillan, 1945.

Shiva, Vandana. *The Violence of the Green Revolution.* London: Zed, 1991.

Shover, John L. *First Majority–Last Minority: The Transforming of Rural Life in America.* 1976. De Kalb: Northern Illinois University Press, 1986.

Simon, Arthur. *Bread for the World.* New York: Paulist Press, 1973.

Simon, Julian, and Herman Kahn. *The Resourceful Earth: A Response to Global 2000.* New York: Basil Blackwell, 1984.

Simpson, D. Harper. *The Soil Conservation Service.* New York: Praeger, 1983.

Slusser, Dorothy M., and Gerald H. Slusser. *Technology: The God That Failed.* Philadelphia: Westminster Press, 1971.

Smith, Frank E. *The Politics of Conservation.* New York: Pantheon, 1966.

——, ed. *Conservation in the United States: A Documentary History (Land and Water, 1900–1970).* New York: Chelsea House, 1971.

Smith, Page. *Dissenting Opinions.* San Francisco: North Point Press, 1984.

Soth, Lauren. *The Farm Policy Game Play by Play.* Ames: Iowa State University Press, 1989.

Stapledon, Sir Reginald George. *Human Ecology.* 2d ed. Edited by Robert Waller. London: Charles Knight, 1971.

Starke, Linda ed. *State of the World 1987: A World Watch Report on Progress Towards a Sustainable Society.* New York: Norton, 1987.

Steiner, Fredrick R. *Soil Conservation in the United States: Policy and Planning.* Baltimore: Johns Hopkins University Press, 1990.

Strange, Marty. *Family Farming: A New Economic Vision.* Lincoln: University of Nebraska Press, 1988.

Stross, Randall E. *The Stubborn Earth: American Agriculturists on Chinese Soil, 1898–1938.* Berkeley: University of California Press, 1989.

Sykes, Friend. *Food, Farming and the Future.* London: Faber and Faber, 1950.

Thirsk, Joan. *Alternative Agriculture: A History, from the Black Death to the Present Day.* New York: Oxford University Press, 1997.

Thompson, John Stuart. *The Chinese.* Indianapolis: Bobbs-Merrill, 1909.

Thompson, Paul B., and Bill A. Stout. *Beyond the Large Farm: Ethics and Research Goals for Agriculture.* Boulder, Colo.: Westview, 1991.

Tobey, Ronald C. *Saving the Prairie: The Life Cycle of the Founding School of American Plant Ecology, 1895–1955.* Berkeley: University of California Press, 1981.

Tossett, Otis. *Land, Water and People: A History.* St. Paul, Minn.: Webb, 1961.

——. *Roosevelt's Revolution: The First Year, a Personal Perspective.* New York: Macmillan, 1977.

Tugwell, Rexford G. *The Battle for Democracy.* New York: Columbia University Press, 1935.

——. *The Diary of Rexford G. Tugwell: The New Deal, 1932–1935.* New York: Greenwood Press, 1962.

——. *The Brains Trust.* New York: Viking, 1968.

Tugwell, Rexford G., Thomas Munro, and Roy E. Stryker. *American Economic Life and Means of Its Improvement.* New York: Harcourt Brace, 1925.

Turner, James S. *The Chemical Feast: The Ralph Nader Study Group on Food Protection and the Food and Drug Administration.* New York: Grossman, 1970.

Van Vuren, J. P. J. *Soil Fertility and Sewage.* New York: Dover, 1948.

Wallace, Henry A. *New Frontiers.* New York: Reynal and Hitchcock, 1934.

Walters, Charles. *Angry Testament.* Kansas City: Halcyon House, 1969.

——, ed. *The Albrect Papers.* Vol. 2. Kansas City: Acres USA, 1975.

Waring, P. Alston, and Walter Magnes Teller. *Roots in the Earth: The Small Farmer Looks Ahead.* New York: Harper & Brothers, 1943.

Watson, G. C. *The Soil and Social Reclamation.* London: P. S. King, 1938.

Weiner, Douglas R. *Models of Nature: Ecology, Conservation, and Cultural Revolution in Soviet Russia.* Bloomington: Indiana University Press, 1988.

White, Graham, and John Maze. *Henry A. Wallace: His Search for a New World Order.* Chapel Hill: University of North Carolina Press, 1995.

White, Morton, and Lucinda White. *The Intellectual Versus the City.* New York: Oxford University Press, 1977.

Whitten, Jamie L. *That We May Live.* Princeton, N.J.: D. Van Nostrand, 1966.

Whorton, James. *Before Silent Spring: Pesticides and Public Health in Pre-DDT America.* Princeton, N.J.: Princeton University Press, 1974.

Wickenden, Leonard. *Make Friends with Your Land.* New York: Devin-Adair, 1949.

Wiley, Harvey N. *The Lure of the Land: Farming After Fifty.* New York: Century, 1919.

Wilford, Harrison. *Sowing the Wind: A Report for Ralph Nader's Center for Study of a Responsible Tomorrow on Food Safety and the Chemical Harvest.* New York: Grossman, 1972.

Willcox, Oswin. *Reshaping Agriculture.* New York: Norton, 1934.

Williams, Edward. *China: Yesterday and Today.* New York: Thomas Crowell, 1927.

Worster, Donald. *Dust Bowl: The Southern Plains in the 1930s.* New York: Oxford University Press, 1979.

———. "Organic, Economic and Chaotic Ecology." In *Major Problems in American Environmental History,* edited by Carolyn Merchant, 465–79. Lexington, Mass.: Heath, 1993.

———. *The Wealth of Nature.* New York: Oxford University Press, 1993.

———. *Nature's Economy: A History of Ecological Ideas.* 2d ed. Cambridge: Cambridge University Press, 1994.

Wrench, G. T. *Reconstruction by Way of the Soil.* London: Faber and Faber, 1943.

ARTICLES AND OTHER PUBLICATIONS

Adams, Nathaniel. "Smithsonian Horizons." *Smithsonian* 24 (1993): 10.

Albrect, William A. "Wastebasket of the Earth." *Bulletin of Atomic Scientists* 17 (October 1961): 335–40.

Appleby, Joyce. "Commercial Farming and the 'Agrarian Myth' in the Early Republic." *Journal of American History* 68 (March 1982): 833–47.

Baskin, Yvonne. "Into the Wild." *Natural History,* October 1999, 34–37.

Beeman, Randal. "Louis Bromfield Versus the 'Age of Irritation.'" *Environmental History Review* 17 (Spring 1992): 77–92.

———. "The Trash Farmer: Edward Faulkner and the Origins of Sustainable Agriculture, 1943–1953." *Journal of Sustainable Agriculture* 4 (Winter 1993): 91–102.

———. "'Chemivisions': The Forgotten Promises of the Chemurgy Movement." *Agricultural History* 68 (Fall 1994): 23–45.

Bishop, F. C. "Entomology in Relation to Conservation." *Journal of Economic Entomology* 31 (February 1938): 1–10.

Blum, Barton. "Composting and the Roots of Sustainable Agriculture." *Agricultural History* 66 (Spring 1992): 171–87.

Bongaarts, John. "Can the Growing Human Population Feed Itself?" *Scientific American,* March 1994, 36–41.

Borlaug, Norman. "The Green Revolution: Can We Make It Meet Expectations?" *Proceedings of the American Phytopathological Society: Symposium on World Food* 1 (1977): 6–8.

Brewer, Richard. "A Brief History of Ecology." *Papers of the C. C. Adams Center for Ecological Studies* 1 (1960): 1–13.
Brown, Lester R. *Foreign Agricultural Economic Report No. 11.* Washington, D.C.: USDA, 1963.
Browning, J. Artie. "Relevance of Knowledge About Natural Ecosystems to Develop Pest Management Programs for Agroecosystems." *Proceedings of the American Phytopathological Society* 1 (1974): 191–95.
Buchele, Wesley F. "Healing This Wounded Earth: An Agricultural Engineer's Proposal." *Webbs Ag World* 1 (December 1975): 1–5.
Bunce, Arthur C. "Using Our Soils for War Production." In *Wartime Farm and Food Policy.* Pamphlet No. 7. Ames: Iowa State College Press, 1943.
Carman, Harry J., and Rexford G. Tugwell. "The Significance of American Agricultural History." *Agricultural History* 12 (April 1938): 100–103.
Center for Resource Economics. *Farm Bill 1990 Revisited: Agenda for the Environment and Consumers.* Washington, D.C.: CRE, 1992.
Christie, Jean. "New Deal Resources Planning: The Proposals of Morris L. Cooke." *Agricultural History* 53 (July 1979): 507–606.
Commoner, Barry. "Summary of the Conference: On the Meaning of Ecological Failures in International Development." In *The Careless Technology: Ecology and International Development,* edited by M. Taghi Farvar and John P. Milton, xxi–xxix. Garden City, N.Y.: Natural History Press, 1972.
Council for Agricultural Science and Technology. *Long-Term Viability of U.S. Agriculture.* CAST Report No. 114. Ames, Iowa: CAST, 1988.
———. *Alternative Agriculture Scientists' Review.* CAST Report No. 16. Ames, Iowa: CAST, 1990.
———. *How Much Land Can Ten Billion People Spare for Nature?* CAST Report No. 121. Ames, Iowa: CAST, 1994.
Danbom, David. "Romantic Agrarianism in Twentieth-Century America." *Agricultural History* 65 (fall 1991): 1–12.
Daniel, Pete. "A Rogue Bureaucracy: The USDA Fire Ant Campaign of the Late 1950s." *Agricultural History* 64 (spring 1990): 91–121.
Egerton, Frank N. "Changing Concepts of the Balance of Nature." *Quarterly Review of Biology* 48 (1973): 322–50.
Ehrenfeld, David. "Beyond the Farming Crisis." *Technology Review* 90 (July 1987): 47–56.
Eisenberg, Evan. "Back to Eden." *Atlantic Monthly,* November 1989, 57–74.
Hall, Darwin C., Brian P. Baker, Jacques Franco, and Desmond A. Jolly. "Organic Food and Sustainable Agriculture." *Contemporary Policy Issues* 7 (October 1989): 47–73.
Hardin, Garrett. "Tragedy of the Commons." *Science,* 30 July 1968, 99.
Hays, Samuel P. "From Conservation to Environment: Environmental Politics in the United States Since World War II." *Environmental Review* 6 (fall 1982): 14–41.
Hilliard, Sam B. "The Dynamics of Power: Recent Trends in Mechanization on the Farm." *Technology and Culture* 13 (January 1972): 1–24.
Hotelling, Harold. "The Economics of Exhaustible Resources," *Journal of Political Economy* 39 (April 1931): 137–49.
Johnson, Sherman E. "Definitions of Efficient Farming." *Land Policy Review* 2 (September–October 1939): 22–23.
Kidd, Charles V. "The Evolution of Sustainability." *Journal of Agricultural and Environmental Ethics* 3 (1992): 2–23.

Kline, Allan B. "What the Farmers Want." *Annals of the American Academy of Political and Social Science* 259 (September 1948): 122–27.

Klinkenborg, Verlyn. "A Farming Revolution." *National Geographic,* December 1995, 66–88.

Lear, Linda J. "Bombshell in Beltsville: The USDA and the Challenge of Silent Spring." *Agricultural History* 66 (spring 1992): 151–70.

Lehman, Tim. "Failed Land Reform: The Politics of the 1981 National Agricultural Lands Study." *Environmental History Review* 14 (spring/summer 1990): 129–49.

Logsdon, Gene. "Death of a Sacred Cow." *Ohio Magazine,* May 1992, 30–49, 56–59.

Long, Cheryl. "Certified Organic: A Guarantee of Pure, Wholesome Food." *Organic Gardening,* November/December 1999, 44–45.

Mitchell, Roger. "Agronomy in a Global Age." In *Agronomy in Today's Society,* edited by J. W. Pendleton, 1–5. American Society of Agronomy Special Publication No. 33. Madison, Wis.: ASA, 1978, 1–5.

Moore, Barrington. "The Scope of Ecology." *Ecology* 1 (1920): 1–13.

Odum, Eugene P. "The Emergence of Ecology as a New Integrative Discipline." *Ecology,* 25 March 1977, 1289–93.

Overfield, Richard. "Charles E. Bessey: The Impact of the 'New' Botany on American Agriculture, 1880–1910." *Technology and Culture* 16 (April 1975): 162–81.

Rasmussen, Wayne D. "Advances in American Agriculture: The Mechanical Tomato Harvester as a Case Study." *Technology and Culture* 9 (October 1968): 531–43.

Reganold, John P. "Sustainable Agriculture in the United States: An Overview." *Proceedings of the First International Symposium in Natural Resource Management,* 1 (1990): 447–48.

Reilly, William K. "Agriculture and the Environment." *Vital Speeches* 53 (December 15, 1986): 136–39.

"The Seven Challenges of Sustainable Agriculture." *The New Farm* 13 (January 1991): 32.

Thomas, V. G. and P. G. Kevan. "Basic Principles of Agroecology and Sustainable Agriculture." *Journal of Agricultural and Environmental Ethics* 3 (1993): 1–19.

Thompson, Paul. "Agrarianism and the American Philosophical Tradition." *Agriculture and Human Values* 7 (winter 1990): 3–9.

Tugwell, Rexford G. "The Resettlement Idea." *Agricultural History* 33 (October 1959): 159–63.

Welsh, Rick. "The Industrial Reorganization of U.S. Agriculture: An Overview and Background Report." Policy Studies Report No. 6. Greenbelt, Md.: Henry A. Wallace Institute for Alternative Agriculture, 1996.

Wilson, R. S. *The Trilogy of American Conservation and the Eternal Question: Two Addresses to Soil Conservationists.* Ankeny, Iowa: Soil and Water Conservation Society of America, 1949.

Wik, Reynold. "Henry Ford's Science and Technology for Rural America." *Technology and Culture* 3 (summer 1962): 247–58.

Worster, Donald. "Transformations of the Earth: Toward an Agroecological Perspective in History." *Journal of American History* 79 (March 1990): 1087–105.

Youngberg, Garth. "The Alternative Agriculture Movement." *Policy Studies Journal* 6 (summer 1978): 524–30.

Youngberg, Garth, and Frederick H. Buttel. "Public Policy and Socio-political Factors Affecting the Future of Sustainable Farming Systems." In *Organic Farming: Current Technology and Its Role in a Sustainable Agriculture,* edited by D. F. Bezdicek and J. F. Power, 167–86. American Society of Agronomy Special Publication No. 46. Madison, Wis.: ASA, 1984.

THESES AND DISSERTATIONS

Beeman, Randal S. "A Green and Permanent Land": Agriculture in the Age of Ecology, 1935–1985. Ph.D. diss., Iowa State University, 1995.
Christie, Margaret M. "Carl C. Taylor, 'Organic Intellectual' in the New Deal Department of Agriculture." M.S. thesis, University of Wisconsin–Madison, 1996. ["Organic" refers to Antonio Gramsci's theory of intellectuals.]
Peters, Suzanne. "The Land in Trust: A Social History of the Organic Farming Movement." Ph.D. diss. McGill University, 1979.
Tjossem, Sara Fairbank. "Preservation of Nature and Academic Respectability: Tensions in the Ecological Society of America, 1915–1979." Ph.D. diss. Cornell University, 1994.

Index